ANN LONG'S
DINNER PARTY
BOOK

Ann Long's DINNER PARTY BOOK

Hodder & Stoughton

LONDON SYDNEY AUCKLAND TORONTO

British Library Cataloguing in Publication Data

Long, Ann
    Ann Long's dinner party book.
    1. Dinners and dining
    I. Title
    641.5'68   TX737

    ISBN 0 340 38608 8

Acknowledgments

My sincere thanks go to my family, Ian and Suzanne, who, with Carol, have loyally supported, helped and encouraged me during the long gestation of this book. I am indebted also to David and Jane and Joan for their help, and to Gayna.

Contents

All recipes serve eight.

The menus are arranged according to main courses.

INTRODUCTION

Good cooking is often thought to be the exclusive province of trained chefs, but this is not so. With the expenditure of time and patience and by paying careful attention to recipe instructions, special dishes can be produced to do honour to special occasions. There are really no 'shortcuts' in cooking well, but it is very rewarding and the end results do show your guests that you care about them.

I cook for a living but I enjoy developing my skills and preparing food which not only looks good but also tastes right. I stress the importance of using fresh ingredients, carefully selected, and of presenting the finished dishes attractively. I like to think my guests and readers will share my pleasure in cooking. However, although cooking is my work, I still experience stage-fright! Before the meals are served I am keyed-up and feel panic, then the show begins and I am exhilarated and afterwards have a marvellous feeling of satisfaction when I know the evening has gone well.

I realise that the housewife has many other domestic duties so I have included some of my well-loved time-and-stress savers. One of the most helpful habits to develop is list-making: a list of things to be obtained and tasks to be done at the early stages and a last minute list will be invaluable. You can see each item crossed off and feel secure! Do read the recipe all the way through to check that you have everything you need. Make sure you have space and the right pans. Forward planning for your own peace of mind is important so that you have time for your own personal appearance.

To pipe a cream decoration over a beautifully prepared cake is daunting, yet just a single line of piped cream set to one side of the cake will create an elegant garnish. You may prefer to decorate the serving plate or stand with the cream and then rest the cake on top: it is easier to wipe a mistake from a plate than from a cake. I have tried to mention the utensils to use in each recipe; for instance, there is no point in creating a light mousse – putting in all that effort – to find that by folding in the whites with a wooden spoon, a lot of the froth disappears. Throughout, unless I have stated otherwise, I use heaped spoonfuls.

8

I cook vegetables quickly in plenty of lightly salted boiling water as I find this retains their colour, flavour and achieves a pleasant crispness. The easiest way is to cook them in a wire spaghetti-basket which can be lifted out when they are ready. These baskets can be bought from most kitchen shops.

I personally prefer to eat meat or fish without bones; presenting it boned and attractively shaped gives me pleasure and enables me to make sure there are suitable portions for each guest. I have described the ways I find helpful in boning, slicing and serving.

Your first course should tempt your guests with a taste of what is to follow.

I like to use the element of surprise: hidden stuffings, mingling two sauces of a similar colour but with a contrasting flavour on a plate. It is important for people to see what they are eating; I use an opaque sauce on the plate but a clear one to glaze.

Good coffee at the end leaves a lasting impression; the last taste is very important.

When you give a dinner party you are really inviting your friends to share your delight in cooking and preparing a meal. Your guests are coming to see you and you want them to go home feeling happy; you will have taken care beforehand and during the cooking and serving and you should feel happy too!

CAULIFLOWER CHEESE SOUP
served with a garnish of crisp radishes arranged around a
bowl of sea salt

BONED TROUT
filled with spinach and crisp bacon stuffing, oven baked and
garnished with orange and lemon

BOILED NEW POTATOES
TOMATO AND BLACK OLIVE SALAD

FIGS MARINATED IN PORT
gently poached, with a pecan nut centre and served with
clotted cream

I enjoy making soup. I have used a very basic method to make all the soups in this book. Once you have tried these recipes, I am sure you will have fun making your own combinations and experimenting with herbs and spices.

Things to bear in mind

Do not season with salt and ground pepper until the soup is ready to serve. The vegetables should be cooked until tender but still slightly firm. There is nothing wrong in using frozen vegetables for soup if no fresh ones are available, but when you do, make sure you have a good stock.

I have found that a sheet of greaseproof paper gently pressed on to the vegetables during their cooking period helps to retain moisture and capture flavours.

A liquidizer is essential when making puréed soup and also a fine sieve to pass the soup through after you have liquidized it. A stainless steel sieve is best as some vegetables, such as spinach and broadbeans, will change colour when they come into contact with other metals.

Cauliflower cheese soup served with a garnish of crisp radishes arranged around a bowl of sea salt

2 lb (900 g) cauliflower
2 ripe tomatoes
8 oz (225 g) onions
4 oz (110 g) butter
½ pint (275 ml) medium dry sherry
1 teaspoon paprika

1 teaspoon cinnamon
3 pints (1.5 litres) chicken stock
4–6 oz (110–175 g) strong Cheddar cheese
Black pepper and salt
Juice of 1 lemon

Garnish

Radishes
Sea salt

Cut the cauliflower into small florets and chop the stalks. Throw away the leaves. Slice the unpeeled tomatoes in half. Top and tail and peel the onions, cut them in half vertically. Slice the halves across into thin slices.

Melt the butter in a large saucepan, add the onions and cook until transparent, but not coloured. Add the cauliflower, tomatoes, sherry, paprika and cinnamon. Give the vegetables a good stir. Turn down the heat as low as possible. Cover the vegetables with a sheet of greaseproof paper and put the lid on the saucepan. Cook for 30–40 minutes, until tender.

Take the saucepan from the heat and pour in the chicken stock.

Have ready, by the liquidizer, a plastic container. You need one large enough to hold the soup and allow a sieve to rest on top. I find a gallon ice cream container with lid, perfect. Ladle the soup, a little at a time, into the liquidizer and work until smooth. Pour the purée into the sieve, coaxing it through into the container with a wooden spoon. For a lighter textured soup, stir in milk, wine or more stock, until you have a consistency which suits your taste. Let the soup cool completely, then refrigerate.

Radishes

Choose medium-sized perfect radishes.

Slice off the leaves, leaving ½ in (1 cm) of stalk and snip away the tapered root. Store them in a polythene bag, and 1 hour before serving, drop them in a bowl of iced water to ensure crispness.

To serve

Pat the radishes dry with kitchen paper and on a plate, arrange them around a small bowl filled with sea salt.

Grate the cheese, using the finest grater. Bring the soup to a gentle bubble, add the grated cheese and using a wooden spoon, stir until smooth. Grind in black pepper and a touch of salt. Taste and if you think it needs a sharper flavour, add the lemon juice. Taste again. Ladle into warmed bowls.

Offer the radishes for your guests to eat with the soup or before the main course.

Variation: Curried cauliflower soup

1 garlic clove
1 level teaspoon curry powder

A pinch of cumin, turmeric, chilli powder,
English dried mustard and coriander
1 eating apple, quartered but not peeled

Crush the garlic clove on to the softened onions, stir in the spices, then add the apple with the cauliflower.

Boned trout filled with spinach and crisp bacon stuffing, oven baked and garnished with orange and lemon

Look for trout that have lovely translucent skins and bright eyes. Ask your fishmonger to let you feel the fish; the flesh should be soft but springy to light pressure. As soon as you get them home, unwrap and lay the fish on a tray, cover loosely with clingfilm to prevent the skins from drying out and place them in the coldest part of the refrigerator for up to 24 hours.

8 trout each weighing 7–8 oz (200–225 g), gutted
Butter for greasing the dishes

8 slices of Canadian-style smoked bacon rashers (they are usually sold without rind)

2 baking dishes that will hold 4 trout comfortably in each.

Stuffing

1 lb (450 g) young spinach
1 medium onion
8 oz (225 g) streaky bacon
A little oil for frying
3 oz (75 g) butter
2 oz (50 g) brown breadcrumbs

½ teaspoon tarragon leaves, chopped. Tarragon is added as a background flavour, so don't be tempted to add any more.
Black pepper and salt
1 egg, beaten

To finish and garnish

½ oz (10 g) butter
8 orange slices. I prefer blood oranges for this recipe.
1 dessertspoon caster sugar
1 oz (25 g) butter

5 fl oz (150 ml) dry vermouth
Juice of 1 lemon
Juice of 1 medium orange
1 tablespoon chopped parsley

Stuffing

Throw away any discoloured spinach leaves and trim the base of each stem. Rinse the leaves in lots of cold water to remove the grit and pat the spinach dry with a tea-towel. Roll bundles of leaves to form cigar shapes and then cut them across into thin slices.

Trim and peel the onion, also discard the first fleshy layer as it is coarse-textured and resists chopping. Cut the onion in half vertically and lay the halves cut side down on a board. Holding one half firmly, make several slices parallel with the cut surface, to within ½ in (1 cm) of the base. Slice down at ¼ in (5 mm) intervals through the onion without cutting the root. Gently re-shape the cut half and then slice across the previous cuts to form squares. Repeat with the other half. For years I had difficulty in cutting perfect squares of onions. It is rather nice to see the uniform shapes in a stuffing, so I have described the way I find easy.

Remove the rind from the bacon slices and cut each rasher into thin strips. Heat a little oil in a large frying pan, swirling it to coat the surface with hot fat, and add the bacon, separating the strips as you do so and fry until crisp. Take the pan away from the heat and using a slotted spoon, transfer the bacon to a plate lined with kitchen paper and leave to drain.

Drop 2 oz (50 g) of the butter into the hot pan and over a low heat sauté the onion until soft. With a slotted spoon, scoop it into a mixing bowl. Heat the rest of the butter in the pan, add the spinach, sprinkle with salt and, using a wooden spoon, stir the spinach over a low heat for about 2 minutes, until tender.

Tip the spinach with juices into the onions, mix in the breadcrumbs, crisp bacon and tarragon. Twist in black pepper and taste, add the beaten egg to the spinach mixture and stir.

Trout

The trout's belly will already have been opened when it was gutted. Using a sharp knife, extend the cut down to the tail of each fish. Hold each trout open with your fingers and, with a small knife, ease the bones away from the flesh. With a pair of scissors, cut through the backbone close to the head and then gently pull out the bone towards the tail and cut it free. Feel over the surface for any bones that may have been missed and pull them out with tweezers. Take the eyes out with the point of a knife. Place the prepared fish to one side.

Rinse the trout briefly in cold water. Pat the flesh and skin dry with kitchen paper. Spoon the spinach stuffing evenly into and along the cavity of each trout and gently press the edges together.

To cook

Set the oven to gas mark 5, 375°F, 190°C. Paint the insides of the dishes with a coating of butter, arrange the trout in place and brush the fish with melted butter.

Lay the smoked bacon on a board. Using the blunt side of the knife and even pressure, run the blade over each slice, just to stretch it a little.

Place a slice on each trout at an angle, tucking the bacon under. Cook them in the oven for 25–30 minutes. The fish will have crispy skins and feel firm to the touch when cooked.

To serve

In a frying pan, heat ½ oz (10 g) butter, add the orange slices, sprinkle with caster sugar and over a high heat, fry them until brown. Using a fish slice, transfer the orange slices to a plate.

Wipe the pan with kitchen paper and while it is still hot, swirl in 1 oz (25 g) of butter. Leave it on a low heat to sizzle while you lift the trout on to warmed plates using the fish slice.

Add the vermouth and the lemon and orange juices to the pan. When the mixture is bubbling, spoon in the parsley and immediately pour a little of the sauce over each fish. Garnish with the browned orange slices.

Present the chilled salad at the table, accompanied with a dish of boiled new potatoes.

Variations

Alternatively the fish may be fried, or cooked in foil parcels.

To fry

Spoon flour on to a plate and spread it out. Brush the trout with a little milk. Dip both sides of the fish in the flour and pat away the surplus. Arrange them on a cake-cooling rack to let the flour dry. I always use this method to prepare fish for frying. Fry the fish, four at a time, in sizzling butter and oil, for 8 to 10 minutes, turning once.

Keep the trout warm on kitchen-paper-lined plates. Wipe out the pan and make the sauce.

Foil-wrapped trout

Finely chop 1 onion and 1 carrot. Cut 8 × 12 in (20 × 25 cm) long oval shapes out of foil. Divide and spread the chopped vegetables on each oval and place the trout on top. Bring the sides of the foil together and pour a tablespoon of dry vermouth in each with a knob of butter. Pleat the foil over at the top to enclose the fish, leaving room for the steam to circulate. Crimp the foil together to form a neat rippled finish. Cook at gas mark 8, 450°F, 230°C, feeling the parcel for firmness after 20 minutes.

Tomato and black olive salad

Tomato salads are usually served at room temperature, but I would suggest you serve this salad chilled as a rather nice contrast with hot trout.

1 lb (450 g) black olives, stoned
24 medium sized tomatoes

Vinaigrette

8 fl oz (220 ml) light olive oil
2 tablespoons red wine vinegar
2 tablespoons white wine vinegar
Sprig of mint

1 teaspoon sea salt
A few twists of black pepper
A long, shallow, white dish

Preparation

Marinate the olives in the oil for about 24 hours. At the same time soak the mint in the combined vinegars.

To assemble

Tip the olives and oil into a sieve placed over a bowl to collect the well-flavoured oil. Slice each olive down in half. Keep 16 halves for decoration and arrange the rest, cut side down, on the dish.
    Cut around the stems of the tomatoes to loosen their skins. Put all the tomatoes in a bowl and pour boiling water over to cover. Slowly count to ten, then tip the water away. Immediately run cold water on to them until the tomatoes are chilled. You will now be able to peel the skins away. Slice each tomato in half horizontally and using your fingertips, scoop out the seeds. Cut the halves into rounds and their caps into thin slices. Arrange the tomato rounds in overlapping slices to cover the olives in the dish and sprinkle the sliced caps evenly over the surface.
    Cover the dish with clingfilm and chill.

Vinaigrette

Pour the strained oil into a jug to check the volume. Before discarding the mint squeeze out its juices into the vinegars. Pour the flavoured vinegars into a small bowl, add the sea salt and black pepper. Stir the vinegars using a wooden spoon until the salt has dissolved and gradually add 8 fl oz (220 ml) oil, stirring to blend together.

To serve

Arrange the 16 cut half-olives, side by side to form a thick band at an angle to the overlapping sliced tomatoes. Using a wooden spoon, blend the oil and vinegar together again, pour it evenly over the salad and serve.

Variation: *Tomatoes with hot basil dressing*

Skin, slice and arrange the tomatoes on a bed of thinly-sliced crisp Iceberg lettuce or Chinese leaves. Gently heat French dressing in a small frying pan, stir in chopped basil leaves, immediately pour this dressing over the salad and serve.

Figs marinated in port, gently poached, with a pecan nut centre and served with clotted cream

I have a small selection of moulded, tall, clear-glass 'fish tanks' in which I serve poached fruit, layered fruit or vegetable salads, their flavours blended together in syrup or vinaigrette. A great deal of time and care is spent on layering fruit or vegetable salads and to present them at the table in the high-sided 'tank' shows off the colours and shapes of the ingredients and makes the time spent well worthwhile.

2 oranges
6 tablespoons of honey
1 ½ pints (1 litre) port

2 lb (900 g – 1 kg) dried figs
1 lb (450 g) shelled pecan nuts
1–2 tablespoons redcurrant jelly

To serve
Clotted cream

Finely grate the oranges and squeeze out the juice. Then in a large saucepan, heat the honey, port, orange rind and juice until they are blended together. Leave to cool.

Place the dried figs in a large mixing bowl and pour the cold flavoured port over them. Leave the figs to soak overnight in a cool place.

The next day, cut a small opening in each fig, carefully push in a pecan nut and, using your thumb and forefinger, press the cut edges together to enclose the stuffing. Place the filled figs in a large saucepan and pour in the port marinade. Cover the pan with a lid and poach the figs in the gently bubbling liquid for 10 minutes. Using a slotted spoon, arrange layers of puffed figs in the tank.

Strain the port through a fine sieve placed over a clean saucepan, add the redcurrant jelly to the pan and using a wooden spoon, stir until the jelly has dissolved. Raise the heat and boil until the liquid thickens a little. Taste. Leave the flavoured port to cool and then pour it over the figs. Cover and seal with clingfilm and keep in the refrigerator.

To serve

You will find that it takes 1 hour for the figs to come to room temperature. Serve them at the table with a bowl of clotted cream.

Variation

The stuffed figs are also pleasant soaked in freshly brewed cold coffee and then gently poached in coffee syrup – see Coffee jelly (p. 125). Serve the flavoured figs with a fruit purée of your choice (p. 211).

Forward preparation

2 days before

Make the flavoured port marinade and leave the figs to soak overnight.

The day before

Prepare

Soak the black olives in olive oil and a sprig of mint in the mixed vinegars.

Make

Soup and when cold, cover and chill.
Fill and poach the figs. When they are cold seal with clingfilm and chill.

The morning

Prepare

Trim the radishes and keep them in a polythene bag.
Finely grate the cheese on to a plate, cover and seal with clingfilm.
Scrape the new potatoes and leave them in water.
Cover prepared tomatoes with boiling water, then cold water. Lay them on a tray lined with kitchen paper to peel later.
Drain and cut the olives.

Make

Vinaigrette.
Spinach stuffing.
Bone and fill the trout. Set them in the prepared baking dishes, cover with clingfilm and chill.

Early evening

Prepare

The tomato salad and chill.
Drop the radishes in iced water.
Chop the parsley.
Take the figs out of the refrigerator and remove the clingfilm.
Dish up the clotted cream.
Set the oven to gas mark 5, 375°F, 190°C.

Have ready

The potatoes in a saucepan, covered with lightly salted water.
Unwrap the fish.
Pat the radishes dry and arrange them on the plate with sea salt.
Set the soup ready to re-heat and have seasoning, cheese and lemon juice close by.
Slice the orange.

Put butter in the frying pan.
Arrange the olives in a band over the tomato slices, cover and chill again.
Dress the salad just before serving.

CAMEMBERT FRITTERS

SOLE FILLETS
spread with smoked salmon pâté rolled and cooked in a light
wine, served with cream sauce, garnished with spinach purée

NEW POTATOES
FRENCH BEANS
garnished with crisp breadcrumbs

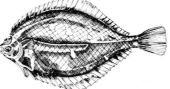

COFFEE HAZELNUT MERINGUE
A purée of strawberries

Camembert fritters

To my mind, this is the best way of serving Camembert. You need to make the
fritter mixture 2 days in advance, then the following day, shape and
breadcrumb them.

4 oz (110 g) butter
3 oz (75 g) flour
14 fl oz (400 ml) milk
½ lb (225 g) ripe Camembert, without the rind
6 egg yolks
2 teaspoons coarse grain mustard
Grated nutmeg to your taste
Flour

1–2 large eggs lightly beaten together with a
pinch of salt
8 oz (225 g) brown breadcrumbs mixed with
2 oz (50 g) sesame seeds for coating the
fritters. (Crisp-fry any leftover breadcrumbs
and use for garnishing the French beans.)
Oil for frying. I prefer to use a light, tasteless
vegetable oil for cooking the fritters to avoid
adding unnecessary flavour.

Melt the butter in a heavy-based saucepan, stir in the flour and cook until foaming.
Gradually add the milk and bring to the boil. Let the sauce simmer for 2 minutes while
you chop the Camembert. Place the chopped cheese with the yolks in the blender and
blend until they are well mixed together. Spoon into the white sauce and over a low
heat, stir until it boils and the cheese has dissolved. Take the pan off the heat, stir in
the mustard and nutmeg.

Line a shallow baking tray with clingfilm and brush it with melted butter. Pour in the
cheese mixture and spread evenly. Chill overnight.

Roll the mixture into 1 in (2.5 cm) balls, then with your fingertips, flatten them into
rounds ½ in (1 cm) high. Dip each one into flour, then coat each one with egg. With
clean dry hands, coat them with breadcrumb mixture, pressing them back into shape
as you do so. Lay them on greaseproof paper and chill for at least an hour, or, better
still, overnight.

Heat ½ in (1 cm) of oil in a large frying pan, and sauté the fritters, a few at a time,
until they are crisp and light brown, turning them once during cooking. Drain and keep
warm on crumpled kitchen paper.

Serve them on crisp lettuce leaves; I suggest Iceberg.

Sole fillets spread with smoked salmon pâté, rolled and cooked in a light white wine, served with cream sauce, garnished with spinach purée

If you buy whole soles, the skin should be shiny and the eyes bright. The flesh on fillets, I can only describe as transparent white in colour, soft, springy and clean to the touch. If they are sticky and yellow at the edges, I wouldn't buy them.

Once you have skinned and filleted the soles, keep them covered with clingfilm and use as soon as possible. Sole cooked without the bones, I find, needs a little extra flavouring, so smoked salmon pâté is an ideal partner. If you have made more than you need, it is delicious on hot toast.

Sole fillets	Smoked salmon pâté
4 lemon soles 1 ½ lb (700 g) each or 8 small soles	5 oz (150 g) butter
A little butter to spread on the bottom of the baking tray. I find it better to use 2 trays	10 oz (275 g) smoked salmon
	2 teaspoons lemon juice
10 fl oz (275 ml) vermouth or white wine	Black pepper
	Grated nutmeg

Cut the butter into small cubes. Roughly chop the salmon, and put into the blender with the lemon juice. Work until smooth, then add the seasoning and the butter pieces. Blend well together.

Wash the fillets in cold water. Lay them out on kitchen paper and, with a cloth, gently dab them dry.

I find that pressing out the fillets at this stage of the preparation prevents them from shrinking during cooking. Use a palette knife for this; lay each fillet on a board, skinned side up. Hold the fish at the tail, and gently run the knife along the whole length. Now spread them with the pâté and roll them up starting at the tail end. Arrange them in serving portions close together in the buttered baking dish or dishes to stop them unrolling as they cook. Pour in the wine, cover with buttered greaseproof paper and seal with foil.

Set the oven to gas mark 4, 350°F, 180°C and cook the fish for 30–40 minutes. When the fish is cooked, it will be white and firm, but moist.

Spinach or sorrel purée

I enjoy serving a purée and a sauce with most dishes, for the look and contrast of texture and taste. Spinach and sorrel complement any fish, and served with the rolled fish and a delicate pink sauce present an attractive combination of colours.

When you buy spinach or sorrel, look for young, glossy leaves. Give each bundle a good shake to remove any dry dirt and insects, rinse well in running water. Wrap the leaves in a dry tea-towel and they will keep for a couple of days in the refrigerator. You do need a non-stick, stainless steel or Pyrex saucepan to cook the purée, to retain the colour and flavour. If you are using sorrel, remember the leaves will not take as long to cook.

4 oz (110 g) onion	Salt and pepper
2 oz (50 g) butter	½ pint (275 ml) dry sherry or chicken stock
¾ lb (425 g) spinach	Sugar to taste
Grated nutmeg	

Finely chop the onion. Melt the butter and add the onion. Cook very gently, without burning the butter, until the onions are transparent.

Roll the spinach leaves together and cut across into thin strips. Add them to the pan, with nutmeg, salt and pepper. Pour in the sherry or chicken stock and give it a good stir. Turn down the heat as low as possible, cover with greaseproof paper and a tight-fitting lid. Cook for 15–20 minutes, but check after 10. Take off the lid and let the spinach cool a little before you put it into the liquidizer. Liquidize until smooth and pass the purée through a sieve. Taste for seasoning, as you may find you would prefer to add a little sugar. Keep in a plastic jug, covered loosely with clingfilm until ready for use.

Cream sauce

½ pint (275 ml) double cream	I teaspoon brandy
Black pepper	½ teaspoon of tomato purée for colour
A shake of Tabasco	I oz (25 g) butter

Reduce the cream by a third, then when the fish is cooked, strain the juices into the cream. Bring to the boil and keep boiling until the sauce thickens slightly. Add the pepper, Tabasco, brandy and tomato purée. Whisk in the butter.

Pour the sauce on to the plates, arrange the rolled fillets on top, then spoon the warm spinach purée over half of each roll.

Variation

As a variation of flavour for this sauce, bring the reduced cream and strained cooking juices to a boil, draw the pan aside and whisk in 1 tablespoon of either pink, or mustard, mayonnaise (see page 211).

Alternative stuffings for rolled sole fillets

The first adds a sharp taste but is a change from lemon, the second has a spiced curry flavour.

Grapefruit stuffing

I grapefruit	2 tablespoons chopped parsley and chives
2 oz (50 g) brown breadcrumbs	Salt and pepper
3 oz (75 g) soft butter	

Peel the grapefruit, separate the segments and skin them. Lay a small piece of grapefruit on each prepared fillet, chop the remainder and mix with the breadcrumbs, butter, parsley and chives. Taste and season. Divide the stuffing between the fillets and roll them up.

Sauce: Reduce the cooking liquid and whisk in a little butter at the last minute.

Spiced stuffing

2 tablespoons minced onions	½ teaspoon ground ginger or grated root
I small clove of crushed garlic	ginger
I dessertspoon oil	4 oz (110 g) thinly sliced white fish or scampi
I tablespoon coriander	2 tablespoons brown breadcrumbs
I teaspoon ground turmeric	I beaten egg
	Touch of salt and pepper

Fry the onions and garlic in oil, add the spices and lower the heat. Cook for five minutes, stirring all the time. Remove the pan from the heat and mix in fish and breadcrumbs. Tip the spiced mixture into a small bowl and stir in the beaten egg. Divide the stuffing between the fillets and roll them up. I suggest you serve the cooking liquid reduced as a sauce.

Spiced fritters

A light sautéed first course can also be made with the above stuffing. Double the ingredients and use the food processor to chop the fish into a fine paste, then prepare as described. Form the mixture into small balls and coat them first with flour, then egg and lastly with breadcrumbs. Chill them for about an hour and then sauté until crisp.

Serve them on crisp lettuce tossed in French dressing and garnished with lemon cream or as a complete contrast, blackcurrant and mint purée.

Coffee hazelnut meringue

A variation of oatmeal meringue, but equally as good. When making a meringue, one must always resist the temptation to add the sugar too quickly. I find by not having all the ingredients to hand enough time is allowed between one addition and the next.

8 egg whites
Pinch of salt
1 lb (450 g) caster sugar
1 teaspoon red wine vinegar
1 tablespoon cornflour
1 teaspoon cinnamon
5 oz (150 g) ground hazelnuts

For filling and decoration

1 pint double cream
2 tablespoons Camp coffee
1 teaspoon caster sugar
2 tablespoons rum

2 11 in (28 cm) loose-bottomed flan tins, lined with lightly greased greaseproof paper.

Set the oven to gas mark 1, 275°F, 140°C.

Start to whisk the egg whites with the salt and continue beating while you line the flan tins and weigh out the sugar.

The whites will now be stiff and dry. Add two-thirds of the sugar, a spoonful at a time. Then collect the vinegar, cornflour and cinnamon, add them to the meringue mixture. Slowly spoon in the rest of the sugar and switch off the machine. Remove the bowl and fold in the hazelnuts with a metal spoon, so you don't break down the volume.

Spread the mixture into the flan cases and bake for 1¼–1½ hours. Cool the meringues in their cases.

Whip the cream and as it begins to thicken add the Camp coffee, caster sugar and rum. Continue beating the mixture until it thickens. Taste for sweetness.

Put about a teaspoon of cream on to the serving dish to stop the cake moving. Take out one meringue from the tin and carefully remove the greaseproof paper. Lay it on the dish, smooth side down. Spread with two-thirds of the cream. Take the other meringue out of its tin. Place on top of the cream, pressing it down a little with your hand, then peel away the paper. Pipe and decorate the top with the rest of the cream.

Cut the meringue into wedges at the table and ladle a little purée over each portion as you serve.

A purée of strawberries

1 lb (450 g) strawberries
6 tablespoons caster sugar
6 tablespoons cassis

Just liquidize everything together, and sieve if you wish. Keep covered in the refrigerator. It also freezes very well.

Forward preparation

Two days before

Make

Camembert mixture and chill.

The day before

Prepare

Breadcrumbs sufficient to coat the fritters and to sauté for garnishing the beans.
Shape and coat the Camembert with breadcrumbs and chill.

Make

Meringue and keep in a cool place.
Spinach purée.
Smoked salmon pâté.
Strawberry purée.

The morning

Prepare

Sole fillets and spread them with the pâté, roll them up and arrange on buttered trays.
Pour in the wine, cover loosely with greaseproof paper and chill.

Vegetables.
Sauté breadcrumbs for garnishing the French beans.

Early evening

Cover the fish with foil, ready to cook.
Fill and decorate the meringue.
Reduce the cream for fish sauce.
Have potatoes ready to cook.

Beans ready in vegetable basket.
Crumpled kitchen paper on plates ready to drain the fritters.

TOMATO CASSEROLES

SMOKED HADDOCK
cooked in individual pastry parcels served on a smooth
Stilton sauce

RED WINE BUTTER-COATED BROCCOLI
garnished with toasted almonds and colourful carrots

POACHED PEARS WITH BLACKCURRANT PURÉE
Clotted cream
Crisp sweet biscuits

Tomato casseroles

These are seasoned layers of sliced tomatoes, peppers and black olives, moulded together in individual ramekins, topped with breadcrumbs and baked until they have brown crunchy coats. This course is light and refreshing, served either hot or chilled.

2 oz (50 g) tinned sweet red peppers
12 medium-sized firm tomatoes
24 stoned black olives
5 fl oz (150 ml) olive oil
1 teaspoon chopped marjoram leaves

2 teaspoons chopped mixed herbs, parsley,
   thyme and tarragon or sage
Black pepper
Brown breadcrumbs

Garnish

Sprigs of parsley
8 ramekins

Set the oven to gas mark 7, 425°F, 220°C.
Drain the peppers in a sieve set over a bowl.
Cut around the stems of the tomatoes to loosen the skins. Immerse them in boiling water, slowly count to 10, then, using a slotted spoon, transfer the tomatoes to a bowl of ice-cold water. With your thumb and finger-tips peel away the skins. Using a sharp, stainless-steel knife, cut each tomato in 6 horizontal slices.
Cut the peppers in half lengthways and with the handle of a teaspoon remove any remaining seeds and slice them into thin strips. Quarter the olives.
Using a pastry brush, paint the insides of the ramekins with a light coating of oil. Place three slices of tomato to cover the base of each mould, top them with three slices of pepper and a few slivers of olives. Divide and sprinkle half of the herbs over the surface and twist in black pepper; continue building up the layers, ending with tomato. Dress the casseroles with the oil and press breadcrumbs evenly over the tops. Transfer them to a baking tray and cook in the pre-heated oven for 5 minutes. Using the back of a spoon press the crumbs into the bubbling oil and continue to cook for 5 more minutes.

22

To serve straight from the oven

Place a warm plate upside down on top of a casserole, invert them together and, with the help of a cloth, lift away the mould. Turn out the rest of the casseroles and garnish each one with a single sprig of parsley.

To serve chilled casseroles

Slide the tray of cooled, filled ramekins, into the refrigerator. Wait until they are quite cold. Run a thin knife around the insides of the ramekins to loosen the casseroles before you place the plates on top to turn them out. Use the same simple but effective garnish.

Variations

There are endless variations for these individual casseroles. They are equally delicious made with slivers of cooked chicken, anchovies, prawns, flaked smoked fish or poached salmon nestling between layers of tomato and pepper.

Smoked haddock cooked in individual pastry parcels, served on a smooth Stilton sauce

½ lemon
2 lb (1 kg) smoked haddock fillets
Milk
8 oz (225 g) long-grain rice
4 hard boiled eggs (for perfect boiled eggs, start them in cold water and cook them for 10 minutes after the water comes to a boil), shelled and chopped
2 tablespoons chopped parsley
¼ pint (150 ml) double cream
2 teaspoons curry powder
Black pepper
Anchovy essence to taste
1 lb (450 g) puff pastry
1 egg white

Stilton sauce

1 oz (25 g) butter
2 tablespoons flour
1 pt (570 ml) milk reserved from cooking the haddock
6 oz (175 g) Stilton, without the rind
Up to ½ pint (275 ml) double cream
Salt
Black pepper

Using a stainless-steel knife, peel the lemon and cut it across into slices. Place the haddock with the lemon slices in a large saucepan, pour in the milk – just enough to cover the fillets. Set the pan over a low heat and simmer for about 4 minutes: do not let the milk boil as such a high heat can toughen the fish. Draw the pan aside, lift the cooked fillets out of the liquid with a large slotted spoon and transfer them to a bowl.

Pour the milk through a sieve set over a plastic tub and reserve 1 pint (570 ml) of the liquid.

As it is easier to remove the skin and bones while the fish is still hot and wet, pull away the skin using your finger tips and take out all the bones and place the prepared fish in a mixing bowl.

Tip the rice into a saucepan and add ½ pint (275 ml) of boiling water. As soon as the water returns to the boil put a tight-fitting lid on the pan and draw to one side. After 5 minutes, remove the lid and give the rice a gentle stir; the grains should be tender but still firm.

Spoon the rice into the mixing bowl. Add the chopped eggs, parsley, double cream, curry powder and twists of black pepper. Carefully stir the assembled ingredients together, taste, add anchovy essence and taste again.

Roll out the pastry as thin as possible on a lightly-floured surface and, using a paper stencil measuring 4 × 4 inches (10 × 10 cm), cut out 8 squares. Use the trimmings to stamp out 8 heart shapes for decoration.

Divide the fish mixture evenly on to the centre of each square. Lightly mould the mixture into diamond shapes and lay them on the pastry with a point of the diamond in the centre of the straight side of the pastry.

With a pastry brush, paint the pastry edges with water and bring the corners to meet in the centre. Using your thumb and forefinger, press the edges firmly together. Trim the sealed edges with scissors and re-crimp into neat ruffles. Brush one side of the pastry hearts with water and press one on each parcel to cover the central joint. Arrange the pastries on a greased, flour-dusted tray and chill for at least an hour.

Stilton sauce

On a low heat, melt the butter in a heavy-based saucepan, add the flour and cook slowly for 2 minutes, stirring with a wooden spoon. Gradually add the reserved milk, raise the heat, whisk until smooth and bring the sauce to a boil. Draw the pan to rest, half over a lowered heat, and simmer the sauce very gently for 15 minutes to lose the flour taste. Stir it often to stop the sauce from sticking to the bottom of the pan.

Crumble the Stilton into the pan with half of the double cream. Raise the heat and stir the sauce until smooth. Taste, add salt, twists of black pepper and stir in more cream if you prefer a thinner sauce. Taste again. Pour the Stilton sauce into a jug and press clingfilm over the surface to stop a skin from forming.

To cook and serve

Set the oven to gas mark 5, 375°F, 190°C.

Using a fork, lightly blend the egg-white together with a pinch of salt and brush it over the pastry.

Cook the parcels near the top of the oven for 20–25 minutes until crisp and brown. Reheat the sauce and ladle it to cover half of the base of each plate. Slide a spatula under each parcel and lift it carefully to rest on the sauce. Serve them accompanied with broccoli coated in red-wine butter and garnished with crunchy toasted almonds. Also offer a dish of hot, crisp carrots.

Red wine butter

Red wine butter lends an unusual, pleasing flavour to cooked vegetables. It also adds an appetizing coat of colour to white cabbage and cauliflower. Whisked into dark sauces at the last minute, it will thicken and give them a lovely sheen. It is very good spread over plain grilled or sautéed meat.

¾ lb (350 g) butter	2 tablespoons chopped parsley
½ pint (275 ml) red wine	Black pepper
2 tablespoons chopped onions	2 oz (50 g) toasted almonds
1 tablespoon lemon juice	

Place the butter in a large mixing bowl and leave it at room temperature until it is soft enough to work easily.

Pour the wine into a saucepan, add the onions, bring the liquid to boil and allow it to reduce to 2 fl oz (55 ml). Strain the flavoured wine through a sieve into a jug and set aside to cool.

Set the mixing bowl on a damp tea-towel and, with a wooden spoon, beat the butter until it is pale and smooth. Stir in the lemon juice, parsley and black pepper, then blend the wine into the butter until evenly flavoured and coloured. Using a pliable spatula, transfer the butter to a small container and cover the surface with clingfilm.

To serve

In a saucepan and over a low heat, melt a small amount of the butter, pour it evenly to cover and glaze the hot broccoli spears, sprinkle over the toasted almonds and serve immediately.

Poached pears with blackcurrant purée

This is a cool and refreshing dessert. I would serve it decorated with chocolate leaves, clotted cream and crisp biscuits.

2 lemons
8 firm Comice pears
½ pint (275 ml) water
5 oz (150 g) caster sugar
3 fl oz (75 ml) blackcurrant liqueur

Blackcurrant purée made with 1 lb (450 g) fruit
    and ¼ pint (150 ml) sugar syrup

8 chocolate leaves

Crisp sweet biscuits

5 oz (150 g) butter
1 egg yolk
1 tablespoon water
1 tablespoon lemon juice
8 oz (225 g) plain flour
2 tablespoons icing sugar
½ teaspoon salt

Poached pears

Pour 2 pints (1 litre) of water together with the juice of the 2 lemons into a mixing bowl. Select a saucepan with a lid, that will hold the pears comfortably together with a little room to turn and baste them during cooking.

Using a sharp stainless-steel knife, trim the base of the pears so they will stand upright, but leave the stems attached. Using light even pressure, slice the skin away in lengthwise strips. Immerse the pears in the lemon water as soon as they are peeled to help prevent discolouration.

Pour the ½ pint (275 ml) water into the pan, add the sugar and set it over a medium heat. Stir the liquid with a wooden spoon until it is boiling and the sugar has dissolved, then lower the heat and leave to cook for a few minutes. Add the pears to the syrup, cover with the lid and cook them very gently for 30–40 minutes, turning and basting them twice. Test whether they are cooked by carefully lifting out a pear, using a slotted spoon, pushing a darning needle into the base and if it slips in easily the fruit is done. Leave the pears in the pan and pour in the blackcurrant liqueur. Mix it in with a wooden spoon and turn the pears to coat them evenly with colour. Use the slotted spoon to transfer the pears, standing them upright in a serving bowl.

Reduce the liquid over a high heat until thick and shiny. Pour a little over each pear.

Crisp biscuits

Cut the butter into cubes. Using a fork, lightly blend the yolk and liquids together in a small bowl. Pass the flour, sugar and salt through a fine sieve set over a mixing bowl, add the butter cubes to the sieved flour and place the bowl on a damp tea-towel. Gently rub the mixture together with thumbs and fingers until you have a very fine crumble.

Make a well in the centre, pour in the liquid and using a spatula, cut and fold it into the mixture. Hold the bowl steady. With your free hand gather the ingredients together and roll them around the base and walls of the bowl, merging the cracks to form a smooth ball. Wrap it in clingfilm and leave in a cool area to rest and settle.

Set the oven to gas mark 4, 350°F, 180°C.

On a lightly floured working surface roll the pastry to a thickness of ⅛ in (3 mm) and prick it all over with an even pronged fork. Using a round large cutter, press out as many shapes as you can and carefully lift away the trimmings. Slide a fish slice under each round and transfer them to a lightly greased baking-tray.

Cook for 12–15 minutes until they are just coloured with a golden border and firm to touch.

Use the fish slice to slide them on to a greaseproof paper lined cake rack and leave to cool. Store them in an airtight tin. They are at their best eaten on the day they are baked.

Variations

Use a smaller cutter and pair together baked biscuits with chocolate ganache filling (see page 61). Paint the golden biscuits with a coat of thin lemon icing, or bake them with a glaze of egg white and sprinkling of coarse sugar.

Chocolate leaves

Always coat more than you need, in case one breaks when you peel away the leaves. Don't choose perfect leaves, I think they look lovely with one or two holes in them.

4 oz (110 g) plain chocolate, Terry's or
    Bournville
10 bay leaves

Break the chocolate into pieces. Put them closely together on a plate that will lie comfortably over a saucepan. Fill the pan half full of water and bring it to the boil. Turn off the heat and lay the plate on top. Leave the chocolate to melt gently, then, using a spatula, blend together until smooth.

Make sure the leaves are dry. Hold the leaf by the stem, and draw it through the chocolate, taking care to coat only the underside. Lay them to dry on greaseproof paper. When the chocolate is hard, peel away the leaf, starting at the stem.

To serve

Dish up the clotted cream.

Arrange the biscuits in a napkin-lined basket. Dress each pear with a touch of blackcurrant purée and pour the rest into a serving dish. Pull the bay leaves away from their coating of chocolate, press the silhouettes into the fruit and serve.

The poached pears are just as delicious served warm with a coating of hot custard.

Forward preparation

The day before

Make

Tomato casseroles. Bake them and when they are cool, keep them in the refrigerator.
Pastry, or allow frozen pastry to defrost in the refrigerator overnight.
Blackcurrant purée.

The morning

Prepare

Carrots and broccoli.
Toast the almonds.
Red wine butter and keep in a cool place.
Hard boil the eggs, peel them and keep in cold water.
Cook the rice.

Make

Haddock parcels and leave them ready to cook on a greased and floured tray.
Stilton sauce.
Poach the pears.
Bake the biscuits.
Chocolate leaves.

Early evening

Turn out the tomato casseroles if you intend to serve them chilled.

Have ready

Beaten egg and pastry brush.
Stilton sauce.
Red wine butter.
Almonds close by.
Carrots and broccoli ready in vegetable-baskets.
Dress the dessert with purée.

Peel the leaves away from the chocolate and decorate the pears.
If you are serving the tomato casseroles hot, set the oven to gas mark 7, 425°F, 220°C and allow 10 minutes for them to warm through. Lower the heat to cook the parcels.

FILLETS OF DUCKLING
and orange segments encased in a clear, sparkling jelly

BUTTER-BRUSHED RED MULLET FILLETS
baked in wine with onions and black olives

CAULIFLOWER AND BROCCOLI
served hot with a coating of French dressing and garnished
with prawns and sesame seeds

A CHEESE AND CREAM DESSERT
glazed with poached redcurrants

Fillets of duckling and orange segments, encased in a clear,
sparkling jelly

Light vegetable oil for coating the ramekins
4 oranges
12 oz (350 g) cooked duck, when taken off the
  bone
2 teaspoons snipped chives
Black pepper

For the jelly

I tablespoon Madeira
½ oz (10 g) (1 packet) gelatine
¼ pint (150 ml) white wine
½ pint (275 ml) chicken stock

To serve

Mustard dressing – see Stilton pâté (page 211).

Garnish

8 sprigs of mint or sage
40 shelled, but not skinned, almonds
8 ramekins, to hold 5 fl oz (150 ml) of liquid

Using a pastry brush, paint the insides of each ramekin with a light vegetable oil.

With a sharp, stainless steel knife, slice away the skin from the top and bottom of each orange. Stand the fruit up on one cut side and slice down to remove the remaining skin in sections round the orange. One at a time hold a peeled fruit in your free hand and position it over a small bowl, cut down each side of the dividing membrane and allow the segments to fall into the bowl. Squeeze the juices out of the skeleton before you segment the next orange.

Drain the segments in a sieve, placed over a bowl to collect the juice. Do not press the fragile orange pieces. Spoon 3 tablespoons of the strained orange juice into a small saucepan and sprinkle the gelatine evenly over the surface, then set aside to soak.

In another saucepan combine the wine, chicken stock and Madeira together and over a low heat bring it to a gentle bubble. Ladle a little of this on to the soaked gelatine and using a plastic spatula stir until all the crystals have dissolved. Pour both liquids into the same jug and leave to cool.

Peel the skin off the duck and pull the flesh away from the bones. Using a small, sharp knife, remove any fat and gristle and slice the trimmings into thin strips. Place them into a large mixing bowl, add the drained segments and chives. Twist in black pepper and with your hands gently toss the ingredients together. Still using your hands lift and arrange the strips in the prepared ramekins and ladle tepid gelatine over, filling each mould to its rim. Arrange the ramekins on a tray, gently press any uncovered meat down into the liquid and slide the tray into the refrigerator. Leave for about 1 hour, or overnight, to allow the jelly to set.

To serve

Run a thin knife around each jelly. Place the ramekin in one hand and cover it with the other. Invert the ramekin and shake it until you feel the jelly fall on to your hand, let it drop back into the mould, then quickly turn it out on to a plate. Turn out the others using the same method.

Set the plates on larger, napkin-lined, plates. Place a sprig of mint, together with 5 shelled almonds on each napkin, tucking the stalks underneath the small plates.

Blend the mustard dressing together and ladle it to cover half of each jelly, allowing it to fall and flow on to the plates. Serve the jellies immediately they have been dressed.

Variation

Use strips of beef instead of duck and garnish each jelly with horseradish mayonnaise.

Butter-brushed red mullet fillets, baked in wine, with onions and black olives

Individual fish are normally already convenient serving portions and if you prefer to serve them whole, red mullet is an ideal choice. They are, to my eye, perfectly formed fish with beautiful, pink, translucent skins. The colour deepens during cooking, making the fish even more attractive and appetising in appearance, especially when they are trimmed and then cleaned through their gills and the livers kept for flavour. Push a finger in and pull out all the innards, together with the gills. Feel inside each one for anything left behind. Separate the livers and throw the rest away.

Rinse the fish with water, replace the livers with a knob of butter and a seasoning of cinnamon. Encase each one in foil and bake them at gas mark 4, 350°F, 180°C for just over 30 minutes. See foil-wrapped trout, page 14. Unwrap the parcels, slide the fish on to individual plates and glaze each one with melted butter.

I do not enjoy eating any cooked meat or fish on the bone as I find it slightly irritating. This is reflected in my cooking; I tend to bone and shape almost everything I serve – it also provides the comfort of knowing that there is the correct amount of parcelled food for each guest.

Fillets of red mullet

8 even-sized red mullets – 8–12 oz (225–350 g)
About 4 oz (110 g) butter, to brush each fillet, 2
   baking dishes and greaseproof paper topping
Cinnamon
Sea salt and black pepper
3 medium onions
40 black olives, stoned
1 pint (½ litre) dry white wine

2 baking dishes of a size to hold 4 fish comfortably in each

Garnish

Chopped parsley

Set the oven to gas mark 5, 375°F, 190°C.

Using a sharp knife slice down both sides of the long back fin of each fish, then with scissors cut it away, cut off the other fins level with the skin. One at a time hold each fish firmly at the tail end and scrape a knife towards the head, releasing the clear, petal-shaped scales.

Wash the board, rinse the fish under cold water and cut off the heads. Slicing through behind the last gill opening, scoop out the livers and put them to one side. With scissors cut down the bellies and pull out and discard the innards. Press your free hand on one mullet to steady it; with the knife, slice along the backbone from head to tail.

Run the knife over the ribs in firm, sharp strokes, releasing the top fillet and putting it to one side. Poke the knife underneath, next to and parallel with the bones and again using firm sliding strokes, release the bottom fillet. Discard the bones, or use them to make fish stock. Bone the rest, using the same method.

Lay the fillets, skin side down, lightly run a finger over the centre of each one to feel for small bones and as you find them pull them out with tweezers. Wash the fillets in cold water, pat them dry with a cloth and lay them out, skin side down on a clean working surface.

In a small saucepan, slowly melt about 4 oz (110 g) butter and, using a pastry brush, paint the delicate white flesh with a thin coat.

Slice and arrange the liver down the centre of 8 fillets, season the surface with a good sprinkling of cinnamon, twists of black pepper and a touch of sea salt. Pair the fillets together, skin sides outside, enclosing the livers and brush the surface of each one with butter. For a neat presentation, cut 8 pieces of string and wrap this loosely around each portion, looping it twice.

Trim and peel the onions, remove the first fleshy layer and cut them in half vertically. Lay them cut side down on a board and cut them across into thin half-moon slices. Brush the dishes with a thin coating of butter and sprinkle the bases with a few slices of onion. Slide a spatula underneath each fish and lay them on top, scatter the olives and the rest of the onions around the fish. Bring the wine to warm in a saucepan and pour it around the mullet, gently press buttered greaseproof paper over the surface and seal with foil. Cook them in the preheated oven for about 30 minutes, basting occasionally. The fish will be firm to the touch and the flesh opaque.

To serve

Cut and pull away the string from each mullet and, with a spatula, lift each one on to a plate. Stir chopped parsley and black pepper into the cooking juices. Use a slotted spoon to transfer the olives and onions over each fish and glaze with the liquid.

Cauliflower and broccoli served hot with a light coating of French dressing and garnished with prawns and sesame seeds

---

2 lb (1 kg) broccoli
1 cauliflower
¼–½ lb (110–225 g) cooked and peeled
   prawns

1 lemon
¼–½ pint (150–275 ml) French dressing
   (see page 211)
Sesame seeds or crisp fried breadcrumbs

Trim and peel away the outer skin from the broccoli stems. Soak the spears in salt water to remove any caterpillars that always seem to hide.

    Bring 2 saucepans of lightly salted water to a boil.

    Cut the cauliflower into florets.

    Pat the prawns dry with kitchen paper and flavour them with the juice of ½ lemon and twists of black pepper.

    Immerse the broccoli in one pan of boiling water, add the rest of the lemon juice and boil the spears, uncovered, for 3–4 minutes. Cook the cauliflower in the other pan, uncovered, for about 3 minutes until tender but still crunchy.

    Stir the prawns into the dressing.

    Drain the vegetables in a colander set over a bowl and gently shake away the water. Quickly place the hot broccoli around the border of a large, warm, serving dish and arrange the cauliflower florets in the centre. Coat them lightly with dressing, sprinkle with sesame seeds and serve immediately.

A cheese and cream dessert glazed with poached redcurrants

This is a version of the Russian Easter dessert, Paskha. A traditional paskha is made in a tall, tapered four-sided wooden box, unmoulded, decorated and taken to church on the evening before Easter to be blessed. It is carried home after the service and eaten at the meal that breaks the Lenten fast and is usually accompanied by a rich fruit cake. This cheese and cream dessert is set in a holed plastic bowl to allow the surplus liquid to drain away. To provide a pleasing contrast, serve the shaped cream at room temperature and the poached fruit chilled.

6 oz (175 g) sultanas
4 tablespoons vodka
1 ½ lb (700 g) cream cheese
12 oz (350 g) soft unsalted butter
6 oz (175 g) caster sugar
2 tablespoons ground almonds

1 plastic bowl, to hold 3 pints (1 ½ litres) of
    water
1 long trussing needle
A very thin tea-towel or a square of muslin

Custard

9 fl oz (275 ml) double cream
3 egg yolks
4 teaspoons caster sugar

Poached redcurrants

1 lb (450 g) prepared redcurrants
½ pint (275 ml) light sugar syrup
Lemon juice or kirsch to flavour, if necessary

To decorate

5 perfect trails of redcurrants

Tip the sultanas into a small bowl and stir in the vodka. Leave overnight to soak.

Hold a long trussing needle at the eye end and pass and twist the tip through a flame until you think it is hot.

Wrap your free arm round the plastic bowl and hold it steady. Quickly pierce the base 5 times, reheating the needle as necessary. Be careful to keep your fingers clear when piercing! I suggest you keep this pierced bowl separately after use.

Rinse the cloth in cold water, wring it out and drape it over the prepared bowl. Gently encourage the damp cloth to fall to the base and press the folds against the walls, leaving an overlap.

Place the cream cheese and butter in a large mixing bowl, set it on a damp tea-towel and, using a wooden spoon, beat until smooth and creamy. Gradually add the sugar and almonds. Lastly stir and blend in the vodka-flavoured fruit.

To make the custard, pour the cream into a medium saucepan and set it over a low heat to boil. In a mixing bowl blend the egg yolks and sugar together, using a wooden spoon. Allow the cream to boil for 2 minutes then pour it on to the beaten egg mixture. Mix together until smooth and then pour it back into the saucepan. Stir the custard over a low heat until little bubbles appear around the edges and immediately pour it back into the mixing bowl. Stir the custard until it cools and then ladle it into a jug.

Gradually stir and blend the cooled custard into the cheese, then spoon it into the lined bowl. Fold the loose ends of the material over the top, rest the bowl on a tray to catch the drips and refrigerate overnight. The dessert can be kept wrapped and chilled for 4 days.

Poached redcurrants

To prepare the currants, hold each stalk over a bowl, press a fork over the top of the berries and run it down to the tip, releasing the redcurrants into the bowl. Poach them gently in the sugar syrup for about 2 minutes. Try not to overcook them as the skins pop easily.

Using a slotted spoon, transfer the berries to a bowl. Taste the syrup and heighten the flavour with lemon juice or kirsch, then taste again. Allow the liquid to cool, then pour it over the berries and chill.

To decorate and serve

Unwrap the loose ends of the material, place a cake stand over the bowl and invert them both. Lift off the bowl and carefully peel away the material to reveal the dessert already partly decorated with imprints of the natural curved folds of the lining. Arrange and press the redcurrant sprays to fall in an interlocking trail over one side of the cream.

32

Pour the chilled liquid and fruit into a bowl.

Use a sharp knife to cut the dessert into small wedges, lift out each wedge with a cake slice and use the knife to slide it on to the plates. Ladle the fruit over each portion.

Variation

Serve the dessert with strawberry purée and decorate it with sliced strawberries.

Forward preparation

2 days before

Flavour the sultanas with vodka.

The day before

Make the dessert.

The morning

Make

Duckling in orange jelly and chill to set.

Prepare

Red mullet. Place them on a tray and keep them chilled, loosely covered with clingfilm. Stone the black olives. Flavour the prawns. Gently poach the redcurrants. Cauliflower and broccoli.

Early evening

Brush the baking trays with butter, slice the onions and set the fish ready to cook. Pour the wine into a saucepan. Unwrap and decorate the dessert. Ladle the redcurrants into a serving bowl and keep in the refrigerator. Preheat the oven to gas mark 5, 370°F, 190°C.

Have ready

2 saucepans of lightly salted water. Colander resting over a bowl. French dressing and prawns. Chopped parsley and black peppers. Decorated napkins. Mustard dressing with a small ladle close by. Unmould the jellies.

SLICED CHICKEN BREAST AND AVOCADO
garnished with Stilton dressing

CRABMEAT
layered with crisp puff pastry

TOMATO AND ORANGE SALAD
LETTUCE
COLESLAW

STRAWBERRIES, CREAM AND LONG FINGERS OF CRISP SHORTBREAD

Sliced chicken breast and avocado, garnished with Stilton dressing

4 boned chicken breasts
2 pints (1 litre) light chicken stock or water
French dressing (see recipe)
4 avocado pears
Stilton dressing (see below)

Marinade for chicken

2 tablespoons rum
2 tablespoons soya sauce
2 tablespoons lemon juice
Just a touch of grated root ginger
½ teaspoon brown sugar
Black pepper

Mix all the marinade ingredients together and stir until the sugar has dissolved. Gently remove the skin from the chicken breasts, trim away the fat and the thread of gristle on the fillets. Lay the chicken on to a plastic, china or stainless steel tray and pour the rum liquid over. Cover loosely with clingfilm and leave to marinate for not less than 3 hours. Remember to turn them occasionally. The acid in some marinades damages aluminium, cast iron or enamel trays.

In a large saucepan, bring 2 pints (1 litre) of light chicken stock or water to the boil, turn down the heat and poach the breasts. The liquid should just bubble and they will take about 15 minutes to cook. Take them out, using a slotted spoon. Lift up the small fillet on each breast and if the flesh is white and firm underneath they are cooked.

Lay them on a plate and brush both sides with a little French dressing. When they are quite cold cover them with clingfilm and chill.

Stilton dressing

Buy mild Stilton. The cheese flavour should be detectable, but should not overwhelm the marinated chicken.

4 oz (110 g) Stilton
3 fl oz (75 ml) red wine vinegar (Dufrais)
Juice of ½ lemon

½ teaspoon coarse grain mustard
3½ fl oz (85 ml) olive oil
3½ fl oz (85 ml) sunflower oil

34

Roughly chop the Stilton and put the pieces into a liquidizer. Add the vinegar, lemon juice and mustard and liquidize them together. Now gradually add the oils until you have a smooth dressing. Taste and add pepper if you think it needs seasoning.

Pour the sauce into a container that has a lid. If you wish to serve the dressing thin as it is now then keep it at room temperature. I prefer the dressing thicker, so I chill it for a few hours. In both cases whisk before serving.

To serve

I found this difficult to describe, but when using simple ingredients that taste so good together I am sure a little time spent on presentation is worthwhile.

Cut the chicken breasts lengthways into very thin slices and divide them into eight portions.

The avocados must be perfect, and a thin, sharp stainless steel knife must be used to cut them, otherwise they will discolour. Quarter the avocados, lengthways, remove their stones and peel away the skin. Lay each piece of avocado, cut side down, on a board, with the tapered end facing you. Starting about ¾ in (2 cm) from the top, slice the pear towards you, at a slight angle, to make 4 or 5 slices, but still joined together at the top. Gently press and push the cut pears with the palm of your hand to fan them out. Using a fish slice, place a fan of avocado against the rim of each plate.

Put the Stilton dressing into a jug and whisk until smooth. Starting at the opposite rim, pour the dressing in a continuous thick stream diagonally across each plate, so that the pear is covered towards the top, forming a ribbon about 1½ in (4 cm) wide.

Bundle each portion of chicken together and, holding the slices at one end, ruffle them out to form a fan. Place these on top of the dressing at a slight angle to the pear.

Crabmeat layered with crisp puff pastry

Crabmeat mousse made with flavoured mayonnaise, and layered with crisp puff pastry is a delight to serve.

Puff pastry

¾ lb (350 g) puff pastry
I egg beaten with ½ teaspoon salt
I tablespoon grated Parmesan

I large plate to hold the slice, or a baking tray, covered with foil
I flat baking tray 16½ in × 12 in (41 cm × 30 cm)

Crabmeat mousse

This recipe will give a generous amount of mousse, which will enable you to produce a slice that has more crab than pastry.

5 fl oz (150 ml) white wine or dry sherry
2 pkts gelatine
2 oz (50 g) butter
2 oz (50 g) flour
I pint (570 ml) fish stock or very light chicken
   stock cubes are fine

I lb (450 g) brown crabmeat
I lb (450 g) white crabmeat
I pint (570 ml) pink mayonnaise (see page 211)
½ pint (275 ml) double cream

You will need two mixing bowls and a saucepan large enough to hold eventually 1 pint (570 ml) of sauce and the brown crabmeat.

Garnish: Cucumber salad

1 cucumber	12 cloves
1 medium onion	½ teaspoon salt

Crabmeat mousse

Pour the wine into a small saucepan, sprinkle the gelatine powder evenly over and leave it to soak in. Turn the oven to its lowest setting and place the saucepan at the very bottom. Allow the gelatine slowly to melt completely. Meanwhile melt 2 oz (50 g) butter in the large saucepan and tip in the flour. Gradually add the stock, stirring all the time, and bring it to the boil. Whisk until smooth. Pour in the gelatine, mixing it in well. Turn off the heat and stir in the brown crabmeat. Leave to cool.

Spoon the white crabmeat into a mixing bowl and stir in the mayonnaise. Pour the cream into the other mixing bowl, place a damp tea towel underneath to keep it steady and whisk until you can see the whisk shapes in the cream.

With a metal spoon, fold the cool brown crabmeat mixture into the crab mayonnaise then, still using the metal spoon, gently mix in the whipped cream. Leave to set in the refrigerator.

Cucumber salad

Using a stainless steel knife cut the cucumber across into very thin even slices or use the fine vegetable slicer on the food processor and put the slices into a deep bowl.

Trim and peel the onion and remove the first fleshy layer. Press the cloves into the prepared onion and bury it in the cucumber slices. Sprinkle the surface with salt and leave the salad overnight in a cool place to flavour and soften.

Puff pastry

Set the oven to gas mark 7, 425°F, 220°C.

Roll the pastry out evenly, on a floured surface, to a size that will slightly overlap the baking tray. Run cold water over the tray, spreading it over with your hands. Place the rolled out pastry on to the baking tray. Using a fork, prick the pastry all over. Chill for 5 minutes.

Brush the beaten egg down one-third of the long side of the pastry and dust this portion of the pastry with Parmesan cheese.

Bake in the hot oven for 10 minutes. When the top is light brown in colour, take it out of the oven. Slide a palette knife between the pastry and the tray to loosen it and gently turn the pastry over. Cook for a further 5 minutes, and then let the pastry and tray cool a little. Trim around the edges and keep the trimmings for decoration.

Cut the pastry into 3 long even strips about 4 in (10 cm) wide and slide them on to a rack to cool completely.

To serve

I always find it easier to assemble the slice on the serving plate. The cheese-coated strip should be kept for the top.

Using a palette knife, spread half the mousse over the first layer of pastry. Place the second slice over and gently press it down. Smooth the sides of the mousse. You now have an oblong box shape 1 in (2.5 cm) high. Evenly spread the rest of the mousse over and top with the cheese pastry, again smoothing the sides.

Crush the pastry trimmings and press them on to the sides and ends. Brush away any loose pastry trimmings. I usually pipe a line of whipped cream around the slice to make it look clean and attractive. Just before serving, squeeze the juices out of the cucumber slices, twist and arrange them into flower shapes on the plate.

As with all savoury or sweet slices when you have assembled the pastry keep it in a cool place. Use within two hours – there is nothing worse than soggy pastry. To serve the crab slice I find I need a sharp, long-bladed knife and a cake slice. Hold the knife and cut through the pastry vertically to prevent squashing it. Slide the portion on to the cake slice and push it off with the knife.

Tomato and orange salad

Choose a large white plate to display this colourful salad.

12 large firm tomatoes
4 oranges

Chopped chives
French dressing or mustard dressing

Cut around the stems of the tomatoes to loosen their skins. Put them in a bowl and pour boiling water over to cover. Slowly count to 10, then tip the water away. Immediately run cold water on to them until the tomatoes are chilled. You will now be able to peel the skin away. Cut the tomatoes horizontally into slices.

Peel the oranges and cut away all the pith. Hold each orange at the top and bottom with your hand and cut across into slices. Remove all the pips. Place the sliced tomatoes, slightly overlapping, around the edge of the plate, then arrange slices of orange, to form a smaller ring. Continue with tomato and oranges.

To contrast the circular appearance of the salad, arrange a straight line of chopped chives down one side.

Seal with clingfilm and pour the dressing over as you serve it.

Coleslaw

1 hard white Dutch cabbage, about 1 lb (450 g) in weight
3 carrots
1 large onion
Juice of 1 lemon

½ pint (275 ml) pink mayonnaise or
¼ pint (150 ml) mayonnaise mixed with ¼ pint (150 ml) French dressing
2 oz (50 g) sultanas
Black pepper

Garnish

Watercress

Peel away any blemished outer leaves of the cabbage. Slice the cabbage in half and cut out the hard core. Shred the cabbage as finely as you can, or use the vegetable slicer on the food processor. Top, tail and peel the carrots and grate them. Finely chop the peeled onion. Mix the lemon juice with the mayonnaise.

Put the cabbage, carrots, onion and sultanas into a large mixing bowl. Twist in black pepper, pour in the mayonnaise and mix everything together with your hands until the vegetables are evenly coated.

Cover with clingfilm and chill until ready to use. Allow about two hours for the cabbage to soak up the flavour of mayonnaise.

To serve

Give the coleslaw a good stir, tip it on to a large dish and garnish with a cluster of watercress to give colour. A large bowl, filled high with whole crisp lettuce leaves, is all you need to complement the flavour of tomato and coleslaw.

Strawberries, cream and long fingers of crisp shortbread

To complete the meal, pour red wine over a bowl of strawberries or, to add more flavour, the red wine can be spiced and sweetened. Clotted cream is an ideal accompaniment for the strawberries, but a mixture of cream and cream cheese flavoured with nutmeg and lemon is also very good.

For a contrast of texture, the strawberries and cream should be served with crisp shortbread.

2 lb (1 kg) small strawberries

Flavoured red wine

½ pint (275 ml) red wine
1 stick of cinnamon
1 teaspoon grated orange rind
3 oz (75 g) caster sugar
1 tablespoon redcurrant jelly

Pour the wine into a saucepan and add the rest of the ingredients. Set the pan on a low heat and gently bring to the boil, stirring until the jelly and sugar have dissolved. Remove from the heat and leave to cool for about 10 minutes. Strain into a jug.

The wine should be served at room temperature.

Rinse the fruit in cold water and leave to dry in a colander. To remove their cores, gently twist the circle of leaves, using your finger and thumb, and pull them away. Serve the hulled strawberries in a plain glass bowl, and pour the wine over them at the table.

Whipped cream cheese

8 oz (225 g) cream cheese
¼ pint (150 ml) sugar syrup
½ pint (275 ml) double cream

For flavouring I use nutmeg and lemon rind, but if you prefer orange, use orange rind and cinnamon powder.

Beat the cream cheese until smooth, add the seasoning and sugar syrup. Gradually pour in the double cream and whisk until you have a thickness you like.

Crisp shortbread

12 oz (338 g) flour
8 oz (225 g) soft butter
4½ oz (130 g) caster sugar

Tip the flour into a large mixing bowl, cut the butter into small pieces and add them with the sugar to the flour. Using your fingertips work the ingredients together to form a dough. Cover with clingfilm and chill for one hour. (The shortbread can also be made in the food processor.)

Set the oven to gas mark 4, 350°F, 180°C.

Lightly grease an 8 in × 12 in (20 cm × 30 cm) baking tray or sandwich tin.

Work the shortbread until you can pat it into an oblong shape, ½ in (1 cm) thick, which will enable you to make about 20 fingers. Prick all over with a fork.

Bake for 30 to 40 minutes until light golden in colour. Allow the shortbread to cool for a minute, then cut it into long fingers. Using a fish slice, slide them on to a wire cake rack covered with greaseproof paper. Leave until cold. Store in an airtight tin.

Forward preparation

The day before

Prepare

Chicken breasts and marinate them
Cucumber salad

Make

Stilton dressing
Puff pastry, or, if using frozen, allow it to defrost overnight in the refrigerator.
Check you have mayonnaise, French dressing and sugar syrup

Crabmeat mousse – remember, when melting gelatine you should always be able to put your hand on the bottom of the saucepan
Spiced red wine
Shortbread – leave to chill overnight

The morning

Poach the chicken breasts
Roll out the puff pastry and chill until ready to cook
Make coleslaw
Bake shortbread

Blanch the tomatoes, but do not peel them yet
Make whipped cream cheese
Bake puff pastry and cut into 3 strips

Early evening

Slice chicken breasts
Prepare salads, strawberries and put whipped cream cheese into a bowl
Assemble the crab slice and garnish with cucumber flowers
Spoon coleslaw into a serving dish and garnish with watercress

Pour the spiced wine into a jug
Arrange shortbread fingers in the folds of a napkin
Have everything to hand for the chicken and avocado

Melon, courgette and tomato casserole

Sliced melon adds a gentle and intriguing contrast to vegetables cooked in wine.

14 oz (400 g) tinned tomatoes	1 teaspoon chopped basil
4 medium onions	4 tomatoes
2 cloves of garlic	6 medium courgettes
5 tablespoons olive oil	8 oz (225 g) honeydew melon
1 pint (½ litre) red wine	1 teaspoon Tabasco
2 pints (1 litre) water	Black pepper
1 teaspoon chopped oregano	

Place a sieve over a small saucepan and, using a wooden spoon, gently pass the tinned tomatoes and juice into the pan. Set the sieved tomatoes on a low heat to reduce slightly, then draw the pan to one side.

Trim and peel the onions, remove the first fleshy layer and halve them vertically. Cut the halves lengthways into thin, equal slices. Peel the garlic cloves and slice them into thin strips.

Heat the oil in a large saucepan, add the sliced onion and garlic and gently sauté them until they are soft, but not brown, stirring them with a wooden spoon to ensure even cooking. Pour in the wine, water and tomato purée. Stir in the herbs and leave the flavoured liquid to simmer for 30 minutes.

Cut around the stems of the tomatoes to loosen their skins, place them in a bowl and pour in boiling water to cover. Slowly count to 10, then immediately tip away the hot water and refresh them with cold water. Peel away their skins, cut them into quarters, scoop out the seeds and slice them into long strips.

Trim the courgettes, cut them in half horizontally and then lengthways into thin even strips. Using a stainless steel knife, peel and cut the melon to form long slices.

Add the sliced vegetables and melon to the saucepan and bring the liquid back to a bare simmer for 1 minute, add Tabasco, taste, test the courgettes and then season with twists of black pepper to give a clean spicy taste before serving in warmed soup plates.

Simmering onions, garlic and herbs in wine and water or stock gives a delicious flavour base for you to add your own choice of ingredients to create a medley of colours and textures.

A fan of avocado with sweetcorn and peanuts, wrapped in butter-brushed and cheese-flavoured pastry, oven-baked until crisp, served on a mild Stilton sauce

---

Filo pastry – paper thin sheets of pastry made with flour and water – is difficult to make, but is now available ready made. It is ideal to wrap round nuggets of unusual combinations to form exciting, crisp and light parcels. Make sure you have the filling ready and the butter melted before you unwrap the pastry, as the sheets dry out very quickly. There are about 12 sheets of pastry in an 8 oz (225 g) packet.

8 oz (225 g) prepared sweetcorn
1 small onion
5–7 oz (150–200 g) butter
8 oz (225 g) salted peanuts
4 large ripe and perfect avocadoes
8 sheets of filo pastry
4–6 oz (110–175 g) grated Parmesan

1 large baking tray, brushed lightly with oil and dusted with flour

Stilton sauce

6 oz (175 g) strong-flavoured Stilton
1 medium onion
2 oz (50 g) butter
3 oz (75 g) flour
2 pints (1 litre) milk
¼ pint (150 ml) red wine
Salt and pepper

Garnish

1 tinned red pepper

Avocado in pastry

Cook the sweetcorn for 12 minutes in lightly salted water, drain them in a sieve and run cold water over them. Pat the corn kernels dry with kitchen paper. Trim, peel and finely chop the onion, cook it gently in 1 oz (25 g) of butter until soft but not coloured. Draw the frying pan to one side and, using a wooden spoon, mix in the sweetcorn and peanuts, and leave until cold.

Using a stainless steel knife, cut the pears into halves lengthways, remove their stones and peel away the skin. On a board, lay each avocado cut-side down, with the tapered end facing you. Starting about 1 in (2.5 cm) from the top, slice the pear towards you to make 5 slices, but leave them still joined together at the top.

Melt the rest of the butter and leave to cool.

Make sure the working table is completely dry, and unwrap the pastry. Peel away 8 sheets and lay them out. Using a pastry brush, cover each sheet with the melted butter and sprinkle the Parmesan over the surface. Fold the pastry in two to form a square and brush with butter.

Fill the stone-cavities in the avocados with the sweetcorn mixture and place the sliced halves at an angle just off centre of each pastry square, then press the remaining stuffing on top of each avocado. Cover the pear with one corner of pastry and start to roll up to the middle. Fold one opposite corner on to the roll to seal the end and continue rolling up to the farthest end, draw and crimp together the loose ends at the top. Using a fish slice carefully slide the parcels on to the prepared tray, brush the pastry with butter and chill.

Stilton sauce

Chop the Stilton. Trim, peel and grate the onion as this will achieve a smooth sauce. Melt the butter in a saucepan and sauté the grated onion until soft, but not coloured. Add the cheese, beat until smooth, with a wooden spoon. Add the flour and cook for one minute, stirring all the time. Gradually add the milk to the pan, stirring to incorporate it, and gently simmer for 5 minutes.

In a small pan, reduce the wine to 2½ fl oz (60 ml) and stir it into the sauce. Taste and season. Pour into a jug and loosely cover the top with clingfilm.

To cook and serve

Set the oven to gas mark 7, 425°F, 220°C.

Cook the parcels on the top rack for 20 minutes until crisp and brown. Reheat the sauce and ladle it to cover the base of the warmed plates. As a rather nice colourful touch, cut the tinned pepper into 8 thin strips and wrap a pepper ribbon around the neck of each parcel. Using a fish slice, gently slide the wrapped avocado on to the sauce.

Serve the sautéed spinach and beansprouts at the table, the marinated sultanas in small bowls to be spooned over the spinach or to be eaten separately before the dessert.

Variation: Wrapped avocado as a first course

Use a quarter of a pear for each portion.

Sautéed spinach and beansprouts

Shredded spinach needs very little cooking and the beansprouts are added at the last minute just to warm through and retain their crisp texture.

1 lb (450 g) beansprouts	½ teaspoon salt
1 lb (450 g) spinach	2 tablespoons Worcestershire sauce
4 tablespoons hazelnut oil	1 oz (25 g) butter
1 peeled garlic clove	2 tablespoons medium sherry

Wash the beansprouts in cold water and leave them to drain in a colander. Throw away any discoloured spinach leaves and trim the base of each stem. Put the leaves in lots of cold water to remove the grit and pat the spinach dry using a tea-towel. Roll bundles of the leaves to form a cigar shape and then cut across into thin strips.

Heat the oil in a large frying pan, crush the garlic clove over and add the spinach. Sprinkle with salt and, using a wooden spoon, stir the spinach for 2 minutes until tender. Mix in the beansprouts, Worcestershire sauce, butter and sherry. Tip the hot sautéed vegetables into a warm dish and serve immediately.

Marinated sultanas

I lb (450 g) sultanas soaked overnight in 8
  tablespoons dry sherry
4 slices of stale bread

Butter for frying
8 spring onions

Remove the crust from the bread and cut each slice into cubes. Heat plenty of butter in a frying pan, add the cubes, spread them out and keep turning the cubes until they are crisp all the way through. Tip the fried bread on to a tray lined with kitchen paper.

Trim and cut the spring onions across into thin rounds.

Just before serving, drain away any excess sherry, pat the sultanas dry and mix them with the onion and crisp cubes of bread.

Chocolate cream encased in a dark chocolate whisked sponge

Whisked sponge

3 large eggs
3 oz (75 g) caster sugar
3 oz (75 g) plain flour
I oz (25 g) Rowntrees cocoa

Swiss roll tin 10 × 14 in (25 cm × 35 cm), lightly greased, lined with greaseproof paper, brushed with melted butter and dusted with flour.

To decorate

½ pint (275 ml) double cream

The filling

3 × 5.28 oz (150 g) bars Terry's plain chocolate
  – 12 oz (350 g) for the cream, the rest
  reserved to make chocolate curls
4 tablespoons cassis
3 eggs
½ pint (275 ml) double cream
3 tablespoons caster sugar

A bowl that will hold 3 pints (1 ½ litres) of water lined with clingfilm, a plate to fit on top of the sponge and a 4 lb (2 kg) weight – see Summer pudding (page 109)

Whisked sponge

Set the oven to gas mark 6, 400°F 200°C.

Warm the bowl and whisk attachment of the mixer and whisk the eggs and sugar together at a high speed until white, light and fluffy. Sieve the flour with cocoa twice. Place the bowl on a damp tea-towel and, using a metal spoon, fold the flour into the whisked eggs. Spoon the sponge into the prepared tin and bake for 12 minutes until the cake is slightly shrinking from the sides and the centre springy to the touch. Let the sponge and tray cool for a minute. Lay a double layer of greaseproof paper over a cake rack and turn the sponge onto it, carefully peel away the lining and leave until cold.

To store, wrap the cake in the greaseproof paper and completely seal with foil.

To line and fill the sponge

Using a long, thin and sharp knife, slice the sponge in half horizontally. Cut a sponge circle to line the base of the bowl and then cut thin wedges of sponge and place round the sides to form the case. Put to one side with the rest of the sponge while you make the filling.

Break the chocolate into a saucepan, add the cassis and over a very low heat, using a wooden spoon, stir until smooth, and then draw the pan aside. Separate the eggs – the whites into a mixing bowl, the yolks into a jug. Blend the yolks, one at a time, into the cooled chocolate mixture. Pour the cream into a mixing bowl placed on a damp tea-towel to keep it steady, add the sugar and whisk the cream into soft, floppy peaks. Whisk the egg whites until stiff. Using a metal spoon, fold the chocolate into the cream and then fold in the whisked egg whites.

Cut a circle of sponge to cover the top and ladle the chocolate into the mould, layering it with sponge and chocolate, finishing with the round sponge. Cover with clingfilm, place the plate on top and press it down with the weight. Refrigerate overnight.

Chocolate curls

Break the reserved chocolate into pieces and put them closely together on a plate that will lie comfortably over a saucepan. Fill the pan half full of water and bring it to the boil. Turn off the heat and rest the plate on top. Leave the chocolate to melt gently. Put the plate down on a tea-towel as the underneath will be wet, and blend the chocolate together, using a palette knife, until smooth. Pour the chocolate on to a dry formica surface and spread it as evenly as possible. Leave until the chocolate has lost its sheen and, using a paint scraper held at 45° angle to the surface, scrape the chocolate away to form long curls. Keep them carefully sealed in clingfilm in a cool place.

To decorate

Whip the cream until it is thick enough to spread. Place a tablespoon of the cream in the centre of a serving dish to prevent the dessert slipping. Remove the weight, plate and clingfilm. Invert the serving dish over the chocolate, turn the dish and chocolate mould over together and carefully unwrap. With a spatula spread the whipped cream over the sponge, using circular strokes to produce a rippled finish. Arrange the chocolate curls on top.

Variations

Use freshly brewed coffee instead of cassis. Just before adding the whipped cream to the chocolate, fold in almond praline made with 5 oz (150 g) chopped or nibbed nuts, 5 oz (150 g) caster sugar and 1 teaspoon lemon juice, ground to a smooth paste (see page 66).

Forward preparation

The day before

Make

Make and cook the whisked
chocolate sponge.
Stilton sauce.
Assemble the chocolate
dessert and leave it weighted
in the refrigerator.

Prepare

The onions and garlic and
simmer with the herbs in the
wine and water for 30
minutes. Leave to cool, pour it
into a large plastic container
and refrigerate.
Sweetcorn and peanut
mixture. Keep covered with
clingfilm in the refrigerator.
Pour sherry over the sultanas
and leave covered in a cool
place.
Crisp fry the bread cubes,
keep them in an airtight tin
lined with kitchen paper.

The morning

Prepare

The spinach and wash it, wrap
the shredded leaves in a
tea-towel and keep in the
refrigerator.
Wrap the avocado in filo
pastry, slide on to the
prepared baking tray and chill.
Make the chocolate curls,
carefully wrap them in clingfilm
and keep in a cool place.

Early evening

Wash the beansprouts and
leave them to drain in a
colander.
Unmould, unwrap and
decorate the dessert.
Prepare the vegetables and
melon for the casserole.
Pour the flavoured liquid into
a large saucepan, reheat it
before adding the vegetables.
Set the oven to gas mark 7,
425°F, 220°C.

Have ready

Gather together the
ingredients for the sautéed
spinach and beansprouts.
Spoon the hazelnut oil into a
large frying pan.
Stilton sauce in a small
saucepan.
Slice the red pepper into 8
strips.
Pat the sultanas dry, place
them in a mixing bowl, and the
bread cubes and spring onions
close by.

```
┌─────────────────────────────────────────────────────────┐
│                                                           │
│            SAUTÉED SPICED LENTILS                         │
│              with a purée of tomatoes                     │
│                                                           │
│                                                           │
│                  COURGETTES                               │
│     filled with beansprouts, oven baked and served on lemon│
│                       butter                              │
│                                                           │
│          MARINATED MUSHROOM SALAD                         │
│            PLAIN BOILED POTATOES                          │
│                                                           │
│                                                           │
│               CHOCOLATE BOXES                             │
│     filled with mint-flavoured and delicately coloured cheesecake│
│                                                           │
└─────────────────────────────────────────────────────────┘
```

Sautéed spiced lentils with a purée of tomatoes

The brightly coloured tomato sauce provides a moist contrast to the almost dry flavour of lentils.

Spiced lentils

12 oz (350 g) lentils
¾ pint (425 ml) water
1 unpeeled onion with a few cloves pressed
  into the skin
1 medium onion
1½ oz (40 g) butter
2 teaspoons cumin
2 teaspoons coriander
2 teaspoons chopped parsley
Salt and pepper
1 egg yolk
Oil for frying

To coat

Brown breadcrumbs
Flour
2 eggs and 1 egg white

Tomato sauce

2 lb (900 kg) ripe tomatoes
1 medium onion
1½ in (4 cm) celery, sliced from the top and to
  include leaves
4 oz (110 g) butter

1 teaspoon chopped basil
1 teaspoon marjoram leaves
¼ pint (150 ml) dry sherry
½ teaspoon honey
Black pepper

Spiced lentils

Wash the lentils under running cold water. Place them in a large mixing bowl and pour boiling water to cover. Leave to soak for 2 hours, or soak overnight in cold water.

46

Drain the lentils, put them with the measured water in a saucepan and add the clove-studded onion. Bring to a boil, turn down the heat and cover the pan with its lid. Gently simmer the pulses for ½–¾ hour until almost all the water has disappeared and the lentils are soft to the touch. Remove the lid and discard the onion, raise the heat and beat the lentils until completely dry. Spoon the mixture into a mixing bowl.

Top, tail and peel the uncooked onion, remove the first fleshy layer and cut the onion in half lengthways. Cut the halves into small even sized pieces. Heat the butter in a small frying pan and sauté the onion until soft, but not coloured. Mix the onion, butter and herbs with the lentils, taste, add salt and twists of black pepper and taste again. Using a small teaspoon, blend the yolk until smooth and mix it in. If you find your lentil paste too wet to handle and mould, add breadcrumbs to firm. Taste for seasoning again.

Prepare 3 separate dishes of flour, breadcrumbs and eggs beaten together with a pinch of salt. Mould the lentils into 24 balls, then with your finger tips, flatten them into ½ in (1 cm) high-rounds.

Dip each one into the flour and then coat each one with egg. With clean, dry hands, coat them with breadcrumbs, pressing them back into shape as you do so. Lay them on a tray lined with greaseproof paper and chill for at least 1 hour, or overnight.

Tomato sauce

Cut each unpeeled tomato in quarters. Peel and chop the onion finely to enable it to cook evenly with the tomatoes. Chop the celery finely. Melt the butter in a large saucepan, add the onion, tomatoes and celery. Stir them together with a wooden spoon, add the herbs and pour in the sherry. Turn down the heat as low as possible. Cover the vegetables with a sheet of greaseproof paper and put the lid on the saucepan. Cook for 25–30 minutes until tender. Take the saucepan from the heat. Have ready the liquidizer and a small sieve set over a container. Liquidize the cooked vegetables in small batches and pass the purée through the sieve with the help of a wooden spoon.

Taste, stir in the honey and black pepper, taste again. Cover with clingfilm when cold.

To serve

Set the tomato sauce to reheat.

Have ready a tray lined with crumpled kitchen paper. Heat ½ in (1 cm) of oil in a large frying pan and sauté the shaped lentils, a few at a time, until they are crisp and light brown, turning them once during cooking. Drain and keep warm on the tray.

Ladle the warmed sauce to cover the base of each plate and place the lentils on top.

Variation: A stuffing for hollowed-out tomatoes

Prepare and cook the lentils. Add the flavourings and beaten egg yolk. Stir in grated cheese until you have a strength of taste you enjoy. Hollow out tomatoes and fill the shells with the stuffing. Top with breadcrumbs and bake them.

Courgettes filled with beansprouts, oven baked and served on lemon butter

16 large courgettes

Beansprout stuffing

6 oz (175 g) beansprouts
1 medium onion
1 small garlic clove
1 stick of celery
1 small red pepper
2 tablespoons mango chutney
Oil
½ teaspoon grated root ginger
Black pepper
Cayenne pepper
1 egg yolk

Lemon butter

4 oz (110 g) butter
Juice of 1 lemon
Black pepper

Beansprout stuffing

Place the beansprouts in a colander, rinse them in cold water and leave to drain.

Top, tail and peel the onion. Remove the first fleshy layer, cut it in half and chop the halves into small, even shapes. Peel the garlic clove and cut it into slivers. Pull the strings away from the celery stick, then finely chop it. Cut the red pepper in half lengthways, cut away the stem, seeds and pith. Slice the flesh into small, even-sized cubes. Liquidize the mango chutney.

Heat the oil in a frying pan and over a medium heat, sauté the onion and garlic for 2 minutes, stirring them with a wooden spoon. Lower the heat and stir in the ginger, celery and red pepper cubes and cook for a further minute. Draw the pan aside and mix in the mango chutney and beansprouts, gently breaking them down with the spoon as they soften with the heat. Tip the stuffing into a bowl, taste, add cayenne pepper and black pepper. Taste again.

Beat the egg yolk with a fork to blend it together and stir it into the stuffing. Put to one side.

Courgettes

Have ready a large saucepan of lightly salted boiling water. Cut a thin slice away from both ends of each courgette to make them all of a similar size. Hold a trimmed courgette in one hand and, using an apple corer, push it through the centre of the cut end and down as far as it will go. Twist out the central core, throw it away, and push the corer into the other end to complete the tube. Repeat with the rest of the courgettes.

Cook the courgettes 8 at a time for 5 minutes in boiling water. Carefully lift them into a container and run cold water over them. Drain and pat the tubes dry with kitchen paper.

To cook

Set the oven to gas mark 5, 375°F, 190°C. Paint the inside of a large baking tray with melted butter, using a pastry brush. Carefully stuff the hollowed courgettes and arrange them in the baking tray. Cover with buttered greaseproof paper and foil. Cook for 30 minutes, then take the courgettes out of the oven, remove the foil and greaseproof paper.

Lemon butter

In a small frying pan and over a low heat, slowly melt the butter, add the lemon juice and twists of black pepper. Blend together using a wooden spoon.

To serve

Pour a little lemon butter on each plate. Using a fish slice, place the courgettes on top.
   Serve a bowl of plain boiled potatoes at the table accompanied with mushroom salad (see page 93).

Chocolate boxes filled with mint-flavoured and delicately coloured cheesecake

---

Part of the fun of these boxes lies in making them, so allow plenty of time to enjoy the satisfaction of achieving perfect cubes of colour balance. I have found it impossible to measure the amounts of essence and colouring you need for the light-textured cheese filling, as just a drop of essence can flavour the cheese to your liking. The bright colour of green is usually more than pleasing in savoury dishes, a spinach purée for instance, but when the same depth of colour is applied to desserts it is off-putting and garish. If, however, the tinting is delicate, so delicate that you are not aware of it until it is contrasted with dark chocolate, then immediately the colour takes on a clean, cool, mouth-watering appearance.
   A crystallised violet placed on the filling and a pale violet-coloured ribbon wrapped around each box would, I suggest, complete the presentation.

2 x 5.28 oz (150 g) bars of Terry's or Bournville
   plain chocolate
A large sheet of waxed paper

Sponge base

4 oz (110 g) plain flour
A pinch of salt
4 eggs
2 oz (50 g) butter
4 oz (110 g) caster sugar

A baking tin 9 x 13 in (23 x 32.5 cm) (it can be a touch larger, but no smaller), brushed with oil, lined with greaseproof paper, brushed again and dusted with flour.

To decorate

4 tablespoons apricot jam
8 crystallised violets
8 x 15 in (38 cm) lengths of thin violet coloured
   ribbon.

Cheesecake

4 tablespoons water
½ oz (10 g) 1 pkt gelatine
2 eggs
8 oz (225 g) cream cheese
2 oz (50 g) caster sugar
½ pint (275 ml) double cream
Mint essence, to taste
A small amount of green essence to colour

Using double sided tape, secure the waxed paper to a working surface set in a cool area and measure a rectangle 9 × 13 in (23 × 32.5 cm). Break the chocolate on to a plate that will fit comfortably over a large saucepan. Half fill the open pan with water and bring it to the boil. Turn off the heat, place the plate on top and leave until the chocolate melts. Put the plate down on a dry tea-towel as the underneath will be wet, and blend the chocolate together with a palette knife until smooth. Pour the chocolate on to the lined surface and, using a pliable spatula, spread it evenly to cover the marked rectangle. Leave it to set and lose its sheen – about 30 minutes.

Sponge base

Set the oven to gas mark 4, 350°F, 180°C.

Warm the mixer bowl and whisk attachment. Sift the flour and salt together. Break the eggs into a small bowl. Over a low heat slowly melt the butter and pour it into a small jug.

Tip the eggs into the warm bowl, add the sugar and at a high speed, beat until thick, white and fluffy, about 8 minutes. Lower the speed, spoon in a third of the flour, then a third of the butter and add the rest in alternate stages. Allow the mixture to blend and quickly pour the sponge into the prepared tin, smoothing over so that it will cook evenly. Bake for 20 minutes until the sponge feels springy. Leave the tin to cool for a few minutes and then turn it on to a greaseproof-paper-lined cake rack. Peel away the cake lining and leave the sponge on the rack until cold.

Cheesecake

Set the oven to the lowest setting. Put the water into a small saucepan and sprinkle the gelatine evenly over. Leave to soak and melt at the very bottom of the oven.

Separate the eggs, putting the whites into a large mixing bowl and the yolks into the food processor or blender with the cream cheese and sugar. Work until smooth. Set the blender in motion again, pour in the double cream and blend. Drip the essence in, blend and taste. When you have a flavour you enjoy, add a drop of colouring and blend.

Set the mixing bowl over a damp tea-towel and whisk the egg whites until stiff. Start the blender and pour in the melted gelatine. Gently fold the mint-cheese into the egg whites, using a metal spoon, and put to one side.

To assemble, decorate and serve

Use a ruler to mark out 1½ in (4 cm) chocolate squares. With a sharp knife cut the chocolate down into strips and the strips across to make squares. Measure and cut the cake into 8 × 1½ in (4 cm) squares. These form the bases of the boxes. Over a low heat melt the jam and pass it through a sieve. Place each square of sponge on a piece of greaseproof paper. Brush the jam over the top and edges of each cake. Using a palette knife, transfer and gently press a chocolate square upright on to each side of each individual base to make empty boxes. Spoon in the cheesecake to fill them. Slide a fish slice underneath the greaseproof paper, transfer each box onto a tray and refrigerate.

To serve

Place a violet on top, off centre, and tie the ribbons around each box, finishing with a floppy bow. Slide the boxes on to the plates.

The day before

Prepare

Soak lentils.

Make

Tomato sauce.
Breadcrumbs.
Mushroom salad (see page
93).
Chocolate squares. Place the
set squares in an airtight tin
and a cool place.
They will keep for 2 days
without discolouration.
The sponge may be made the
day before, but try not to
squash the texture when
completely sealing it to store.

The morning

Prepare

Potatoes.
Courgettes, cook and drain
them. Keep the courgettes
refrigerated on a
kitchen-paper-lined tray and
covered with clingfilm.
Lemon butter.

Make

Sponge if not made earlier.
Spiced lentils. Place the
breadcrumbed shapes on
greaseproof paper and chill.
Beansprout stuffing and chill.
Cheesecake – and have fun
assembling the boxes!

Early evening

Fill the courgettes and set
them ready to cook.
Spoon the mushrooms into a
large bowl.

Have ready

Potatoes to cook.
Tomato sauce in a small pan.
Oil in a frying pan.
Crumpled kitchen paper on a
tray.
The oven set to gas mark 5,
375°F, 190°C.
Lemon butter in a small pan.
Using a fish slice, slide the
boxes on to plates and keep
them cool.
Violets and ribbons close by.

CAULIFLOWER CURRY
garnished with toasted coconut and sultanas

MARROWS
filled with a nutty stuffing baked in light white wine garnished
with yellow pepper purée

FRENCH BEANS
LIGHTLY COOKED CARROTS

SALAD
with Stilton dressing

PINEAPPLE UPSIDE-DOWN CAKE
CHOCOLATE SAUCE

Cauliflower curry, garnished with toasted coconut and sultanas

2 onions
3 tablespoons olive oil
1 teaspoon grated fresh ginger
1 teaspoon coriander
½ teaspoon turmeric
½ teaspoon ground cloves

24 trimmed cauliflower florets
¼ pint (150 ml) dry sherry
2 oz (50 g) creamed coconut
3 fl oz (75 ml) double cream
Black pepper and salt
Lemon juice

Garnish

4 oz (110 g) sultanas, soaked in water overnight
   and then dried on kitchen paper
1 tablespoon chopped mint
2–3 tablespoons toasted coconut
Butter to fry sultanas

Peel the onions, cut them in half lengthways, and then across into thin slices. Heat the oil in a large saucepan, add the onions, cook gently for a few minutes and then stir in the grated ginger, coriander, turmeric, cloves and lastly cauliflower. Mix well to coat the florets with colour and flavouring. Pour in the sherry and cook over a low heat for 10 minutes, when the cauliflower should be just tender. Now stir in the creamed coconut and cream. Taste, add twists of black pepper, a touch of salt and lemon juice. Taste again and bring the curry slowly to the boil, stirring gently.

   Sauté the sultanas in a little butter and keep warm.

To serve

Mix the toasted coconut with the chopped mint.

Place three cauliflower florets on each plate and pour the liquid over them, arrange the plump sultanas around one side of the plate and spoon the mint and coconut over the cauliflower. Serve immediately.

Marrows filled with a nutty stuffing baked in light white wine, garnished with yellow pepper purée

A large oval platter spread with a glaze of yellow pepper purée, marrows gently shaped to follow the curve of the dish and then, in the centre, vegetables piled high, produces a pleasing, colourful meal. The moistness of the marrow contrasts perfectly with a garnish of crisp, golden-brown cubes of bread.

2 medium sized marrows
1 oz (25 g) butter
½ pint (275 ml) white wine

Stuffing

8 sticks of celery
2 onions
12 oz (350 g) button mushrooms
1 avocado
3 firm tomatoes
1 oz (25 g) butter to cook celery and onions
2 teaspoons yeast extract
8 oz (225 g) mixed nuts roughly chopped.
  Brazils, almonds and a few walnuts are a
  good choice, not too many walnuts as they
  can be overpowering and slightly bitter
2 teaspoons mixed herbs
4 oz (110 g) brown breadcrumbs
2 eggs, beaten

Garnish
Day-old brown bread
Oil for frying

Yellow pepper purée

6 yellow peppers
1 onion
2 oz (50 g) butter
¼ pint (150 ml) medium sherry

Crisp garnish

Fry ½ in (1 cm) cubes of day-old brown bread in oil until golden. Drain them on a tray lined with kitchen paper and then store them in a paper-lined airtight tin.

Nutty stuffing

Cut the celery into cubes. Peel and roughly chop the onions, put them in the food processor/blender and chop them finely. Wipe the mushrooms, using a damp cloth and cut them into thin slices. Peel the avocado with a stainless steel knife and then cut into cubes. Remove the stalks from the tomatoes to loosen their skins and place them in a small bowl. Pour boiling water over, count to ten, tip away the hot water and replace with cold. Peel each tomato and then cut into four, remove the seeds and slice the flesh into long strips.

Heat 1 oz (25 g) butter in a frying pan and gently cook the onions and celery until soft. Turn them into a mixing bowl and stir in the yeast extract. Mix in the mushrooms, avocado, nuts, tomato strips, herbs and breadcrumbs. Taste for seasoning and fold in the beaten eggs.

Heat the oven to gas mark 4, 350°F, 180°C.

Marrow

Peel the marrows, cut them in half lengthways and, using a metal spoon, scoop out the seeds. Have ready a large saucepan of boiling salted water and cook the halves two at a time on a low heat for 2–3 minutes. Drain them thoroughly and lay the marrow on kitchen paper.

Fill the marrow halves with the nut stuffing and reshape. Tie them up with tape or string, looping at 2 in (5 cm) intervals. I use tape as it will not cut into the flesh.

Heat 1 oz (25 g) of butter in a roasting tin that will hold the marrows comfortably, put in the prepared marrows and pour the wine over. Cover the marrows with greaseproof paper and foil and cook for 25 minutes. Remove the paper and foil, spoon the cooking-liquid over the marrows and return to cook for a further 30 minutes until tender, basting occasionally.

Pepper purée

Make the pepper purée while the marrows are cooking. Cut each pepper in half, cut away their stems and remove their seeds and pith, slice the flesh into even sized cubes.

Peel the onion, slice it in half and cut it into pieces about the same size as the peppers; this will ensure even cooking. Melt the butter in a saucepan and, over a low heat, gently cook the onion, add the peppers and pour in the sherry. Give the vegetables a good stir and then cover them with a sheet of greaseproof paper and the saucepan lid. Turn down the heat as low as possible and cook for 30 minutes until tender. Liquidize into a purée and, with the aid of a wooden spoon, push it through a sieve. Taste and season.

To serve

Strain the cooking liquid from the marrows into a saucepan and reduce by half. Untie the marrows and keep warm. Add the purée to the reduced wine and bring it slowly to the boil. Taste in case any extra seasoning is needed and then pour it to cover the base of a large serving dish, serving the rest of the sauce in a jug. Set the marrows on top, bending them slightly to follow the curve of the dish. Then spoon crisply cooked carrots in the centre with French beans and put the fried bread garnish on top.

Follow with a salad tossed with Stilton dressing.

Variations

Tint homemade pasta to a gentle colour using tomato purée. Serve the marrows on tomato sauce and in the centre arrange butter-tossed pink noodles. Again the crisp fried bread cubes will provide contrast of texture.

The stuffing can be baked in a lightly buttered dish, turned out and served on perhaps a sherry and cream sauce.

Pineapple upside-down cake

Topping	Sponge
1 small pineapple	8 oz (225 g) self-raising flour
2½ oz (60 g) butter	½ teaspoon salt
4 tablespoons brown sugar	2 teaspoons ground ginger
	½ teaspoon grated nutmeg
	8 oz (225 g) soft butter
	8 oz (225 g) caster sugar
	Grated rind and juice of 1 lemon
	4 eggs

1 deep 10 in (25 cm) baking tray

Preheat the oven to gas mark 4, 350°F, 180°C.

First prepare the topping. Peel the pineapple and then cut across into rings, remove the core and cut each slice in half. Cream the butter and sugar together and, using a spatula, spread it over the bottom of the dish. Arrange the sliced pineapple on top to form a neat overlapping layer.

Sponge

Sieve the flour and add the salt and spices.

Put the butter, sugar, lemon rind and juice into a large mixing bowl, rest the bowl on a damp tea-towel and using a wooden spoon, cream until fluffy with air and almost white in colour. Beat in the eggs one at a time, making sure each egg is thoroughly mixed in before you add the next. Tip in the spiced flour and fold in, using a metal spoon.

Using a spatula, spread the mixture evenly over the pineapple and cook for 40–45 minutes until the sponge feels bouncy and begins to shrink from the sides of the dish. The cake is cooked when a needle, inserted into the centre, comes out clean.

Leave the cake to cool and settle for 10 minutes, then place a large serving plate upside down over the cake, invert the two and carefully lift away the dish. Rearrange pieces of pineapple that may have come adrift.

To serve

Serve the cake warm. Tie a small bunch of mint together with a long ribbon of lemon rind and place this simple but effective decoration on the plate. Pour the hot chocolate sauce over each portion at the table. For hot chocolate sauce recipe see pineapple and melon oatmeal meringue (page 191).

Forward preparation

The day before

Prepare

Soak sultanas.
Breadcrumbs.
Check you have chocolate sauce.
Toast coconut.
Cut bread into cubes, crisp fry and when cold wrap in kitchen paper and put in an airtight tin.

Make

Yellow pepper purée.
Stilton dressing.

The morning

Prepare

Stuffing, except for the avocado; mix it in just before cooking.
Blanch the marrow, keep covered with clingfilm in the refrigerator.
Carrots and beans.

Lettuce for the salad – keep the leaves in polythene bags.
Pineapple upside-down cake. Mix the sugar and butter topping, spread it over the base of the cooking tin and layer pineapple slices on top.

Collect all the ingredients, equipment and garnishes together in preparation to cook cauliflower curry.
Work out your cooking times for the evening.

Early evening

Set the oven to gas mark 4, 350°F, 180°C.
About 2 hours before the main course is due to be served, mix the sponge and spread it over the pineapple. Set it in the preheated oven.
Chop the avocado and mix it with the stuffing. Fill the marrows, re-shape and tie them up. Prepare them for cooking.
When the sponge is cooked, take it out and in its place start to cook the marrow.

Let the cake cool and settle, then turn it out.
Have the mint, lemon ribbon and jug for sauce close by.
Prepare the salad. The dressing will need to be whisked just before serving.

Have ready

Saucepan, sieve and pepper purée.
Chocolate sauce to heat.

Start to cook the curry.

Leek and Coriander Soup

Boned Chicken
filled with a light pork forcemeat cooked on a bed of oranges,
sliced on to a Madeira sauce and garnished with apricot purée

SLICED WHITE CABBAGE WITH BACON
COURGETTES

A CAKE COATED WITH CHOCOLATE ICING
AND FILLED WITH CHOCOLATE GANACHE

Leek and coriander soup

2 lb (900 g) leeks
½ lb (225 g) onions
4 oz (110 g) butter
2 tablespoons dried powdered coriander

½ pint (275 ml) medium dry sherry
3 pints (1.5 litres) chicken stock
Salt and pepper to finish
1 teaspoon honey

Trim away the roots and very dark green leaves of each leek. Wash the trimmed leeks to remove any grit and then cut them crossways into thin slices. Top and tail the unpeeled onions and cut them in half vertically. Cut the halves across into thin slices. If you try to make the slices about the same size as the leeks you will find the soup will then cook evenly.

Melt the butter in a large saucepan, add the onions and cook until transparent, but not coloured. Add the leeks, coriander and sherry. Give the vegetables a good stir.

Turn down the heat as low as possible. Cover the vegetables with a sheet of greaseproof paper and put the lid on the saucepan. Cook for about 40–45 minutes, until tender. Take the saucepan from the heat and pour in the chicken stock.

Have ready by the liquidizer, a plastic container. You need one large enough to hold the soup and allow the sieve to rest on top. I find a gallon ice-cream container, with lid, perfect.

Ladle the soup, a little at a time, into the liquidizer and work until smooth. Pour the purée through the sieve into the container and stir with a wooden spoon.

Taste. Add salt and pepper and stir in the honey.

Let the soup completely cool and then refrigerate until ready to reheat.

Preparing chicken

To cook a plain roast chicken for 8 people, you need to buy an oven ready chicken weighing 5 lb (2.25 kg) or up to 8 lb (3.5 kg) if you want some left over for later use. Wash the chicken under cold water and dab it dry with a cloth. Carefully remove the wishbone, it will make carving easier. I often put a quartered unpeeled apple inside, to add moisture and flavour. This also works well with turkey but you will need more than one apple. Spread butter over the skin to help it crisp during cooking.

I tend to cook chickens at a constant heat – gas mark 3, 325°F, 170°C. A 5 lb (2.25 kg) bird will usually take 2 hours. Divide the cooking time into four. For the first quarter cook the chicken breast side down, the second on one side, the third the other side and lastly, breast side upwards. Baste the bird each time you turn it. To make sure the bird is cooked, pierce the thigh with a skewer; the juices should run clear. If not, cook a little longer.

Place the chicken on to a warm serving dish and allow the meat to rest for 15 minutes, while you make the gravy. Add ½ pint (275 ml) chicken stock to the cooking juices in the baking tray and bring to the boil. Skim off any surface fat. Stir in a little brown sauce to thicken and colour slightly. Season to taste and if you wish add 2 fl oz (55 ml) medium dry sherry. Whisk until smooth and strain into a jug.

Boned chicken, filled with a light pork forcemeat, cooked on a bed of oranges, sliced on to a Madeira sauce and garnished with apricot purée

As with learning any skill, poultry-boning becomes easy with care and practice. Although it looks difficult it is really straightforward. You require only patience and a sharp knife.

I am sure you will enjoy boning any poultry and filling it with layers of different stuffings to make the dish look spectacular with the first slice. A boned and stuffed bird, cooked and served cold, is very good for a buffet. Sliced, as you would a loaf of bread, there are no carving problems.

1 5 lb (2.25 kg) chicken, boned
4 boned and skinned chicken breasts
3 oranges, sliced
Greaseproof paper
Foil
String and needle

Pork forcemeat

1 lb (450 g) trimmed pork fillet
7 fl oz (205 ml) double cream
Salt and pepper and grated nutmeg

Madeira sauce

2 oz (50 g) butter
1 onion, chopped but not peeled
1 bay leaf
1 teaspoon chopped thyme
12 fl oz (330 ml) Madeira
1 pint (570 ml) beef stock
¼ pint (150 ml) brown sauce (see page 209)
½ oz (10 g) butter to finish

Apricot purée

This is delicious served with any poultry and meat. It will keep covered in the refrigerator for a week and freezes well. Serve it cold with toast at breakfast.

1 ½ lb (700 g) fresh apricots. If you have to use dried, soak them in water with a few lemon slices overnight.
½ pint (275 ml) white wine

2 teaspoons brown sugar
Juice of 1 lemon
1 teaspoon curry powder

The boning

Remove any trussing string. Straighten out the wings. Cut the skin free at the bottom of the legs. With your fingers, find the wishbone and carefully cut it away. Place the chicken, breast-side down on to a board. With a sharp-pointed knife, cut the skin down the centre of the underside of the chicken. Cut away the flesh and skin from the carcass, holding the meat away as you work towards the leg joint. With your fingers, feel for the sinew between the ball and socket joint that joins the bone to the carcass and cut through it. Keeping the knife edge against the carcass, work your way towards the bone and cut through to release it. Repeat this process on the other side.

Again, keep the knife edge against the ribs, cut away the breast on both sides. Then carefully cut free the flesh from over the breastbone. This perhaps is the most difficult part as you want to end up with both sides of the chicken attached. Lift away the carcass and lay the chicken out flat.

Legs: Hold the end of the joint in one hand and push it up towards you so you can see the end of the bone. Cut away the flesh, scraping the thighbone clean. Put down the knife and pull the bone out. Repeat the same process with the other leg.

Wings: Cut each wing off at the centre joint, scrape around the rest of the bone and pull out.

Pork forcemeat

Chop the trimmed pork fillet and place it in the blender. Work until the meat is smooth and add the seasoning. Set the blender in motion again and gradually pour in the cream. When the cream is completely mixed in, spoon the forcemeat into a bowl. Cover with clingfilm and chill.

To prepare and cook

Lay the boned chicken out flat. Carefully remove the breasts without cutting the skin and put them with the other trimmed breasts.

Cut away the rest of the flesh from the leg and wing area, trim this and mix into the forcemeat.

Cut the small fillets away from the 6 breasts and put to one side. Lay 3 chicken breasts down the centre of the skin, lengthways. Top them with the forcemeat, smoothing it out with wet hands to form a long sausage. Press 3 of the small fillets lengthways on either side of the sausage and arrange the other breasts on top of the shaped forcemeat to cover and enclose.

Cut the sides of the skin so they will overlap slightly down the centre of the breasts. Tuck and fold in the skin at both ends to cover the meat and sew the bird neatly together. Tie around with string, looping it at ½ in (1 cm) intervals; it will then keep its shape during cooking.

Cutting the breasts and spreading the stuffing as I have described will ensure the bird is cooked evenly and every slice will look similar.

Weigh the bird and calculate the cooking time, allowing 25 minutes to the 1 lb (½ kg). Lay a piece of foil, large enough to wrap up the chicken, in a baking dish and cover the foil with a sheet of greaseproof paper. Put a line of orange slices down the centre. Brush the chicken with a little melted butter and place it on top of the oranges, sewn side down. Arrange the rest of the slices on top. Wrap the chicken up and fold the edges over to seal. Bake in the centre of the oven at gas mark 3, 325°F, 170°C. Be careful when you unwrap the parcel; the steam will be very hot.

The rolled chicken will be cooked if the centre feels very firm. Do not pierce the skin at this stage as you will see there is a lot of juice bubbling underneath; leave it to settle for a minute or two, then use a skewer to check that the juices are clear.

After resting the chicken for 15 minutes, gently lift it on to a board and untie the string. Cut off and discard a thin slice at either end, then slide the bird on to the serving dish, pouring a little of the cooking juices over. If the cooked orange slices still look good, arrange 3 of them to one side with a sprig of parsley for colour.

Serve the Madeira sauce and apricot purée separately.

Variation: A boned duck filled with pork forcemeat

1 5 lb (2.25 kg) duck	Pork forcemeat
2 single duck breasts or 2 boned and skinned	
chicken breasts	

Bone and prepare the duck, using the same method as for chicken.

Set the oven to gas mark 5, 375°F, 190°C. Cover a wire rack with foil and, using a fingertip, push 4 or 5 holes through and rest it on a baking tray. Place the duck on the covered rack. To give the skin an appetising golden glaze, brush the surface with a mixture of melted butter and honey.

Cook for 1 hour, turning the bird once. Check that the juices run clear, transfer the duck to a dish and leave it to rest and settle. Scoop the fat away from the roasting juices that have collected in the tray and then you have a delicious base left for gravy.

Madeira sauce

Melt the butter in a saucepan and lightly cook the onion, add the bay leaf, thyme and Madeira, bring to the boil and then, on a low heat, reduce by half. Pour in the brown beef stock and reduce by a third. Stir in the brown sauce and slowly bring to the boil. Strain into a jug.

When ready to serve, heat the Madeira sauce through and whisk in the butter to give a lovely sheen.

Apricot purée

Cut the apricots in half, remove the stones and wrap them in muslin. Put the apricots with the parcel of stones in a saucepan, pour in the wine, add the sugar and cook over a low heat until tender. Stir in the lemon juice and curry powder.

Leave the apricots to cool a little, then take out the stones. Liquidize the apricots and juices and pass them through a sieve for a smooth purée.

Sliced white cabbage with bacon

1 white cabbage	2 teaspoons red wine vinegar
8 oz (225 g) bacon	Salt, black pepper
1–2 tablespoons sunflower oil	

Peel away any blemished outer leaves of the cabbage. Slice the cabbage in half and cut away the hard core. Shred the cabbage as finely as you can, or use the vegetable slicer on the food processor.

Cut away the rind of the bacon. Cut the bacon into strips and fry in a large frying pan until crisp, adding a little oil if there is not enough fat from the bacon. Take the pan off the heat and add the vinegar, cabbage, salt and pepper. Return to a high heat. Fry for 4 to 5 minutes, shaking the pan and stirring often. Serve immediately.

A cake coated with chocolate icing and filled with chocolate ganache

This is a classic filling and if you love chocolate there is none better.

1 10 in (25.5 cm) diameter chocolate cake. For this recipe it needs only to be 1 in (2.5 cm) thick. I usually make an average sized cake, slice it horizontally and use one half, spread with jam, for tea.

1 10 in (25.5) cm cake tin.

Chocolate ganache

8 oz (250 g) plain chocolate, Bournville or Terry's
8 fl oz (¼ litre) double cream

Chop the chocolate in small pieces and put it with the cream into a large saucepan. Stir it with a wooden spoon over a low heat for 10 minutes until dark and smooth, but do not allow the chocolate to boil. Pour the mixture into a bowl. Chill for at least an hour or, better still, overnight.

Tip the chilled chocolate cream into the mixer bowl and whisk it at a high speed for 5 minutes until the chocolate has doubled in volume. The colour will now be pale and the texture fluffy. If you whisk by hand, it will take about 15 minutes. While the chocolate is whisking, lightly grease the inside of the cake tin and line it with plenty of clingfilm.

Cut the cake in half horizontally and lay one piece at the bottom of the tin. Spoon the ganache on top and spread it smooth. Place the other slice of the cake on top. Cover with clingfilm and chill for about 2 hours, to allow the filling to firm up.

Chocolate icing

4 tablespoons of strong freshly made coffee
6 oz (175 g) plain chocolate
1 oz (25 g) butter

Pour the coffee into a saucepan and place over a low heat, break the chocolate into the pan and add the butter. Stir with a wooden spoon until smooth and do not let it boil.

Pour the icing into a jug and leave it to cool for just under an hour.

To serve

Unmould the cake, peel away the clingfilm and place the cake on a serving dish. Pour the cooled chocolate icing over to cover the top and let it fall down the sides.

The cake needs very little decoration; a small cluster of crystallized violets to set off the centre is simple but elegant.

The day before

Prepare

White cabbage. Use a stainless steel knife for shredding it and keep in a bowl, sealed with clingfilm.

Make

Soup and chill.
Pork forcemeat.
Madeira sauce.
Apricot purée.
Chocolate cake.
Chocolate ganache.

The morning

Prepare

Bone and fill the chicken. Calculate cooking time – 25 minutes per pound (½ kg). Lay it ready in the foil parcel, but do not seal.

Make

Whip up the chocolate ganache and put the cake together. Refrigerate. Chocolate icing and leave at room temperature.

Early evening

Unmould the cake, pour the icing over and decorate – keep in a cool place.
Seal the chicken completely with foil, ready to cook.
Fry the bacon until crisp and leave in the frying pan until you are ready to sauté the cabbage.
Have the soup, Madeira sauce and apricot purée ready in the saucepan.
Cut the courgettes thinly and have them ready in the vegetable-basket to cook at the last minute, as they take only seconds to cook when plunged into boiling water.

SAUTÉED SCALLOP AND VEGETABLE SALAD
garnished with coral mayonnaise

CHICKEN BREAST
filled with chestnut and grapes, wrapped around with bacon,
oven baked, sliced on to sherry and cream

GREEN SALAD WITH HERBS AND FRENCH DRESSING

LIGHTLY COOKED CAULIFLOWER FLORETS
NEW POTATOES

A RICH CHOCOLATE CREAM WITH ALMOND PRALINE

Sautéed scallop and vegetable salad garnished with coral mayonnaise

Once you have prepared and gathered all the ingredients together, this is an elegant last-minute sauté dish, which is very light and clean in appearance. Make sure you have everyone sitting at the table, waiting, as it must be served immediately.

The carrots are good for colour, but it is not imperative to use mangetout as I have. Leeks are also very good and, like the carrots, should be blanched. Do try thinly sliced white cabbage or beansprouts instead but there is no need to blanch these.

Brown breadcrumbs and butter	Black pepper
24 scallops, defrosted overnight if frozen	4 carrots
5 fl oz (150 ml) stock or wine to cook the corals	24 mangetout
5 fl oz (150 ml) hazelnut oil	Chopped spring onions and parsley to garnish

Sauté the breadcrumbs using plenty of butter (they seem to absorb a surprising amount) until they are crisp and brown. If you want to add extra flavour, add a crushed garlic clove.

Cut the corals away from the white muscle and prick them with a needle to stop them bursting while cooking. Carefully remove the thin white skin around the scallop and cut each scallop into 3, downwards, with the grain.

Gently poach 8 of the corals in a little stock or wine, drain and put to one side for the mayonnaise.

Sprinkle a little of the hazelnut oil over the scallops, season with pepper, cover with clingfilm and chill.

Peel the carrots and cut them into thin 2 in (5 cm) strips, put them into the vegetable-basket; then into boiling water. As soon as the water returns to the boil, lift the basket out and dip the carrots into cold water. Drain and dry on kitchen paper. Repeat with the mangetout.

Now make the coral mayonnaise.

Coral mayonnaise

½ teaspoon root ginger, grated
8 cooked scallop corals
½ pint (275 ml) mayonnaise
½ teaspoon chilli powder

1 clove of garlic, crushed
Salt and pepper
½ teaspoon coriander

I find it easy to keep peeled root ginger cut into about 1 in (2.5 cm) cubes in the deep freeze. Grate it while it is still frozen. It works very well.

Cut the corals in half and with a wooden spoon pass them through a fine sieve. Mix them with the rest of the ingredients until smooth.

Keep the mayonnaise chilled.

To cook and serve

Heat the hazelnut oil in a large frying pan, add the sliced scallops and cook for a few seconds, shaking the pan to keep them moving. When they turn white, tip in the carrots and mangetout. Carefully and quickly mix them in until they are hot. Take the pan away from the heat, then add the spring onions and parsley.

Spoon on to the plates and scatter the buttered crumbs over. You can either put a little of the scallop mayonnaise on the plates or serve it at the table. Don't try to arrange the scallops and vegetables. Just tip them out of the pan with the help of a large spoon, so they fall into the centre of the plates.

Chicken breasts filled with chestnut and grapes, wrapped around with bacon, oven baked, sliced on to sherry and cream

To wrap chicken breasts in smoked bacon, and then to oven bake them gives the flesh a delicate flavour, which is complimented by chestnuts and grapes. I like to serve them with sherry and cream, but you may prefer lemon butter (see page 49).

Stuffing

12 oz (350 g) unsweetened chestnut purée
Salt and pepper
8 oz (225 g) seedless grapes
1 teaspoon dry sherry

8 chicken breasts
8 to 10 rashers of smoked long back bacon
Oil to sauté
8 sheets of foil
Small bunches of grapes for garnish

Sherry and cream sauce

8 fl oz (220 ml) double cream
½ pint (275 ml) dry sherry
2 oz (50 g) butter

2–3 tablespoons Worcestershire sauce
Black pepper

To make the stuffing beat the chestnut purée until smooth, add the seasoning and sherry, then fold in the grapes. Remove the skin from the chicken, cut away the wings and gently slice the breast from the bone. Trim off any fat and the little white thread from the fillet. Lay the breast on the table and put your hand flat on the breast so it doesn't move, while you cut a deep horizontal slice along the thick edge of the breast with a sharp, pointed knife. Be careful not to go through to the other side.

Fill with the stuffing and press the edges of the pocket together with your fingertips. Roll the breast sealing in the stuffing, so it looks like a sausage.

Take the rind off the bacon and stretch each rasher a little with the blunt edge of a knife. Roll the bacon around the breast, slightly overlapping each roll. This may take a little practice to do, but by the time you have got to the last one it should be easier. Try to make sure the ends are covered with bacon. Tie the breasts up with string so they keep their shape during cooking.

Heat ¼ in (5 mm) depth of oil in a frying pan and on a high heat seal the breasts 4 at a time.

Shape each sheet of foil to make a tray with ½ in (1 cm) lip to hold one chicken breast. Arrange the filled trays on a baking tray as far away from each other as possible. Chill for one hour or more.

Sherry and cream sauce

To make the sauce, heat the butter in a small frying pan and when it is very hot, pour in the sherry. Stand back, it may flame at this stage, but don't worry. Reduce until the sauce thickens. Add the Worcestershire sauce and black pepper, pour in the cream, and mix well together and reduce again. It should now be thick and creamy, medium brown in colour.

To cook and serve

Set the oven to gas mark 7, 425°F, 220°C. Bake the chicken breasts for 20 minutes, turning after 10 minutes. Take the breasts out of the oven, cut away the string and let them rest a little.

Gently reheat the sauce.

Cut each breast into 3 at an angle. Pour the sauce on to the plates, arrange the slices on top and garnish with a small bunch of grapes.

As the chicken with chestnut has a mild flavour, I suggest you serve it with a green salad that has been flavoured with chopped chives, watercress, tarragon and garlic.

Variations

Make cream cheese and herb pâté, using the method described in the recipe for chopped lamb (see page 138). While the pâté is still soft, mix in fine strips of smoked ham, divide the mixture into eight sausage shapes and chill. Fill the chicken pockets with the firm pâté, then wrap in bacon.

A rich chocolate cream with almond praline

This is a very rich and delicious dessert, so don't be tempted to serve too much.

To make the cream look as good as it tastes, set it in a bowl lined with lightly greased clingfilm. Turn it out and pour chocolate over to give a beautiful shiny coat. Decorate with almond-flake flowers.

Praline

5 oz (150 g) caster sugar
1 teaspoon lemon juice
5 oz (150 g) chopped/nibbed nuts

Chocolate cream

18 oz (500 g) plain chocolate – Bournville is
  very good
Juice and grated rind of 1 orange with strong
  coffee added to make up to 7½ fl oz (210 ml)
4½ oz (125 g) butter
15 fl oz (425 ml) double cream

Chocolate coating

2 oz (50 g) butter
8 oz (225 g) plain chocolate
5 tablespoons of strong coffee

Praline

Put the sugar into a small heavy-based saucepan. Set it on a very low heat until the sugar has melted, but resist the temptation to stir it; this was one of my first mistakes. Have the lemon juice to hand, and when the sugar turns golden brown in colour, pour it in. Take the pan off the heat and stir in the nuts.

Brush a thin layer of oil onto a large flat baking tray and spread the praline over it. It will now be cool enough for you to pull it apart into small pieces. Leave it to harden.

Put the praline in a plastic bag, wrap the bag in a tea-towel and using a rolling pin, crush the praline coarsely. The bag and teatowel will stop the praline flying everywhere.

Store in an airtight container.

Chocolate cream

Having made the praline, you come to the easy part.

Break the chocolate into a saucepan, add the coffee and orange. Melt over a low heat until smooth. Remove the pan from the heat. Add small pieces of butter a little at a time, stirring until blended with the chocolate. Leave to cool, then add the praline.

Whip the cream in a large mixing bowl until it forms soft peaks. Pour in the cooled chocolate and fold in with a metal spoon. When you have mixed them together, spoon it into the prepared bowl and refrigerate.

Leave for at least 2 hours to set.

Chocolate coating

Use this to coat cakes, biscuits or eclairs. As you should use the chocolate straight away, have the cake ready.

Chop the butter into small pieces.

Break the chocolate into a small saucepan and add the coffee. Place over a low heat and stir until melted and smooth. Take off the heat and whisk in the butter, little by little. Pour the icing over the cake slowly and spread it over, using a spatula.

Keep the cake in a cool place, not in the refrigerator, otherwise it will lose the lovely shine.

Forward preparation

The day before

Prepare

Scallops.
Cook the corals.
Breadcrumbs, keep in a plastic bag in the refrigerator.

Make

Chocolate and praline cream.
Mayonnaise.

The morning

Prepare

Blanch the vegetables for scallop salad.
Chicken breasts ready to bake.
Chop the herbs for the salad and keep sealed with clingfilm.
Chop the spring onions and parsley for the scallops. Seal also.

Make

Coral mayonnaise.
Sauté the breadcrumbs.

Early evening

Turn out the cream and coat with chocolate.
Make sherry and cream sauce, pour into a jug ready to reheat.
Prepare the green salad, sprinkle the herbs over, but leave the dressing till the last minute.
Potatoes ready to cook.
Cauliflower florets in the vegetable-basket.
Hazelnut oil ready in a frying pan.
The oven set to gas mark 7, 425°F, 220°C for the chicken.

GRAPEFRUIT WITH MINT ICE

CHICKEN BREASTS
spread with crabmeat, cooked in puff pastry and served on a
smooth curry sauce

BRAISED CELERY HEARTS
SAUTÉED RICE AND CAULIFLOWER

STILTON AND PEAR MOUSSE
BISCUITS
SELECTION OF NUTS
AND A GLASS OF PORT

Grapefruit with mint ice

A clean tasting and appetising beginning.

1 pint (570 ml) water
6 oz (175 g) caster sugar
Grated rind and juice of 3 limes

8 grapefruit

3 handfuls of mint leaves
2½ fl oz (60 ml) creme de menthe
2 egg whites

To serve
8 small, neat sprigs of mint

Combine the water, sugar and lime juice in a saucepan. Bring gently to a boil and simmer for 5 minutes. Draw the pan to one side, stir in the mint leaves, rind and creme de menthe. Leave the mint to mingle with the syrup for 10 minutes, then pour the liquid through a sieve into a bowl. Lightly press the rind and leaves with a wooden spoon to ensure all the flavours pass into the bowl. Taste for sweetness.

To make the initial freezing process quicker, pour the mint liquid into two shallow plastic trays and place them in the freezer. After an hour the liquid will be frozen around the edges; using a fork, mix it into the liquid and return the trays to the freezer. Repeat this process every 30 minutes two or three times, until the mixture has an even, slushy consistency.

Tip the egg whites into a large mixing bowl set on a damp tea-towel and whisk them until they form soft, floppy peaks.

Using a plastic spatula, quickly scrape the ice into the blender and work briefly until smooth, then pour it on to the floppy peaks. With a metal spoon, fold the whites from the bottom of the bowl over to the top and continue folding until you have an evenly coloured mixture.

Transfer the ice to an ice cream container that has a lid, cover the surface with

68

clingfilm and rest the lid on top. Return the mint ice to the freezer and allow 4 hours to set.

Grapefruit

Using a stainless steel knife, cut a thin slice from the top and bottom of the grapefruit to show the flesh. Place the fruit, cut side down on a board, hold it steady with your fingertips and slice away the skin in vertical strips to reveal the fruit. Trim away any remaining pith. One at a time, hold a grapefruit over a bowl and cut down both sides of each segment, close to the membrane, releasing the fruit.

To serve

On each plate, arrange the segments to form a neat open fan of translucent grapefruit and set them on larger, napkin-lined plates. Using light, even pressure, run a tablespoon over the surface of the ice to form pale green curls and transfer them to rest at one side of the fan; tuck a sprig of mint underneath the smaller plate and serve.

Chicken breasts spread with crabmeat, cooked in puff pastry and served on a smooth curry sauce

To wrap and seal plump white chicken and crabmeat together will encourage a delicate merging of flavours. To provide a lively complementary contrast, they are served on a smooth curry sauce.

8 skinned and boned and completely trimmed
   chicken breasts
2 oz (50 g) butter

1 lb (450 g) puff pastry
1 egg
Salt

Crabmeat stuffing

5 oz (150 g) white crabmeat
5 oz (150 g) brown crabmeat
1 teaspoon chopped marjoram leaves
1 teaspoon lemon juice
1 egg yolk
Black pepper

Garnish
1 lemon
Cayenne pepper

Curry sauce

2 oz (50 g) butter
1 onion, chopped
1 small garlic clove, peeled and chopped
1 tablespoon curry powder
4 tablespoons mango chutney
1 apple, chopped
1 banana, sliced
½ pint (275 ml) dry white wine
2 slices of lemon
1 teaspoon peanut butter
Double cream or chicken stock

W. H. HARVEY & SONS

Crabmeat stuffing

Place the white and brown crabmeat in a mixing bowl, add the marjoram, lemon juice, egg yolk and twist of black pepper. Using a wooden spoon, carefully blend in the flavourings.

Chicken

Peel the skin from each breast and place one, skinned side up, on a board. Feel for the wish bone and using a sharp pointed knife, cut away the flesh to uncover it completely and gently pull it out. Cut through the flesh to one side of the breast bone and cutting against the bone, slice off the breast, leaving the wing behind. Repeat with the other breasts. Trim off the fat and the white thread from the small fillet.

In a large frying pan, slowly melt the butter and when it is bubbling gently add the breasts, four at a time. Lightly seal them and using a spatula and your fingertips, turn the chicken over to seal the other sides. Lift them with the spatula, transfer them to a kitchen-paper-lined tray and leave to cool.

Cut each chicken breast in half widthways, place one half on top of the other and trim the ends until they are neatly paired. Lift away the top halves, spread crabmeat over the revealed surfaces and gently replace the chicken. Divide and spoon the remaining mixture over the tops.

On a floured surface, roll out the pastry as thin as possible. Using your thumb and fingertips as a ruler, cut the pastry into 8 rectangles just over 3½ times the width and twice the length of each chicken portion. For each pastry parcel, lay the rectangle with the short end facing you, place one chicken breast near the bottom, in the centre. Brush the edges with water and fold the top end of the pastry over the breast towards you, gently patting it round the shape. With thumb and fingers, lightly crimp the edges together. Brush the insides of the open ends of the roll with water and cut, fold and pinch them together, making neat, tidy ends. Trim the crimped edge of the pastry with scissors and re-crimp into neat ruffles.

Cut 24 small leaf shapes out of the pastry trimmings, brush one side with water and lightly press 3 close together on each pastry parcel. Using a fish slice, transfer the parcels to a prepared baking tray and slide it into the refrigerator to chill.

Curry sauce

Melt the butter in a large saucepan and sauté the onion and garlic until they are soft but not coloured. With a wooden spoon, stir in the curry powder, then the mango chutney, apple and banana. Pour in the wine and continue stirring until the liquid comes to a boil. Lower the heat, add the lemon slices and gently cook the sauce until the onions can be easily squashed between your fingers.

Remove the slices of lemon and add the peanut butter. Transfer the sauce a few ladlefuls at a time to the liquidizer and liquidize until smooth. Place a sieve over a bowl and using a wooden spoon, press the liquidized sauce through the sieve. At this stage the cooled, puréed sauce can be covered and stored in the refrigerator for one week.

To reheat and finish, return the purée to the cleaned saucepan and stir it continuously over a medium heat until hot. Whisk in enough chicken stock or double cream to give the sauce a pouring thickness, taste, adjust seasoning and taste again.

Variations

Sauté prawns and sliced crisp apples in butter in a saucepan, stir in a few flaked almonds to soak up the juices and remove the pan from the heat. Spoon in curry sauce, return the pan to the heat and stirring with a wooden spoon, gently warm the sauce through. Swirl in double cream and serve it on squares of brown toast or in hot, crisp bread boxes (see page 75).

To cook, serve and decorate

Set the oven to gas mark 7, 425°F, 220°C.

Using a fork, lightly blend an egg and a pinch of salt together in a bowl, brush it evenly over the chicken parcels and cook them near the top of the oven for 20 minutes until golden brown.

Cut the lemon into 8 thin-round slices and with the tip of the knife, remove the pips. Using the handle of a teaspoon, place a very small mound of cayenne in the centre of each slice.

Reheat the sauce and ladle it to cover half of each plate. Using a spatula, transfer the parcels to rest on the sauce and place a lemon slice on each rim.

Serve the chicken accompanied with the dishes of braised celery and sautéed rice and cauliflower.

Variation

Sliced bananas or mango set between the chicken pieces instead of crabmeat.

Braised celery hearts

The perfume of finely grated lemon rind on the surface of hot, braised celery is a perfect finishing touch.

4 heads of celery
2 tablespoons light olive oil
½ pint (275 ml) beef stock

Salt and black pepper
3 oz (75 g) Parma ham
1 lemon

1 heavy-based frying pan with a lid

Trim the celery heads to about 5 in (13 cm) from the base, shave away any brown discolouration from the bottoms and scrub the trimmed hearts clean. Immerse the heads in boiling water for 10 minutes. Drain them in a colander, rinse them with cold water and pat dry. Using a sharp knife, cut the celery in half lengthways.

Heat the oil in the frying pan, put in the celery pieces rounded side down and leave them to colour. With a spatula and with fingertips, turn each over to brown the cut sides. Pour in the stock, season with a sprinkling of salt and bring the liquid to a boil. Lower the heat, cover with the lid and gently simmer for about 40 minutes until tender.

Slice the Parma ham into very thin strips. Using a slotted spoon, transfer the hearts to a butter-brushed, warm serving dish. If the braising liquid needs to be a little thicker, return the pan to a high heat and reduce it. Stir in twists of black pepper, taste, and ladle it over the celery. Sprinkle the strips of ham on top and using the fine side of a grater, grate the lemon, allowing the rind to fall evenly over the surface and serve.

Variation

Sauté onion and bacon in the oil before adding the celery.

Sautéed rice and cauliflower

12 oz (350 g) small cauliflower florets
12 oz (350 g) Uncle Ben's long grain rice
Salt
¾ pint (425 ml) water
1 onion

1 peeled garlic clove
1 in (2.5 cm) root ginger
2 oz (50 g) butter
½ teaspoon cayenne pepper
½ teaspoon cumin

Garnish

4 oz (110 g) yoghurt
Small bunch of watercress

Cook the florets in boiling water for about 3 minutes; they should be tender but still crisp. Using a slotted spoon, lift and transfer the cauliflower florets into a colander and rinse them with water until they are cold. Carefully tip the florets on a tea-towel and pat them dry, as any moisture will lower the temperature of the cooking fat.

Put the rice in a large saucepan with a pinch of salt. Pour in ¾ pint (425 ml) boiling water and as soon as it begins to boil in the pan, put on a tight-fitting lid and switch off the heat. After 8 minutes, take away the lid, stir the rice with a wooden spoon and transfer the grains to a container.

Peel the onion, remove the first fleshy layer and cut it in half. Place the halves, cut side down, on a board and cut them across into thin slices. Finely chop the garlic. Slice the ginger into fine slivers.

Melt the butter in a large frying pan and sauté the onions, garlic and ginger until they are soft, but not coloured, add the spices and stir them in with a wooden spoon. Tip in the rice and cauliflower, shake the pan backwards and forwards to keep the vegetables moving, at the same time stirring them with a spoon. After a few minutes, tip the butter-coated mixture into a warm serving dish, spoon the yoghurt down one side and tuck a cluster of watercress in the corner to give colour.

Stilton and pear mousse

A Stilton mousse set with finely chopped pear, served with savoury biscuits, a selection of nuts and a glass of port.

7 fl oz (200 ml) milk
3 fl oz (75 ml) port
1 oz (25 g) butter
1 oz (25 g) flour
8 oz (225 g) ripe Stilton
Black pepper

1 tablespoon of aspic, dissolved in 8 fl oz
   (200 ml) boiling water
2 eggs, separated
5 fl oz (150 ml) double cream
2 firm dessert pears

1 lightly greased small pudding basin that will hold 2½ pints (1¼ litres) water, the inside brushed with tasteless vegetable oil

To serve

Savoury biscuits
A selection of nuts

A bottle of good port, but not necessarily the
   very dearest

Mix the milk and port together in a jug.

Melt the butter in a saucepan and tip in the flour. Gradually stir in the milk and port, stirring all the time. Bring to the boil, whisk until smooth and leave to cool.

Cut the Stilton into cubes, put them into the food processor or blender and work until smooth. Using a pliable plastic spatula, scrape the paste down on to the base of the blender bowl, twist in black pepper and replace the lid. Slowly blend in the sauce, liquid aspic and egg yolks and continue working until smooth.

Pour the cream into a mixing bowl, place a damp tea-towel underneath and whisk until you can see the whisk shapes in the cream. Using the spatula, scrape and pour the cheese on to the cream then, with a metal spoon, bring the cream from the bottom of the bowl over to the top and continue folding until the ingredients are blended together.

In another mixing bowl, whisk the egg whites until light and fluffy and gradually fold them into the cheese and cream.

Quickly peel and core the pears, using a stainless steel knife. Chop the flesh into even-sized cubes and fold them into the mixture.

Transfer the mousse to the prepared bowl and chill until stiff.

To serve

Place a large cold plate upside down on top of the mousse, turn them over together and still holding the bowl and plate securely, gently shake to release the mousse. Carefully lift the bowl away and arrange the biscuits on the plate around the mousse to form an overlapping border.

Serve the mousse with a selection of nuts and offer a glass of port. Don't forget the nutcracker.

Forward preparation

The day before

Make

Mint ice.
Curry sauce.

Puff pastry, or allow frozen pastry to defrost in the refrigerator overnight.

The morning

Prepare

Cook the rice.
Cut the cauliflower into florets and blanch them.
Trim and blanch the celery.

Store both vegetables on kitchen-paper-lined trays, covered with a tea-towel.

Make

Stilton mousse.
Chicken parcels and leave them ready to cook on a greased and floured tray.

Early evening

Cut the grapefruit into segments
Slice the ham.
Start to braise the celery.
Heat the butter in a frying pan, cook the onion, garlic, root ginger, stir in the spices and turn off the heat.
Sauté rice and cauliflower at the last minute.

Have ready

Beaten egg and pastry brush.
Curry sauce in a saucepan, cream or chicken stock.
Lemon garnish.
Set oven to gas mark 7, 425°F, 220°C.
Turn out the mousse.
Biscuits, nuts and port.
Nutcracker.

PRAWNS AND CREAM CHEESE PÂTÉ
garnished with pineapple chutney

CHICKEN BREASTS
with smoked salmon and asparagus, coated with
breadcrumbs, then sautéed

PUFF PASTRY POTATOES
CRISP STICKS OF CELERY WITH SLICED CHICORY

A LAYERED BLACK CHERRY AND
BRANDY TRIFLE

Prawn and cream cheese pâté, garnished with pineapple chutney

Cream cheese beaten with a wooden spoon until smooth, soft and creamy is an ideal base for so many ingredients. The flavour and texture can be altered so easily by adding cream, eggs and fruit or vegetable purées to make sweet or savoury cheesecakes, or folding in butter, egg yolks and freshly chopped herbs to provide a tasty pâté or stuffing. The mild-tasting cheese is also enhanced by adding prawns and a fragrance of marjoram, as in this recipe.

I enjoy not only working out the versatility of one particular recipe, but also the eye-catching edible containers in which it can be presented. I have often served cheese pâté wrapped and sautéed in wafer-thin filo pastry parcels, cheese pâté served chilled in hot, buttered crisp bread boxes, or mixed with breadcrumbs and cooked in large tomatoes. The pâté is also delicious when blended with chopped avocado flesh and baked in the shells, topped with a coating of crisp crumbs.

All these dishes can be made even more attractive in taste, appearance and colour when served with a complementary mayonnaise or dressing.

1 lb (450 g) cooked and shelled prawns
Black pepper
Juice of 1 large lemon
1 onion
5 oz (150 g) butter
1 lb (450 g) cream cheese
1 egg yolk
1 tablespoon chopped marjoram

Garnish

8 shell-shaped crisp lettuce leaves
Marjoram flowers

Pineapple chutney

1 large pineapple
1 tablespoon olive oil
2–3 oz (50–75 g) caster sugar
1 teaspoon sea salt
2 tablespoons sultanas
1 teaspoon cornflour mixed with 2 fl oz (55 ml) water
1–2 tablespoons coarse-grain mustard

74

In a small bowl season the prawns with black pepper and flavour them with the lemon juice.

Trim and peel the onion, remove the first fleshy layer and cut it in half vertically. Lay the halves, cut side down, on a board and, using a sharp stainless steel knife, cut each half into small, even-sized squares. On a low heat, melt a tablespoon of the butter, add the chopped onions and sauté them until soft but not coloured. Cut the rest of the butter into cubes, add to the pan and stir gently until completely melted. Draw the pan off the heat, blend in the lemon-flavoured prawns and leave to cool.

Place the cheese in a large mixing bowl with the egg yolk and rest the bowl on a damp tea-towel. Using a wooden spoon, vigorously beat the cheese until you have a smooth and soft texture. Gradually blend in the onions, butter, and prawns and lastly fold in the marjoram. Taste, twist in black pepper and taste again. Cover the surface with clingfilm and chill.

Pineapple chutney

Using a stainless steel knife, slice off the leaves and stems and cut the pineapple across into 1½ in (4 cm) thick sections. Slice away the skin in vertical strips and with the tip of the knife, remove the brown spikes from the flesh. Cut each section down at ½ in (1 cm) intervals, hold the slices together with your free hand and cut across the strips, again at ½ in (1 cm) intervals, to form elegant cubes. Separate the core strips from the flesh.

Heat the oil and gently cook the woody core strips to flavour the oil, then, using a slotted spoon, remove and discard them.

Add the pineapple flesh to the pan with the sugar, salt and sultanas. Mix the cornflour and water to a smooth paste and, using a wooden spoon, stir the paste into the pineapple without damaging the strips. Continue stirring until the paste has been evenly dispersed and the chutney has thickened. Remove the pan from the heat and gently mix in the mustard. Taste, adjust seasoning and taste again. Spoon the chutney into a container that has a lid and leave it to cool. Pat a sheet of clingfilm over the surface of the cooled fruit, secure the lid and refrigerate.

To serve

I rather like to serve the pâté at room temperature and the chutney chilled as a contrast, so about half an hour before serving, take the pâté out of the refrigerator. Spoon the pâté into lettuce shells placed on individual plates, garnish with a sprinkling of marjoram flowers and a small mound of chutney placed to one side.

Alternatively garnish the pâté with colourful nasturtiums.

Variation: Hot bread boxes filled with prawns and cream cheese pâté

If you plan to serve the boxes near Christmas time, as a thoughtful seasonal decoration, cut Christmas tree silhouettes out of thin slices of stale bread. Brush the trees with butter and bake them until crisp. For Valentine's Day, serve crisp bread hearts.

1 white tin loaf, 2 to 3 days old
A generous amount of butter
A baking tray with a lip

Set the oven to gas mark 3, 325°F, 170°C.

Slice away the crusts and cut the bread into 8 rectangular shapes, measuring 1½ in (4 cm) square and 2½ in (6 cm) long. Cut an oblong ¼–½ in (5 mm–1 cm) inside the bread shape, down to within ¼–½ in (5 mm–1 cm) from the base. Insert a small pointed knife horizontally ¼–½ in (5 mm–1 cm) above the base and slide the knife to one cut side, draw the blade out, then replace it with the blade facing the opposite way and slide it towards the other cut side to release the centre and carefully lift it out. Slowly melt about ½ lb (225 g) of butter in a small saucepan. Dip in the boxes, one at a time, using your fingertips to turn and soak each side and set them, standing upright, on the tray.

Bake them for about an hour, turning them at regular intervals to allow the boxes to crisp and colour evenly. If the tray fills with excess butter, tip it away each time you turn the boxes. Transfer them to a cake rack to cool.

Store them in a kitchen-paper-lined, airtight tin, or, I have found that they freeze very well. Rest them on a cake rack to heat them through in the oven for a few minutes just before serving.

I prefer to serve very thin, crisp boxes, and I have found that they have got thinner over the years, so perhaps this comes with practice, or perhaps I now use a firmer baked stale loaf and a sharper knife.

Chicken breasts with smoked salmon and asparagus, coated with breadcrumbs then sautéed

Skinned and boned chicken breasts, beaten flat to form escalopes, topped with wafer thin slices of smoked salmon and rolled around asparagus. They are then coated with crumbs, sautéed and served either hot or cold.

The delicate flesh complements the distinctive flavour of smoked fish and I think the lively addition of lime juice is all that is needed to complete the dish.

8 asparagus stems
8 chicken breasts
8 wafer thin slices of smoked salmon – about
    4 in (10 cm) square.
Butter

To garnish
3–4 limes
Parsley

Coating ingredients

Flour
Fine breadcrumbs
2 eggs

Have salted boiling water in a tall saucepan with a vegetable-basket to hand. Using a stainless steel knife, trim off the white, almost woody base from each asparagus stalk and then peel away a thin layer of skin, starting at the bottom and working to the tips. Tie the asparagus stems in a bundle, all the heads together. Place the stalks in the basket and immerse them in the boiling water to just below the heads. Cook them for about 8–10 minutes until tender but still firm. Lift the basket, shake away the excess water and remove the string. Lay the cooked stems on a kitchen-paper-lined tray to dry and cool.

Peel the skin from the breasts. Using a sharp pointed knife and cutting against the bone slice off each breast. Trim away the fat and remove the white thread from each small fillet. This fillet is connected to the breast with fine membrane on one side; open it out to make it easier for you to beat the chicken to an even thickness. Brush a large sheet of clingfilm with water, lay a single breast on it and fold the film over to cover the flesh. Using a lightweight rolling pin, beat the flesh, working from the centre outwards, making the pieces wider rather than longer. Continue beating with gentle, even strokes until the breast is ¼ in (5 mm) thick. Flatten the others in the same way, brushing the film with water each time.

Place the escalopes, skinned side down on the board, lay a slice of salmon on each and near to one side an asparagus tip with a very small knob of butter to moisten the meat from within during cooking. Start rolling the escalope at the end with the asparagus, tucking in the sides to make a neat, tight, cigar-shaped package.

Assemble the coating ingredients: 2 shallow dishes, one filled with flour and the other with fine breadcrumbs. Break the eggs into the third dish, add a tablespoon of water and using a fork, blend them lightly together. Roll the breasts in flour and press each dusted chicken roll in the palms of your hands to squeeze all the air out. Secure the seams of the chicken with a toothpick. Dip each one in the egg, brushing the surface to cover it completely. Finally, place the rolls, one at a time, on the breadcrumbs and sprinkle the crumbs over to coat. To ensure an evenly coated surface, press and mould the chicken breasts in the palms of your hands before placing them on a greaseproof-paper-lined tray. Leave the coating to dry for at least an hour in a cool place.

To cook and serve

Heat a generous ½ in (1 cm) of oil in two frying pans. Shake one prepared chicken portion over the surface of the fat and if the crumbs that fall in immediately sizzle the oil is hot enough. Lay 4 breasts in each pan and over a high heat, roll them over with a spatula to brown them evenly. Turn down the heat and continue to cook the browned chicken for 8 minutes, rolling them several times. Lift them from the pan with the spatula, using your fingers to support each one and place them on a kitchen-paper-lined plate. Leave the chicken to rest and settle while you cut the lime wedges and take the puff pastry potatoes with the salad to the table.

Place the chicken rolls on to a carving board. Carefully feel for the toothpicks and pull them out with a pair of tweezers. Slice each roll across into 5 at a slight angle. Gently press the slices down to form overlapping rounds, slide a spatula underneath each portion and transfer them to the plates. Garnish each with a cluster of parsley and 3 lime wedges.

Variations

An avocado, peeled, sliced into long strips and rolled with the salmon instead of asparagus.

Chopped lamb, flavoured with marjoram and parsley, shaped to represent a sausage, then rolled with the chicken escalope. The sautéed, crumbed chicken, when sliced, will have a pink and lightly cooked centre.

Both are delicious served with lemon butter (see page 49).

Puff pastry potatoes

Sliced potatoes cooked with a coat of puff pastry. This dish tastes best when served warm rather than hot.

2 lb (1 kg) potatoes	Chopped chives or the green strips of spring
2 oz (50 g) butter	onions
1 lb (450 g) prepared puff pastry	Sea salt and black pepper
Grated nutmeg for flavouring as it complements	3 tablespoons of double cream
smoked salmon	1 egg white

1 12 in (30 cm) shallow casserole dish with a lip

Have salted boiling water ready in a large saucepan.

Peel and thinly slice the potatoes, drop them in the bubbling water and cook for 4 minutes. Drain the potatoes into a colander and rinse the slices with cold water, moving the potatoes around with fingertips to ensure every slice is cooled.

In a small saucepan, gently melt the butter and, using a pastry brush, paint the inside of the dish with a thin coating of butter. Divide the pastry into two portions, one slightly larger than the other. Roll out the larger piece on a lightly floured surface to a thin layer about 1½ in (4 cm) wider and longer than the dish. Fold the pastry in half and lift it into the buttered casserole. Unfold the pastry and gently press it into place, leaving the overlap. Arrange the potatoes over the pastry, brushing each layer with the melted butter, seasoning them with nutmeg, chives, salt and twists of black pepper. Continue to stack and season until all the slices are used. Coat this layer of potatoes with the double cream.

Sprinkle the working surface with more flour and roll the rest of the pastry out to a size that will cover the dish. Wash the pastry brush and coat the rim of the lining with water. Roll the pastry around the rolling pin, set it into position over the potatoes and gently pat it down. Using your thumb and forefinger, firmly crimp the two pastries together. Cut off any surplus pastry and re-crimp the pastry to form a neat, ruffled edge. Cut 3 small slits in the pastry.

To cook

Set the oven to gas mark 6, 400°F, 200°C.

Using a fork, gently blend an egg white with a touch of salt and brush it over the pastry. Cook the casserole in the preheated oven for 35–40 minutes. Press a trussing needle through the golden brown pastry and potatoes to check that the dish is cooked. Leave to cool before serving.

Variation

If you enjoy the flavour of garlic, squeeze 1 or 2 cloves into the melted butter and omit the nutmeg. Although very delicious, the flavourings are too overpowering for this menu, but would be perfect served with cold meat.

Crisp sticks of celery with sliced chicory

Crisp contrasting celery sticks arranged with chicory around a bowl of avocado sauce that is blended with a hint of lime to provide a continuation of citrus flavours. I suggest 2 heads of celery so the crisp sticks can be eaten with the main course, then finished up before the trifle is served.

2 heads of celery	1 tablespoon hazelnut oil
8 heads of chicory	Sea salt and black pepper
2 large ripe avocados	A few shakes of Tabasco
4 fl oz (100 ml) lime juice	1 teaspoon dry sherry

Using a stainless steel knife, cut off each celery base and remove any damaged stalks. Pull away their strings and leaves, keeping the pale green ones for decoration. Wash the celery in cold water and pat dry with kitchen paper. Slice the stalks into 3 in (7 cm) lengths.

78

Wipe the chicory and pull away any damaged leaves. Cut a thin slice away from the base and using a pointed knife, cut out the bitter core at the bottom. Slice them in four lengthways, wash them in cold water and pat dry with kitchen paper.

Cut the avocados in half, remove the stones and, using your fingers, peel away their skins. Place the flesh in the food processor or blender with the lime juice, oil, salt and pepper and a touch of Tabasco. Work until you have a smooth purée and taste. Scoop the avocado into a container that has a lid, carefully spoon the sherry to lie on the surface and cover with the lid.

To serve

Stir and spoon the avocado sauce into a bowl and set it in the centre of a large plate, surround it with rows of celery and chicory and arrange a hedge of celery leaves to one side.

Serve the salad accompanied with a dish of sea salt.

A layered black cherry and brandy trifle

What a pity trifles have such a bad name. Even today they seem to be used as a vehicle for stale sponge, packet fruit jellies and bought custard and yet a trifle made with loving care is a truly delicious and traditional way to bring a meal to a close. Make this trifle the day before to give the flavourings time to mingle.

2 lb (1 kg) black cherries
6 tablespoons water
2 pkts gelatine
6 oz (175 g) caster sugar
3 tablespoons redcurrant jelly
15 fl oz (425 ml) red wine
1/4 pint (150 ml) ginger wine

The custard

1/2 pint (275 ml) double cream
2 egg yolks
2 tablespoons caster sugar

The base

6 oz (175 g) fruit purée – I suggest gooseberry,
    strawberry or raspberry
6 oz (175 g) whisked sponge, or macaroons
3 tablespoons brandy

Syllabub topping

1 lemon
2 oz (50 g) caster sugar
5 fl oz (150 ml) sherry
3/4 pint (420 ml) double cream
Nutmeg or powdered cinnamon

To decorate

5 cherries with stalks
1 metre of thin pale pink or lemon ribbon

1 4–5 pint (2–2 1/2 litre) clear glass bowl so that the layers of colours can be seen.

Using the fine side of the grater, grate the lemon rind into a china bowl. Cut the lemon in half. Squeeze out the juice and pour it onto the rind and set it to one side.

Pull the cherries from their stalks and using a cherry or olive stoner (often there is one at the end of the garlic crusher), push out the stones.

Make the purée for the base.

The jelly, custard and base

Pour the measured water into a small saucepan, sprinkle the gelatine over the surface and leave it to soak in.

Put the caster sugar, redcurrant jelly and the wines into a large saucepan, set it over a low heat and stir with a wooden spoon until the sugar has dissolved. Add the cherries and gently poach them for 30 minutes.

Ladle a little of the boiling, flavoured liquid on to the soaked gelatine and using a plastic spatula, gently stir it until all the crystals have disappeared. Pour the smooth gelatine into the wine, stirring it in to blend. Ladle the cherries and juice into a large container, leave to cool and almost set. It will take about 2 hours to thicken, so if you have ice to spare, set the bowl of jelly in a larger bowl of crushed ice and stir it until it starts to thicken. Throw the ice away and leave the jelly in a cool place while you prepare the custard and arrange the base of the trifle.

Pour the cream into a medium saucepan and set it over a low heat to boil. Put the egg yolks and sugar in a mixing bowl. Using a wooden spoon, mix until almost white in colour. Allow the cream to boil for 2 minutes then pour it on to the beaten eggs. Mix together until smooth and then pour it back into the saucepan. Do not let the mixed cream boil as it will separate. Stir the custard over a low heat until you can see little bubbles appear around the edges and immediately pour it back into the mixing bowl. Stir gently to make sure you have a smooth custard. Taste, add a little more sugar if necessary and taste again. Leave it to cool, stirring occasionally.

It needs only a minor distraction while heating the custard for it to boil and separate. If this does happen, quickly pour the custard back into the mixing bowl. Gently whisk in a touch of very cold double cream with a knob of butter – just enough for it to blend together again. The custard will not be quite perfect, but definitely still very good to use as flavouring in the trifle.

Cover the bottom of the bowl with a thin layer of purée. Add half of the sponge and sprinkle it with brandy. Cover it with 1 or 2 ladles of custard, then the rest of the sponge and moisten it with all the brandy. Ladle in the rest of the purée and custard and using a pliable spatula, gently mingle them together, creating long pastel-coloured swirls. Cover the surface with almost-set cherry jelly and place it in the refrigerator until firm.

The topping

Strain the juice and rind through a sieve into a mixing bowl and press the grated skin against the sieve to ensure all the flavours pass through. Using a wooden spoon, stir in the sugar and continue stirring until the crystals dissolve. Gradually blend in the sherry and then the double cream, taste, add the cinnamon or grated nutmeg and taste again. Whisk the syllabub until it forms soft floppy peaks and spread it over the set jelly.

To decorate and serve

Using the back of a metal spoon, ripple the surface of the syllabub. Set the trifle on a large, napkin-lined plate. Tie the tips of the cherry stalks together with ribbon, forming a tight and small bow. Place it so that 3 cherries rest on the syllabub and 2 fall over the glass rim. Allow the trails of ribbon to fall in natural folds on to the napkin.

Variations

Poach 3 lb (1½ kg) stoned cherries in the sweetened wine together with a stick of cinnamon. Serve them chilled accompanied with whipped cream and sugar-dusted biscuits.

Rum, raspberry and banana trifle

Stir raspberries and sliced bananas into the almost-set jelly. Use rum to flavour the sponge and syllabub. Make an apple purée, lightly tint it with raspberry juice and swirl it into the custard.

Forward preparation

2 days before

Grate the lemon and leave it to flavour the juice in preparation for the syllabub.

The day before

Make

Trifle.
Pineapple chutney.
Puff pastry, or leave frozen pastry in the refrigerator to defrost overnight.
Cook and flavour the prawns, or leave frozen ones, tipped into an open container, in the refrigerator to defrost overnight.

The morning

Prepare

Celery, chicory and lettuce and keep them in polythene bags.
Chicken, place the rolls on greaseproof-paper-lined trays.

Make

Prawn pâté.
Puff pastry potatoes and chill.
Blend and flavour the avocados.

Early evening

Heat the oven to gas mark 6, 400°F, 200°C.
Work out the cooking times for the potatoes; remember they taste better warm.
Blend the egg white with salt.
Bring the pâté to room temperature.

Gently fold the sherry into the avocado and put it into a dish.
Arrange the celery and avocado.
Decorate the trifle and leave it in a cool place.

Have ready

Have ready the oil in frying pans, parsley, limes and a kitchen-paper-lined plate.
Have tweezers close by.
Dish up the first course.

KIPPER FILLETS
marinated in wine and flavoured with tomato

ROAST CHICKEN
with vegetable and cheese stuffing

ROAST POTATOES
FRENCH BEANS WITH LEMON BUTTER AND PINENUTS

MELON
filled with spiced peaches and served with coffee sauce

Kipper fillets marinated in wine and flavoured with tomato

A light fish dish that can be made well ahead of time. Use frozen fillets and skin them when the fish is half frozen.

1 ½ lb (700 g) frozen kipper fillets
1 lb (450 g) button onions
¼ pt (150 ml) dry white wine
¼ pt (150 ml) water
2½ oz (60 g) caster sugar

2½ oz (60 g) sultanas
2 tablespoons olive oil
2 tablespoons red wine vinegar
2 tablespoons tomato purée
Salt, pepper and cayenne

Garnish

Chopped parsley
Iceberg lettuce

Gently pull the skin away from the kippers and slice each fillet across at a slight angle into thin strips ½ in (1 cm) wide. Lay them in a shallow plastic tray.

Top and tail the onions and put them into boiling water for about a minute. Drain the onions and run cold water over them. Carefully peel them and at the same time remove the thin slippery layer beneath the skin. Slice them across into thin slices. Pour the wine and water into a saucepan, add caster sugar, sultanas, oil, red wine vinegar and tomato purée. Bring slowly to the boil, stirring until the sugar and purée have dissolved. Tip in the sliced onions and bring to the boil again. Pour the flavoured liquid with the onions and sultanas into a plastic or china mixing bowl. Season and leave to cool. Spoon the cold marinade over the kippers, cover with clingfilm and let the flavours mingle into the fillets for not less than twelve hours, but use within two days.

To serve

Stir the parsley into the kippers. Have plates ready with a little shredded crisp Iceberg on each and brown bread spread with butter, or orange butter. Serve the kippers at the table from a glass dish, using a ladle.

Orange butter

4 oz (110 g) soft butter	½ teaspoon anchovy essence
1 teaspoon orange rind	Black pepper
Pinch of mace	

Put the butter into a small bowl, gradually mix in the orange rind, mace and anchovy essence. Beat until smooth. Taste and stir in black pepper. Cover with clingfilm and keep chilled.

Roast chicken with a vegetable and cheese stuffing

This dish is cooked with the stuffing placed between the skin and the meat to give the flesh flavour and to keep it moist. For the stuffing use spinach, celeriac, parsnips or courgettes. Sprinkle celeriac and parsnips with lemon juice to stop discolouration.

I think the flavour of cheese and marjoram is complemented by gooseberries made into a purée; they also add a delicate colour to chicken.

5 lb (2.25 kg) oven ready fresh chicken	Pepper
1 apple	Soft butter

Stuffing

Gooseberry purée

Stuffing	Gooseberry purée
1 lb (450 g) prepared vegetables	1 lb (450 g) frozen gooseberries
3 oz (75 g) butter	2 oz (50 g) butter
1 onion, chopped	1 tablespoon water or Madeira
4 oz (110 g) cream cheese	Salt and pepper
2 oz (50 g) brown breadcrumbs	Honey to sweeten to taste
1 teaspoon chopped marjoram	
1 egg yolk	
1 tablespoon grated Parmesan	
Salt and pepper	

Gooseberry purée

Allow the gooseberries to defrost and then cook them with the butter and liquid until tender. Chop them roughly in the liquidizer or blender. Taste, season and sweeten.

Stuffing

The vegetables should be very quickly blanched for this stuffing, so have ready a saucepan with boiling water and a sieve placed over a container large enough to hold the hot water. Chop the prepared vegetables in the food processor and put them into the saucepan. As soon as the water boils again carefully pour the water and vegetables into the sieve. Throw away the hot water and run cold water over the vegetables until they are chilled. Shake the sieve and tip the vegetables into a bowl. Using your hands, squeeze out all the juices and, when you think you have finished, squeeze again – you will be surprised by the amount of liquid, especially if you are using spinach. Melt the butter in a frying pan and sauté the onions, without browning. Add the vegetables and mix them well. Take off the heat. Beat the cream cheese in a mixing bowl using a wooden spoon and gradually add the vegetables, breadcrumbs, marjoram, egg yolk and Parmesan. Taste and season. Leave to cool completely while you prepare the chicken.

Variation

This stuffing wrapped and cooked in individual parcels of puff pastry makes an excellent vegetarian dish.

Roast chicken

Wash the bird under cold water and dab it dry with a cloth. Then remove the wishbone to make carving easier. Lay the chicken breast-side up and gently pull back the neck skin until you can see the wishbone. Using a small knife, cut through the flesh underneath the bone, just enough to free it, work until the bone is attached only at one end, hook your finger around it and pull it away. Now slip your fingers between the skin and flesh, carefully working your way towards the tail and freeing the skin over the breast. You should now be able to get all your hand in to free most of the skin over the legs. Take your time over this process as, if the skin is damaged, the stuffing will ooze out while the bird is cooking.

Now fill the space between the flesh and skin. I find it easier to start by covering the legs first and then from the tail to the neck, pressing most of the stuffing over the breast. Pull down the flap of the neck, fold it underneath and sew it in place. Cut the unpeeled apple into quarters and carefully put them inside the bird.

Weigh the chicken to calculate the cooking time. Allow 20 minutes per pound (½ kg), plus 20 minutes, and 15 minutes' resting.

Season the chicken and spread it with butter. Lay it on a baking tray and cook in a pre-heated oven on gas mark 4, 350°F, 180°C, basting it frequently with its own juices. Push a skewer into the thickest part of the thigh; if the juices run clear the bird is ready, if they are pink it will need a little more cooking.

To serve

Transfer the chicken to a serving dish, remove the string and let the bird rest. Pour 6 tablespoons of water or dry sherry into the roasting tin and bring it to the boil, stirring with a wooden spoon. Season and pour the juices over the chicken.

Roast potatoes

Boil the peeled potatoes for 10 minutes, drain and dry them thoroughly. Put them in hot fat to roast. Raise the heat while the chicken is resting if they need more colour.

French beans with lemon butter and pinenuts

Lay pinenuts on a baking tray; as they are served only as a garnish I suggest four tablespoons. Sprinkle them with salt and bake them in the oven until golden brown.

French beans

Cook the beans until crisp, drain them and throw away the water. Return the beans to the pan and toss them over a high heat to dry. Switch off the heat and pour in the lemon butter (see page 49), shaking the pan until they are coated. Add the pinenuts and tip the buttered beans into a warm serving dish ready to take to the table.

Melon filled with spiced peaches and served with coffee sauce

8 small Ogen or Charentais melons
8 sprigs of mint for decoration

Coffee sauce	Filling
1 tablespoon arrowroot	8 peaches
4 tablespoons water	½ to 1 teaspoon cinnamon
1 pint (570 ml) fresh coffee	2 tablespoons caster sugar or honey
6 oz (175 g) caster sugar	4 tablespoons white wine
¼ pint (150 ml) Camp coffee	
3 tablespoons Tia Maria	

Prepare the coffee sauce first and allow to chill. Mix the arrowroot with water and make a smooth paste. Heat the coffee, sugar and Camp coffee, stirring until the sugar dissolves. Add the paste and stir until thick. As soon as the sauce boils remove from heat, mix in the Tia Maria, and chill.

Find a dish that will hold the peaches in a single layer and pour boiling water over them. Slowly count to ten, drain and cover the fruit with cold water. Free the skin at the stem and carefully pull it away in strips. Using a stainless steel knife, cut each peach in half, then into four. Lift each quarter away from the stones. Slice the peaches into a bowl, sprinkle them with sugar or honey and cinnamon and pour in the wine. Shake the bowl until the slices are coated. Cover and seal the bowl with clingfilm.

To serve

Cut a thin piece from the bottom of each melon to help it stand up. Slice away the tops and scoop out the seeds. Fill them with sliced peaches and divide the juice between them. Lay a sprig of mint on each plate, tucking the stem under the base of each melon. Pour the sauce into a jug and serve separately.

Forward preparation

The day before

Prepare

Kipper fillets and marinate
them.
Vegetable and cheese stuffing,
keep it chilled, covered with
clingfilm.

Make

Orange butter for first course.
Gooseberry purée.
Coffee sauce.

The morning

Prepare

Chicken and set it ready to
roast.
Work out the cooking time.
Vegetables.
Brown the pinenuts.
Iceberg lettuce and keep in a
polythene bag.

Early evening

Take the orange butter out of
the refrigerator.
Mix parsley into the kippers
and spoon them into a serving
bowl.
Slice the peaches, spice and
chill them.
Melons should be served at
room temperature to bring
out their flavour, and
by serving them with chilled
peaches you have a good
contrast. Prepare them and
cover the tops with clingfilm.

Have mint garnish close by.
Coffee sauce in a jug.
Start to roast the chicken in
the preheated oven.
Parboil the potatoes and have
the fat ready to heat in a
baking tray.
Have the purée ready to
reheat.
Brown bread and butter.
Arrange the lettuce on plates.
Let the chicken rest and the
potatoes brown while you eat
the kippers.

Melon, avocado and mango salad with curry mayonnaise

Lemon cream, mixed with the fruits, creates a beautiful light contrast for curry mayonnaise. Melon and avocado always go well together, but I have also used crisp eating-apples, apricots and prawns instead of mango.

4 oz (110 g) Iceberg lettuce
1 Charentais or ½ large honeydew melon

3 avocados
2 mangoes

Lemon cream

1 sprig of mint
Juice of 1 lemon
A little sea salt
Black pepper
½ pint (275 ml) double cream

Curry mayonnaise

1 tablespoon tomato purée
2½ fl oz (60 ml) boiling water
1 tablespoon olive oil
1 tablespoon chopped onion
½ clove garlic, chopped
1 level tablespoon curry powder
1 teaspoon mango chutney
2 slices of lemon
2 teaspoons redcurrant jelly
½ pint (275 ml) mayonnaise (see page 210)

Lemon cream

Soak the mint in lemon juice for about half an hour. Strain the juice into a china mixing-bowl and place a damp tea-towel underneath. Add the salt and pepper; I tend to use quite a lot. Stir the ingredients together with a wooden spoon, until the salt has dissolved. Gradually pour in the double cream, stirring until thick. Keep the cream chilled.

Curry mayonnaise

Dissolve the purée in boiling water. Heat the oil in a small saucepan and add the onion and garlic. Cook gently until the onion is transparent and stir in the curry powder.

Pour in the tomato water and slowly bring to the boil, add the chutney, lemon and redcurrant jelly. Stir until the jelly has dissolved. Take the pan off the heat and strain the liquid into a jug.

Put the mayonnaise into a mixing-bowl and stir in the curry sauce. Pour the curry mayonnaise into a container that has a lid.

To serve

Use a stainless steel knife to cut the lettuce and fruit and place in a large china mixing-bowl. Cut the melon in half and scoop out the seeds. Remove the skin and cut the flesh into long thin slices.

Score the skin of the mangoes into four lengthways and gently pull or peel each section of skin away. As mangoes have a large flat stone, stand the fruit upright on the board, cut the flesh down as close as you can, either side of the stone, and cut away the rest of the fruit. Cut the sections of fruit into thin slices.

Cut the avocados in half and remove their stones. Place the cut sides down on the board and cut them across at a slight angle into thin slices.

Spoon the lemon cream into the mixing-bowl and if it is a little thick, stir it gently with a wooden spoon. Add the lettuce, melon, avocado and mango. Lightly toss the salad together using a metal spoon. Tip the salad on to the plates and garnish with the curry mayonnaise to one side. Serve immediately.

Poached chicken breasts with mussel sauce

For this menu, I have chosen mussels to serve with chicken.

Variations

Please try poached chicken with curry sauce (see page 70), garnished with prawns, sliced banana or mango. Lemon butter with grapes and toasted almonds makes a good combination, or perhaps any of the fruit purées.

Smoked mussels are also very good used in the sauce (they can be bought from Loch Fyne Oysters Ltd.) but remember the sauce will then need little flavouring. Do not feel you have to marinate the chicken, though it does add a delicate taste to the breasts.

8 boned chicken breasts
4 pints (2 litres) light chicken stock

Marinade

2 oz (50 g) butter
1 bay leaf
2 tablespoons white wine
1 teaspoon soy sauce
½ pint (275 ml) chicken stock
A sprinkle of dried tarragon and English
   mustard powder
6 peppercorns

Mussels

2–2½ lbs (1 kg) mussels
1 onion, chopped
1 bay leaf
Sprig of thyme
¼ pint (150 ml) water
¼ pint (150 ml) white wine

The sauce

½ oz (10 g) butter
1 tablespoon flour
½ pint (275 ml) milk
5 fl oz (150 ml) double cream
Mussel stock
A pinch of saffron soaked in cold water
Salt, pepper and a little grated nutmeg

Chicken preparation

Gently remove the skin from the breasts, trim away the fat and the thread of gristle on the fillets. Lay the chicken on to a plastic tray.

Melt the butter and leave to cool. Mix the rest of the marinade together, stir in the butter and pour it over the chicken. Cover the tray loosely with cling film and leave the chicken in the liquid for not less than two hours. I tend to let them marinate overnight. Turn them occasionally.

Mussels

Their shells should be closed, any open ones usually mean that the fish inside are dead, so throw them away.

Clean the mussels under cold running water, using a brush or blunt knife to scrape them. Cut away their beards and leave them to soak in salt water for about an hour. Change the water if it becomes cloudy.

To cook them you need a large saucepan with a lid. Place the mussels into the pan and add chopped onion, a bay leaf and thyme. Pour in the water and wine. Put the lid on top and cook them over a high heat for about 5 minutes until the shells open. Shake the pan every so often. Using a slotted spoon take them out. Strain the cooked liquid and rinse out the pan. Pour the liquid back into the pan and reduce by half over a high heat. You now have a super stock for the sauce.

Remove the mussel flesh from their shells.

Sauce

Melt the butter in a saucepan, tip in the flour and stir together with a wooden spoon. Cook gently for 1 minute. Raise the heat and gradually pour in the milk, stirring all the time until the sauce starts to boil. Reduce the heat and simmer for 20 minutes, stirring it often (I hate washing burnt pans!). Pour in the double cream and mussel stock, and stir or whisk it until smooth. Bring the sauce gently to the boil and add the saffron. Taste, season and strain into a jug.

Just before serving add the mussels to warm through.

Poaching and serving the chicken

Use 2 saucepans to poach 4 breasts in each. Heat 2 pints (1 litre) of light chicken stock in each pan and, when boiling, turn down the heat until the stock is just bubbling. Drop 4 of the breasts into each pan and cook them very, very gently for 15 minutes. Lift them out with a slotted spoon and lift up their fillets. If the flesh is white and firm underneath, they are cooked.

Heat the sauce. Lay the breasts on a board, skinned side up and the tapered end facing you. Starting ¾ in (2 cm) from the top, slice the chicken towards you at a slight angle, to make 4 or 5 slices, but still joined together at the top. Gently press the slices to fan them out. Using a fish slice, place a chicken breast against the rim of each plate. Spoon the mussels in a group next to them and pour the sauce to cover the fish and a little of the chicken.

I suggest a bundle of crisp, cooked carrots on each plate, to give colour and garnish. Serve broccoli with toasted almonds and new potatoes at the table.

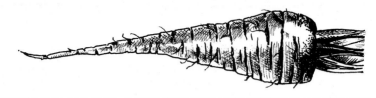

Chocolate cheesecake

This is a light mousse cheesecake, which is served in a crisp dark chocolate case. A dark chocolate case gives an added elegance to any dessert; it is also an ideal container for strawberries, raspberries, mousse or whisked sponge cake.

Chocolate case

2 × 5.28 oz (150 g) plain chocolate – Terry's or
   Bournville
10 in (25.5 cm) cake tin, with a loose bottom
Foil
Clingfilm

To decorate
Piped cream or chocolate leaves (see page 26)

Cheesecake

2 tablespoons rum
4 tablespoons water
½ oz (10 g) gelatine
6 oz (175 g) chocolate, again Terry's or
   Bournville
2 tablespoons Camp coffee
3 eggs
8 oz (225 g) cream cheese
2 oz (50 g) caster sugar
½ pint (275 ml) double cream

Chocolate case

Line the cake tin with foil making sure to push it to the edges and with your fingertips press it firmly against the sides to create flat folds (do not tear).

Break up the chocolate and put the pieces close together on a plate that will fit comfortably over a large saucepan. Half fill the open pan with water and bring it to the boil. Turn off the heat, place the plate on top and leave until the chocolate melts. Put the plate down on a dry tea-towel as the underneath will be wet, and blend the chocolate together with a palette knife until smooth. I have found it easier to pour all the chocolate into the lined tin and then spread it over, using a pliable plastic spatula or the back of a spoon. Pay particular attention to the sides where the chocolate will run back down until it begins to set. The chocolate should form a thick covering with no foil showing through. Leave the case to set for two hours, or better still overnight, in a cool place but not in the refrigerator.

Carefully lift the case out of the cake tin and place on a cold working surface. Peel the foil downwards to the base in strips, making sure that every fold is left foil-free. Take your time over this process as the case is very delicate. If your hands get hot leave it until they cool down, otherwise the chocolate will become a sticky mess with personalised fingerprints. Place your hand in the case and, using your fingers as a support, turn it over so that you can peel the foil away from the base. Slide the chocolate case on to a cake rack where you will be able to see the pattern on the outside created by folding the foil. Line the cake tin with clingfilm and return the chocolate case.

Now make the filling.

Cheesecake

Turn the oven to the lowest setting. Put the rum and 2 tablespoons of water into a small saucepan and sprinkle the gelatine evenly over. Leave to soak and melt at the very bottom of the oven – you should always be able to put your hand on the bottom of the pan as gelatine must melt slowly and not get too hot. Leave alone for about five minutes and it will be ready to use.

Break the chocolate into a small saucepan and add the rest of the water and Camp coffee. Melt the mixture over a low heat, stirring all the time until you have a smooth chocolate cream. Remove from the heat, stir in the melted gelatine and pour the chocolate into a jug. Separate the eggs, putting the whites into a large mixing bowl and the yolks into the food processor or blender with cream cheese and sugar. Work until smooth. Set the blender in motion again, pour in the double cream and blend. Whisk the egg whites until stiff. Start the blender and pour in the chocolate and work until smooth. Gently fold the cheese chocolate into the egg whites, using a metal spoon to prevent breaking down the air bubbles. Pour the mixture into the chocolate case.

Leave it to set in the refrigerator.

To decorate and serve

Carefully unwrap the chocolate cake and, to stop it from sliding about, put a little whipped cream in the centre of the serving dish and place the cake on top. Keep the decoration simple – either a single line of piped cream or three chocolate leaves placed together off-centre.

Leave the cake at room temperature for two hours before serving.

The day before

Prepare

Chicken breasts and marinate them

Make

Chicken stock.
Chocolate leaves for decoration.
Chocolate case.
Curry mayonnaise.
Toast almonds and keep them in an airtight tin.

The morning

Make

Cheesecake.
Mussel sauce.
Lemon cream.
Prepare vegetables.

Early evening

Unwrap the cheesecake, decorate and leave at room temperature for two hours. The potatoes can be cooked ahead of time. Put the cooked potatoes into a dish, spread them with butter, cover and seal with foil, keep them warm in a low oven.
Cook the carrots until crisp, drain and wrap them completely in foil. Place the parcel in the oven with the potatoes.
You now have more room on top of the stove to cook the rest of the meal.
Pour chicken stock into the pans and set them over a low heat to boil.

Have ready

Have sauce ready to reheat, mussels nearby.
Broccoli in the basket ready to cook – don't forget the almonds.

MUSHROOM SALAD
served with a garnish of cucumber cheese wedges

DUCK BREASTS
wrapped in bacon, oven baked, sliced on to red wine sauce
and garnished with blackcurrant purée

SPICED WHITE CABBAGE
BROAD BEANS WITH MUSTARD SAUCE

PINEAPPLE SHORTBREAD

Mushroom salad served with a garnish of cucumber cheese wedges

These white button mushrooms are prepared well ahead of time, allowing the flavours to mingle. I suggest that you serve the salad at room temperature and the cucumber chilled, as I think it provides a pleasant contrast.

Mushroom salad

2 lb (1 kg) button mushrooms
6 button onions
4 tablespoons hazelnut oil
Salt and pepper
1 pint (570 ml) red wine
2 sprigs of fresh thyme or 2 teaspoons of dried
3 tablespoons French dressing

Cucumber cheese wedges

2 cucumbers
Soft cream cheese and herb pâté made with:
   ½ lb (225 g) cheese – see page 138 for
   method

Mushroom salad

Wipe the mushrooms clean, using a damp cloth. Trim the stalks level with the caps and slice each stalk down into quarters.

Top and tail the onions and put them in boiling water to loosen their skins. Drain the onions and run cold water over them. Carefully peel them and at the same time remove the thin, slippery layer beneath the skin. Cut them across into thin slices.

In a large frying pan heat the oil and sauté the onions for 1 minute. Using a wooden spoon, stir in the mushrooms and cook them over a low heat for 2 to 3 minutes to soften them slightly. Sprinkle in the salt and a few twists of black pepper. Take the pan away from the heat and with a slotted spoon transfer the onions and mushrooms to a mixing-bowl.

Return the pan to a high heat, pour in the wine and reduce it to just under ½ pint (275 ml). Draw the frying pan to one side, add the herbs and spoon in the French dressing. Carefully pour the flavoured wine over the mushrooms and leave them to cool.

Cover the cold mushrooms with clingfilm, patting it over the surface and chill for 24 hours.

Cucumber cheese wedges

Peel the cucumbers and cut them in half lengthways. Scoop out their seeds by running a small teaspoon down the length of each piece. Fit a ½ in (1 cm) plain nozzle to a piping-bag and spoon in the soft pâté. Pat the peeled cucumber dry with kitchen paper. Using firm even pressure, pipe the soft cheese into the cucumber halves, slide them on to a tray and chill for 1 hour to allow the pâté to set.

To serve

30 minutes before serving, take the mushrooms out of the refrigerator. Using a slotted spoon, divide the mushrooms into dishes and ladle the liquid over each portion. Slice the cucumber into 1½ in (4 cm) wedges. Arrange them on two plates and serve.

Duck breasts wrapped in bacon, oven baked, sliced on to red wine sauce and garnished with blackcurrant purée

Today you can buy individual, boned duck breasts. They are usually large, so allow one breast for 2 people. However, if you buy whole ducks you have bones for stock and the legs can be poached, then frozen for later use, served in orange jelly, as an addition to sautéed smoked mussels and bacon or crabmeat and avocado parcels. Buy fresh ducks as it is impossible to see how plump the breasts are on a frozen bird. Look at the feet, they should be soft and pliable.

4 × 5 lb (2.5 kg) ducks
8 slices middle back bacon
String

Stock

2 fl oz (55 ml) olive oil
Duck bones, chopped
1 stick of celery, chopped
1 onion, sliced but not peeled
1 carrot, chopped
Sprig of thyme

Blackcurrant purée

¾ lb (350 g) blackcurrants, fresh or frozen
1 tablespoon caster sugar
5 tablespoons red wine vinegar
5 tablespoons redcurrant jelly
2 tablespoons crème de cassis
8 fl oz (200 ml) chicken stock
2 oz (50 g) butter

Red wine sauce

½ pint (300 ml) red wine
½ pint (300 ml) stock
¼ pint (150 ml) brown sauce
1 teaspoon redcurrant jelly
½ teaspoon Worcestershire sauce
Black pepper

Ducks

Place the ducks, breast side up on a board. Gently pull one leg from the body, cut the skin and feel for the ball and socket joint. Using a pointed knife, cut down between the two to release the leg. Remove the other legs and put them to one side to poach later. Cut through the skin to one side of the breastbone and, cutting against the bone, slice away the breast. Repeat with the other breasts. Brush a plastic tray with oil and

94

sprinkle a touch of wine over, add the breasts, laying them fat-side up. Cover with clingfilm and chill.

The stock

Take any skin off the carcasses and throw it away with the tails. Chop the bones.

Heat the oil in a large saucepan, add the bones, vegetables and thyme. Keep stirring them over a high heat until they take on a colour. Cover with water and bring it to a boil, scraping the bottom of the pan to loosen any residues. Lower the heat until the liquid is just bubbling. Scoop away the scum using a slotted spoon, pour a little cold water into the centre to encourage more scum to rise and when it does, scoop it away. Leave the stock to simmer and flavour for 4 hours.

Set a sieve over a large bowl. Remove any large bones and then pour the liquid through the sieve. Wash the saucepan and sieve. Set the sieve, lined with a thin, damp tea-towel, over the clean pan and strain the stock again into the saucepan. Reduce the liquid to 1 pint (½ litre).

Refrigerate the stock overnight. Having reduced the stock if you have time, measure the ½ pint (300 ml) liquid you need for the sauce and refrigerate. Tip the rest back into the saucepan and gently poach the legs. Let both the stock and cooked meat get completely cold, then freeze the legs in the liquid.

Blackcurrant purée

The purée will keep well for 5 days, covered and in the refrigerator. This recipe will make ¾ pint (425 ml) and it freezes well.

Put half the blackcurrants, one tablespoon of water and the sugar in a saucepan. Cook until tender.

In a smaller saucepan reduce the vinegar and redcurrant jelly to a syrup. Pour this over the cooked blackcurrants, add the cassis and the chicken stock. Remove from the heat, liquidize and sieve. Add the rest of the blackcurrants and keep covered with clingfilm in the refrigerator.

Variation

Flavour the purée with chopped mint and serve it with lamb; delicious (see page 129).

Red wine sauce

In a small pan reduce the wine to just under ¼ pint (150 ml).

Take the fat off the stock and throw it away. Add the stock to the reduced wine and stir in the brown sauce, redcurrant jelly and Worcestershire sauce, whisking until smooth. Pour the flavoured sauce into a jug and cover with clingfilm.

To wrap, cook and serve

Cut the rind off the bacon. Using the blunt side of a knife, run it over each rasher to stretch it gently.

With your fingers and a small knife, carefully pull and roll away the skin from each breast, cutting the tissues to release it. Trim off the fat, slice away the tubes and the white thread in each fillet. Cut one breast in half widthways and fold it over. Wrap a rasher around the skinned breast. Repeat with the others and tie each roll up with string. Brush them with oil, then cover loosely with clingfilm.

Preheat the oven to gas mark 6, 400°F, 200°C. Heat a little oil in a large frying pan, add the wrapped ducks and brown the bacon. Lift and arrange them on a baking tray. Cook near the top of the oven for 20–25 minutes. The cooked breast will feel firm to the touch and the juices will run pink. Untie the string and leave the meat to rest while you heat the sauces.

Season the red wine sauce with black pepper and taste. Swirl a touch of butter into the blackcurrant to give a lovely sheen.

Slice each breast across the grain into 3. Ladle the sauce on each plate, place 3 wrapped duck slices on top and spoon the purée to one side.

Serve the cabbage at the table, accompanied with beans tossed in a light mustard sauce.

Spiced white cabbage

Once you have all the ingredients together this is a very easy, quick vegetable dish and also delicious.

1 medium sized Dutch white cabbage	½ teaspoon chilli powder
1 onion	½ teaspoon coriander
2 cloves of garlic	½ teaspoon cumin
2 tablespoons light vegetable oil or hazelnut oil	1 heaped tablespoon sultanas
1 teaspoon salt	1 tablespoon coconut, desiccated

Remove the outer leaves of the cabbage, cut the cabbage into quarters and cut away the hard centre. Slice the wedges as thinly as possible. Slice the onion and garlic.

Heat the oil in a large frying pan, add the onion, garlic and all the spices. Tip in the cabbage and keep turning until glossy. Add sultanas and coconut. Fry for a few minutes. The cabbage should be served crisp.

Mustard sauce

1 oz (25 g) butter	1 tablespoon red wine vinegar
2 tablespoons flour	1 teaspoon caster sugar
1 pint (570 ml) milk	Salt and pepper
1 tablespoon English dried mustard	

Over a low heat melt the butter in a heavy-based saucepan. Using a wooden spoon, stir in the flour and cook for 1 minute, stirring all the time. Raise the heat and gradually add the milk, blending until it boils and is smooth. Reduce the heat and simmer for 15–20 minutes, stirring it often to prevent the sauce sticking to the bottom of the pan. Draw to one side. Mix the mustard, vinegar and sugar together until smooth and whisk it into the white sauce. Pour into a plastic jug and keep covered with clingfilm.

To serve with broad beans

Cook the beans in boiling, salted water until tender, about 2 minutes if they are young.
Reheat the mustard sauce.

Drain the water away from the beans, set the pan back over a high heat and toss the beans dry. Draw to one side and add the mustard sauce. Using a wooden spoon, carefully blend the vegetables and sauce together. Tip into a dish and serve.

Pineapple shortbread

12 oz (350 g) butter
14 oz (400 g) plain flour
Pinch of salt
6 oz (175 g) caster sugar
3½ oz (90 g) ground almonds or rice flour

1 ripe medium sized pineapple
Caster sugar to sweeten the fruit
¾ pint (425 ml) double cream
8 oz (225 g) plain chocolate

3 lightly greased baking trays.

Set the oven to gas mark 2, 300°F, 150°C.

Cut the butter into small cubes. Sift the flour with a pinch of salt into a large mixing-bowl and add the sugar, almonds and butter. Using your fingertips and thumbs rub the mixture together and continue rubbing until the shortbread is evenly crumbled. Now start to press the crumble together to form a dough and divide it into 3 even sized balls. Knead each one on a working surface until smooth.

Transfer the balls to the baking trays and roll or press each one into rounds, 10–11 in (25–28 cm) diameter, ⅛ in (3 mm) thick. Using an even-pronged fork, prick over the surface of the rounds and pinch around the edges for a tidy finish. Bake each round in the preheated oven for 10–12 minutes until the shortbread is pale golden.

With a sharp knife cut one warm round in 8 wedge-shaped portions. Leave the shortbreads to settle for 10 minutes and then carefully slide them on to wire racks to cool.

Cut the top and bottom off the pineapple. Cut it in half horizontally and place the halves, cut side down, on a board. Slice away the skin in vertical strips and, with the tip of the knife, remove the spikes.

Now cut the flesh across in thin slices and cut each slice into three wedges. Arrange the wedges on a plate, sprinkle with caster sugar and cover with clingfilm.

To serve

Whip the cream into soft peaks. Using a spatula, spread a little cream over the serving dish to stop the dessert slipping and place one round of shortbread on the dish. Spread a little cream over, then arrange half of the pineapple on top. Spread cream over the other round and place it, cream side down, on to the pineapple, pressing it down gently. Repeat with cream, pineapple and cream.

Break up the chocolate and put the pieces close together on a plate that will fit comfortably over a large saucepan. Half fill the open pan with water and bring it to a boil. Turn off the heat, place the plate on top and leave the chocolate to melt. Dip one side of each wedge of shortbread into the melted chocolate and arrange them on top of the cream at a slight angle, chocolate side up.

Forward preparation

The day before

Prepare

Shortbread and chill.

Make

Mushroom salad.
Cream cheese and herb pâté.
Blackcurrant purée.
Spiced white cabbage.
Mustard sauce.

The morning

Prepare

Wrap duck breasts.
Take the cream cheese pâté
out of the refrigerator and
leave it in a cool place to
soften.
Broad beans. Young beans
bought in the spring and early
summer are lovely and tender.
They need very little cooking.
However, as the beans get
older, they only eat well if each
bean is skinned, a long job. On
the other hand, cooked frozen
young broad beans are to my
mind the only frozen vegetable
really good enough to eat as a
vegetable.
Red wine sauce.

Make

Bake the shortbread.
Cut up the pineapple and
cover with clingfilm.
Turn the spiced cabbage out
into a serving casserole, cover
with buttered greaseproof
paper and seal with foil.

Early evening

Prepare

Cucumber and chill.
Dish up the mushrooms and
bring them to room
temperature.
Heat a little oil in a frying pan
and seal the duck breasts,
arrange them on a baking tray
ready to cook.
Make up and decorate
pineapple shortbread.
Have the beans ready in the
vegetable-basket.
Set the oven to gas mark 6,
400°F, 200°C.

Allow 30 minutes for the
cabbage to warm through,
20–25 minutes for the duck
breasts, plus cooling time.
Slice the cucumber into
wedges and arrange them on a
plate.

HOME SPICED TURBOT
served sliced with smoked salmon

TRIMMED, BONED LOIN OF PORK
marinated in rum, served sliced with ginger sauce

SAUTÉED MUSHROOMS
POTATO CASSEROLE

TARTLETS
coated with chocolate and filled with apples

Home spiced turbot served sliced with smoked salmon

Turbot marinated in a similar way to the traditional Scandinavian method is delicious. Sliced as you would smoked salmon, it is transparent and almost blue in colour, delightful to eat and when garnished with smoked salmon even better. Buy the fillets from one fish, they will then fit well together for marinating. Also ask for the bones, they are full of gelatine and make a very rich stock. Make it as soon as possible and freeze for later use. I have tried many mayonnaises to serve with the fish and find avocado the best.

Spiced turbot

4 skinned fillets of turbot weighing 1 ½ lb–2 lb (700 g–900 g)
2 tablespoons sea salt

2 tablespoons caster sugar
2 tablespoons brandy
Lots of black pepper

A plastic tray that will hold the paired fillets comfortably, and a board slightly smaller that will rest on top
Weights or a couple of tins that will press the board down on to the fish
Clingfilm.

Avocado Dressing

1 avocado
2 fl oz (55 ml) lime juice or lemon juice
2 egg yolks
1 teaspoon red wine vinegar
Touch of sea salt
Black pepper
½ pint (275 ml) warm olive oil

To serve and garnish

Chopped crisp lettuce for each plate
8 slices of smoked salmon
Brown bread and butter.

Spiced turbot

Mix the sea salt, caster sugar, brandy and black pepper together and spread a third of this over the base of the tray. Place 2 fillets skinned side down on top and spread another third over the fillets, rubbing it in well with your fingers. Place the matching fillets on top, skinned side up. Rub in the rest of the mixture.

Cover the fillets, first with clingfilm, then with the board and finally the weights. Leave the turbot to press for at least 2 days, but not more than 5. Turn the fish twice a day. Keep in the refrigerator.

Variations

If you want to pickle salmon use the same method, but add a tablespoon of fresh dill for flavouring.

A rather pleasant variation of flavour I use successfully is spiced rum instead of brandy.

Avocado dressing

Cut the avocado in half with a stainless steel knife, remove the stone and scoop the flesh into the blender. Add the lime or lemon juice, egg yolks, red wine vinegar, salt and pepper. Set the blender working and blend until smooth. Slowly pour in the warm oil and let it mix well together. Check for seasoning.

Keep the dressing in a jug covered with clingfilm and lid. Keep refrigerated.

To serve and garnish

An hour before serving, take the fish from the marinade. Although the fish has been skinned, there is still a layer of flesh that seems to form a second skin. Slice the fish as thinly as possible, parallel with this skin and put the slices back into the marinade.

Arrange the lettuce in a small pile at the side of the plates. Cut each slice of smoked salmon in half to form triangles. I don't like to see the sliced fish laid flat on the plate, so try to let the salmon and turbot slices fall naturally in waves on to the plates to create a fan shape of fish, with the pointed end on the lettuce.

Just before serving, spoon the avocado dressing on to the lettuce. Serve the bread separately.

Trimmed, boned loin of pork marinated in rum, served sliced with ginger sauce

When you buy pork you should look for a firm but not hard skin, pure white fat and pale pink flesh. The neck and shoulder will be a little darker. Butchers will bone and score the joint for you, but I prefer to buy it boned and score the rind myself.

As with all meats, pork should be kept in the coolest part of the fridge. Unwrap the joint and store it on a cake rack that has been covered with foil. Make about a dozen holes in the foil to let the air circulate around the meat. Place the pork and rack over a 1 in (2.5 cm) deep tray to catch any drips from the meat and brush the rind with oil. Pork treated this way will keep for up to 4 days.

To stop the skin from shrinking during roasting and to make it easier to serve, it should be scored. To do this, use a single-sided razor blade and cut the rind lengthways down the centre about ⅛ in (3 mm) deep and also crossways at ½ in (1 cm) intervals.

If you are going to serve the pork plain roasted, pour boiling water into the baking tray under the joint on the cake rack. The cooking juices are collected in the water and will make an excellent stock for gravy. Cooking the joint at a very high heat at the start of roasting will achieve crisp crackling. Start cooking the pork at gas mark 8, 450°F, 230°C for 15 minutes, then lower the heat to gas mark 3, 325°F, 170°C and cook for 25 minutes per pound. Also allow 15 minutes for the meat to rest. Don't forget that if you stuff the joint it must be weighed afterwards to calculate the cooking time accurately.

To be sure the meat is cooked, pierce it with a skewer and the juices should run clear with no trace of pink. Try not to do it too often, otherwise the meat will look like a pin-cushion. A picture comes to mind of my first roast pork! One of the delights of plain, roast pork is the traditional accompaniments of crackling and apple purée. To add a little more interest try using any of the fruit purées included in this book. The plum for instance is super (see page 120). I enjoy cooking pork as it can be complemented by many flavours. Also it can be marinated in a variety of liquids, rum being an excellent example.

6 lb (3 kg) boned middle loin of pork. Middle cuts are sometimes sold with the kidney intact. Carefully remove it, peel away the skin and cut out the core, slice it into thin strips and lay them along the meat before you roll up the loin.
I teaspoon grated root ginger
I teaspoon grated lemon rind
I garlic clove, crushed
Black pepper
6 tablespoons soy sauce
Juice of 2 lemons
I tablespoon brown sugar
6 tablespoons rum
2 oz (50 g) butter
8 slices of lemon for garnish
A little oil for sealing

Ginger sauce

2 oz (50 g) butter
½ pint (275 ml) ginger wine
2 tablespoons lemon juice
Black pepper
6–8 fl oz (175–230 ml) double cream

Loin of pork

Cut off the rind and then trim away as much fat as you wish – I tend to take it all off, down to the thin skin protecting the flesh. Lay the loin on the table, boned side up. Rub in the ginger, lemon rind, garlic and pepper. If you have the kidney, lay the strips along. Roll the meat into a cylinder shape and tie it up with string, looping it at ½ in (1 cm) intervals. Place the meat into a long dish, deep enough to hold the marinade.

Mix the soy sauce, lemon juice and brown sugar together. Put the rum into a small saucepan and set it on the heat to flame. As soon as the liquid is alight, pour it over the pork. When the flames have died away, add the other liquids. If you have the rind, set this on top, if not, use greaseproof paper. Cover the meat and dish with a tea-towel. Marinate at room temperature for 5 hours, or better still overnight, remembering to turn it often.

Take the meat out of the marinade and dab it dry with a cloth. Weigh it to calculate the cooking time, allowing 30 minutes per pound (450 g). Heat a little oil in a frying pan and brown the loin.

Lay a piece of foil, large enough to wrap up the meat, in a baking dish. Spread butter over the top of the loin and place buttered side down on the lined dish. Bring up the sides of the foil to trap the juices. Pour in 3 fl oz (75 ml) of the marinade, then crimp the foil together to form a parcel. Cook the loin at gas mark 3, 325°F, 170°C.

Ginger sauce

Now make the ginger sauce. Heat the butter in a frying pan and when it is hot, pour in the ginger wine, cook for 4 or 5 minutes until the wine is syrupy, then lower the heat. Stir in the lemon juice, pepper and cream and simmer for a few minutes to thicken slightly.

To serve

Remove the pork from the oven and carefully open the parcel. Check that the juices run clear and leave for a minute to cool. Using the string, lift out the meat and untie it, then put it back into the foil tray to rest while you make the sauce.

Strain the cooking juices into a small saucepan to reheat, slice the meat thinly. Pour the juice onto the plates. Arrange the meat on top and then pour the ginger wine sauce down over half the meat. Garnish with a lemon slice.

Alternative method

You may portion the loin before cooking, and both marinate and cook the pieces individually. By doing this, you will allow each portion to absorb more of the marinade, and will be more aware of the flavours of rum and lemon.

Cut out 8 × 10 in (25.5 cm) squares of double foil, seal the pork as directed, and put each piece in the centre of a foil square. Bring up the sides and pour a little of the marinade in each one, with a knob of butter.

Set the oven to gas mark 5, 375°F, 190°C. Completely seal the pork, crimping the tin foil together, and cook for 25–30 minutes. Take out the pork parcels, carefully unseal each at the top, and leave them to rest in their cooking juices for 15 minutes.

As you will now be cooking the potato casserole at a higher heat, put it in the oven 5 minutes before the pork. Raise the heat to gas mark 6, 400°F, 200°C and leave in the oven for the 15 minutes that the pork is resting.

Sautéed Mushrooms

2 lb (900 g) mushrooms
3–4 tablespoons olive or hazelnut oil
2 oz (50 g) brown breadcrumbs
2 tablespoons chopped parsley

Pepper and grated nutmeg
2 oz (50 g) mangetout or 4 oz (110 g) French runner beans, blanched

Wipe the mushrooms clean with a damp cloth. If they are very dirty, just before cooking, wash them in cold water and dry them as well as you can. Trim the stalks level with the caps and cut the stalks into 4 lengthways. Heat the oil in a frying pan and fry the mushrooms with the breadcrumbs over a high heat, turning them constantly. Cook them for 4 minutes, add the seasoning and parsley. Mix well together, tip them into a warmed casserole and serve.

Mushrooms are very good served with the marinated pork, but I find they could do with a little more colour. Although spring onions would look right, their strong flavour would detract from the rum and ginger, so don't be tempted to use them. I usually add the blanched 1 in (2.5 cm) strips of beans or mangetout peas to the mushrooms at the last minute to heat through.

102

Potato casserole

3 medium onions
I pint (570 ml) of stock; I prefer beef
I teaspoon butter
3 lb (I kg 350 g) peeled potatoes

Salt and pepper
I teaspoon dried thyme
Butter or dripping to finish

Slice the onions as thinly as possible. Heat the stock in a saucepan, add the onions and butter, cook them for one minute, strain and reserve the stock.

Cut the potatoes into slices ⅛ in (3 mm) thick and put them immediately into boiling water, cook for 4 minutes, strain and rinse them with cold water. Arrange the potatoes in a flat casserole dish, layering them with onions, seasoning and thyme, finishing with potato. Don't forget to overlap the top layer neatly, as this will be on show to your guests. Pour in the stock to come just under the top layer of potatoes. Cover with clingfilm until ready to cook.

Set the oven to gas mark 3, 325°F, 170°C and cook the potatoes for 1½ hours. Take the casserole out and raise the oven to gas mark 7, 425°F, 220°C. Using a potato masher, press the potatoes down into the stock, dot them with butter or dripping and cook for a further 15 minutes at the high heat, so that the top layer browns.

Tartlets coated with chocolate and filled with apples

To create a perfectly cooked pastry shell was for me always a worry. But by cooking them stacked, to stop the pastry shrinking, I now find them a delight to make as they are ideal for any amount of fillings, cheesecakes, mousses, buttercream and fruit. Here I have chosen apple.

Pastry

3 oz (75 g) butter
I oz (25 g) icing sugar
4 oz (110 g) plain flour
I egg yolk
A little lemon juice

12 3½ in (9 cm) pastry tins, lightly greased on
the top and bottom

Chocolate coating

8 oz (225 g) plain chocolate – Bournville or
Terry's
I oz (25 g) butter
I teaspoon coffee (liquid)

Apple filling

I pint (570 ml) water
8 oz (225 g) caster sugar
½ lemon

3 lb (I kg 350 g) eating apples
¼ pint (150 ml) double cream
Vanilla essence

Pastry

Chop the butter into the blender, add the sugar and flour. Mix the dry ingredients until smooth and keeping the machine in motion, pour in the egg yolk and ½ teaspoon lemon juice. Turn the pastry onto a floured board and work lightly until smooth. Wrap in clingfilm and chill for one hour.

Roll out the pastry to a thickness of ⅛ in (3 mm) and using a round cutter or saucer that is about 1 in (2.5 cm) larger than the moulds, stamp or cut out 8 circles. Gently press each circle into a mould. Put one lined mould on top of another and then an empty mould on top. Chill for 5 minutes.

With the pastry left over, cut out 8 star shapes. Prick them with a fork and arrange them on a greased and floured tray. Chill until you cook them. Set the oven to gas mark 3, 325°F, 170°C and cook the stacked moulds for 10 minutes. Separate them carefully and cook for a further 5 minutes. They should now be a pale gold colour.

When they are cool enough to handle, take out the pastry shells and put them on a cake rack. While the moulds are still warm, wipe them clean with a dry cloth. Cook the stars until golden, about 5 minutes.

Chocolate coating

Find a Pyrex dish that will fit well over a saucepan, fill the pan two-thirds with water. Bring to the boil, lower the heat. Break the chocolate on to the dish and put it on top of the saucepan. Let the chocolate melt without touching it, then turn off the heat. Using a spatula, mix in the butter and coffee until smooth. Brush the chocolate over the insides of the cases – I use a pastry brush. Start from the centre and brush outwards, then leave to dry on the cake rack.

Apple filling

Pour the water into a saucepan, add the sugar and lemon, bring to the boil and cook until you have made a syrup, and then, lower the heat. Peel 2 apples and cut them into thin slices. Poach them in the syrup while you peel and slice another 2. Cook and peel them 2 at a time. When the slices turn clear in the syrup, scoop them out. I use a spoon with holes in. Leave them to cool and then cover them with clingfilm.

Whip the cream with the vanilla essence until thick. Spoon a little into each chocolate case. Put the apple slices on top. I usually arrange them in layers to look like a pinwheel.

Dust the stars with caster sugar, and put a star on each tart slightly off centre. Arrange the tarts on a large serving dish with a small doily under each.

Forward preparation

A few days before

Prepare

Marinate turbot.

The day before

Prepare

Marinate pork.

Make

Pastry.

The morning

Prepare

Seal pork – weigh it and work out your timetable. Leave the pork ready, but not covered with foil.
Potato casserole.
Mushrooms, unless you have to wash them.

Make

Tartlets and coat with chocolate.
Cook apples.
Avocado dressing.
Blanch mangetout or beans for sautéed mushrooms.
Breadcrumbs.

Early evening

Assemble tarts.
Slice turbot.
Start to cook the pork and potato casserole. The potatoes can be browned at a high heat while the pork is resting.
Arrange turbot and salmon.
Bread and butter.
Just before serving, spoon the avocado on to the lettuce.

Have ready

Have everything to hand for sautéed mushrooms and ginger sauce.
A small saucepan to reheat cooking juices.

PEPPER, MUSHROOM AND WALNUT SALAD
garnished with yellow pepper dressing

ESCALOPES OF PORK
spread with mint and apple mustard, sautéed and served with
a cream sauce

CRISP BUTTERED POTATOES
FRENCH BEANS

A SUMMER PUDDING
with blackcurrant purée

Pepper, mushroom and walnut salad, garnished with yellow
pepper dressing

Peppers have a sweet, mellow flavour when they are cooked, and to mix them
with sliced raw peppers that will be crisp and white button mushrooms, gives a
delightful contrast of texture and a bright medley of colours. Small and
perfectly formed button mushrooms are ideal for this salad as they always look
too good to cook. Prepare them as soon as you bring them home to ensure
they keep their shape.

12 oz (350 g) baby-sized button mushrooms
Juice of 1 lemon
3 tablespoons light olive oil
8 peppers – 3 green, 3 red, 1 yellow and 1
   black
4 tablespoons French dressing
8 oz (225 g) Iceberg lettuce
24 walnut halves

Yellow pepper dressing

3 small yellow peppers
1 medium onion
2 oz (50 g) butter
¼ pint (150 ml) medium dry sherry
3–5 fl oz (75–150 ml) French dressing
Salt and pepper

Mushrooms

Cut away the earthy base from the stalks and wipe the caps clean with a damp cloth.
Place them in a container that has a tight-fitting lid, add the lemon juice and oil, secure
the lid and give the container a good shake to coat all the mushrooms with flavouring.
Shake the mushrooms occasionally during the day to make sure they are evenly
soaked.

106

To roast and peel the peppers

Heat the oven to gas mark 7, 425°F, 220°C.

Lay 2 red and 2 green peppers on a baking tray and cook them in the oven until their skins blister and blacken, turning them occasionally. Have a damp tea-towel ready and wrap the peppers in this as soon as you take them out of the oven. When the peppers are cool enough to handle, start the messy job of peeling them. I find it easier to cut each pepper in half and then peel the skin away using my fingers. Peel them one by one over a plate to catch the drips; keep the juices. Lay the peppers out, cut away the stems and clusters of seeds, then scrape away any loose seeds.

Mix 2 tablespoons of French dressing with the pepper juices. Arrange the peppers in a single layer on a tray, spoon the dressing evenly over them, cover loosely with clingfilm and leave the peppers to soak in the flavours for about 2 hours.

Yellow pepper dressing

Cut the peppers in half, cut away their stems, seeds and pith. Slice the flesh into small even-sized squares. Peel the onion, slice in half and then into pieces of about the same size as the peppers.

Melt the butter in a saucepan and, over a low heat, gently cook the onions, add the peppers and pour in the sherry. Give the vegetables a good stir, cover them with a sheet of greaseproof paper and a lid. Turn down the heat as low as possible and cook for about 20 minutes until tender.

Liquidise the peppers into a purée and then, to make it very smooth, pass it through a sieve. Keep the cooled purée covered until ready to use.

To finish and serve

Cut the lettuce in half and lay it cut side down. Using a thin, stainless steel knife, finely slice the lettuce into thin shreds.

Cut each raw pepper in half, lengthways, remove the core and seeds and slice the flesh into long thin strips. Slice the cooked peppers the same way.

Place the shredded lettuce, peppers and walnuts in a large bowl. Using a metal spoon, gently mix in the mushrooms and pour over just enough dressing to give the salad a shiny coat, then divide between the plates.

Whisk the French dressing into the yellow purée, taste, season, and whisk until it is smooth. Pour the dressing to fall at an angle over each plate and salad, to form a wide yellow ribbon.

Variations

In place of mushrooms mix in sliced, crisp eating-apples.
Chicken breasts cut into long wafer thin strips.
Sautée prawns in butter and while they are still hot spoon them on to the prepared and ready-to-serve salad.

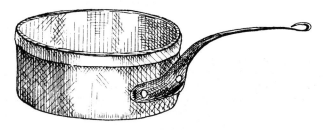

Escalopes of pork spread with mint and apple mustard, sautéed and served with a cream sauce

When meat is fried, the juices that are drawn out turn brown with the heat in the frying pan. These rich residues, with wine, apple and mustard, form a delicious sauce that needs only the addition of cream to perfect it. Pork fillets do not need to be pounded to tenderise as the meat already has a delicate texture, they just need a gentle hand to smooth them into attractive escalopes.

Apple mustard	Pork
4 eating apples	2½ lb (1.25 kg) pork fillet or pork tenderloin
6 tablespoons coarse grain mustard	A little oil and butter, for frying
1 level tablespoon of ground ginger	2 oz (50 g) butter
2 teaspoons olive oil	½ pint (275 ml) dry white wine
1 heaped tablespoon chopped mint	½ pint (275 ml) double cream
	Black pepper

Garnish

2 apples cut into slices

Apple mustard

Peel and core the apples and slice them into a heavy-based saucepan, add a tablespoon of water and cover the fruit with a double layer of greaseproof paper. Cook the apples over a medium heat until tender, shake the pan often to stop the fruit sticking. To make the purée, spoon the apples into the food processor or blender and chop them until smooth.

Mix the mustard, ginger, oil and mint together in a small mixing bowl and stir in the apple purée. Keep the apple mustard in a container that has a lid and refrigerate. Do not use it just to flavour this sauce, it is a very pleasant alternative to plain mustard.

Pork

Trim the fillets removing the thin skin, all the fat and sinew. Cut each fillet across into 4 even-sized medallions and flatten them slightly in the palms of your hands. Place a folded, damp tea-towel underneath a board. On top lay the medallions, one at a time between two sheets of wet clingfilm, and using a rolling pin, gently spread the pork to an even thickness of ½ in (1 cm). Arrange the prepared escalopes on a tray and cover loosely with clingfilm. Keep them in the refrigerator.

To cook

Bring the pork to room temperature. Heat the oil and butter in two frying pans and, when it starts to sizzle, add the pork. Using a pliable spatula, spread a little apple mustard on each escalope, lower the heat and cook the pork on each side until browned lightly – about 4 minutes. Transfer the escalopes to a warm plate and cover them with foil.

To one hot pan add the wine and to the other, butter. Bring the wine to the boil, scraping the residue from the bottom of the pan using a wooden spoon and then carefully pour this on to the bubbling butter. Allow the wine to reduce over a high heat until it begins to turn syrupy, stir in the cream and lower the heat. Add the apple mustard, a spoonful at a time, stirring it in until it blends with the sauce. Taste after each addition until you have a strength of flavour that you enjoy. Leave the sauce on a low heat while you dish up the pork. Put one escalope on each plate and pour the sauce over it, lay a second escalope just overlapping to one side with a fan of sliced apples on top.

A bowl filled with green, clean looking French beans will add colour and texture to the pork, and crisp potatoes complete the meal.

Variations

Flavour the prepared escalopes with 3 tablespoons of olive oil, the juice of 1 lemon, chopped parsley and 1 crushed clove of garlic. Leave them in the marinade for about 4 hours. Pat the pork dry before frying. Use sherry, instead of wine and add sliced mushrooms to the sauce.

Pork with raspberries

10 oz (275 g) raspberries, puréed and passed through a fine sieve, mixed with the juice of 1 lemon. Reduce the wine and cream, blend in the purée and twist black pepper over the sauce just before serving.

Crisp buttered potatoes

You need a heavy-based pan with a lid to cook these potatoes.

Small new potatoes – allow 3 per person
3 oz (75 g) unsalted butter

Scrape the potatoes and put them into a saucepan with enough lightly salted water to cover, and bring to the boil. Draw the saucepan to one side and drain away the water. Melt the butter in the heavy-based pan, add the potatoes, cover them with the lid and cook for 20 minutes, when they will be golden brown. Shake the pan occasionally during cooking, but do not remove the lid for 15 minutes.

A summer pudding with blackcurrant purée

Lightly cooked summer fruit, wrapped in a bread coat is served with a dressing of blackcurrant purée to complete this very English pudding.

Select a pudding basin, or mixing bowl, that holds 2½ pints (1½ litres) of water. You also need a flat plate that will just fit inside the bowl and rest on top of the pudding. Have a selection to hand as I always seem to spend more time looking for the right plate than in making the dessert.

3 tablespoons of lemon juice
1 pkt gelatine
4 fl oz (110 ml) water
6 oz (175 g) caster sugar
2 lb (900 g) prepared mixed fruit –
   strawberries, raspberries, blackberries and
   stoned cherries

10–12 slices of white bread with the crusts
   removed
Blackcurrant purée made from 1 lb (450 g)
   blackcurrants and ¼ pint (150 ml) sugar
   syrup

Measure the lemon juice into a small saucepan and sprinkle the gelatine evenly over the top. Leave it to soak.

In a large saucepan heat the water and sugar. When the sugar has dissolved, add all the fruit and simmer over a gentle heat for 5 minutes. Take out 4 tablespoons of liquid and reserve. Melt the soaked gelatine over a low heat and stir it into the fruit. Leave to cool.

To form and fill the bread coat

Cut a round of bread to fit the base of the bowl and lay it in place. Cut the slices of bread in half lengthways and then trim them into wedge shapes to line the sides of the bowl. Using a slotted spoon, lift the fruit from the pan and into the bread shell, pressing it down well. Completely seal the fruit with the rest of the bread, cutting it to fit. Ladle the juice left in the pan over the pudding, letting it soak into the bread. Place the bowl on a tray deep enough to catch the juices that overflow. Place a plate to rest on the pudding and weight it down with a 2 lb (1 kg) kitchen weight. Refrigerate the pudding overnight.

To unmould and serve

Remove the plate and weight, run a palette knife between the bread and the bowl. Unmould the pudding on to a serving dish that has a lip to catch any juice. Ladle the reserved liquid over parts of the pudding that have escaped soaking. Chill until ready to serve.

Pour a little blackcurrant purée over the top of the pudding, letting it fall down the sides. Cut the pudding into wedges at the table, and hand the rest of the purée round separately.

Forward preparation

The day before

Make

Yellow pepper purée.
Mint and apple mustard.
Blackcurrant purée.
Summer pudding.

The morning

Prepare

Mushrooms.
Pork.
Potatoes.
French beans.
Skin the peppers.
Shake the mushrooms.

Early evening

Prepare

Lettuce, keep in a mixing-bowl
covered with clingfilm.
Slice the skinned and raw
peppers. Don't mix them
together until the last moment.
Check that you have
everything to hand for the
salad and dare I say, shake the
mushrooms.
Fill a small bowl with water
and lemon juice.
Core the apples and, using a
stainless steel knife, slice them
into the water.
Turn the summer pudding out
and have the blackcurrant
purée, ladle and jug close by.

Have ready

Butter in a heavy-based pan
with lid, to crisp cook the
potatoes.
2 frying pans ready, with oil
and butter.
Collect the ingredients for the
pork dish together with foil to
cover the pork.
The oven set on a low heat.
Whisk the French dressing into
the yellow pepper purée.

OVEN BAKED STUFFED TOMATOES
HORSERADISH AND ORANGE MAYONNAISE

BONED LEG OF PORK
marinated in wine and herbs, slowly cooked and served with
reduced wine sauce, garnished with a delicate tinted
gooseberry purée

CABBAGE IN MUSTARD SAUCE
NEW POTATOES

CURD CAKE

Oven baked stuffed tomatoes

Beef tomatoes form ideal cases to be filled with flavoured crisp buttered crumbs.

6 anchovy fillets	8 oz (225 g) brown breadcrumbs
A little milk	4 tablespoons sultanas
4 tablespoons shelled pistachio nuts	1 tablespoon of chopped parsley
2 tablespoons hazelnut oil	Black pepper
2–3 oz (50–75 g) butter	8 firm, but ripe, beef or Mediterranean
1 peeled clove of garlic	tomatoes

Cover and soak the anchovy fillets in milk.

Bring ¼ pint (150 ml) water to boil in a small saucepan, add the nuts and cook them for 1 minute to loosen their skins. Tip the nuts into a sieve placed over a bowl and shake away the excess water. Peel off their skins and place the delicate-coloured pistachios on a tea-towel, wrap them up and rub the nuts dry.

Rinse the anchovies in cold water, pat them dry with kitchen paper and then cut each anchovy across into squares.

In a large frying pan heat the oil and butter, crush the garlic clove over, add the breadcrumbs to the pan and fry them over a gentle heat, stirring with a wooden spoon until they are crisp. It is surprising how much oil the crumbs absorb during cooking, so add a touch more if you think they need it. Transfer the crisp crumbs to a mixing-bowl, stir in the nuts, sultanas, parsley and anchovies (separating the squares as you do so). Taste, twist in black pepper and taste again. I always taste again as I find the pairing of sultanas with anchovies rather pleasant.

To fill and cook

Set the oven to gas mark 5, 375°F, 190°C. Brush a baking tray lightly with oil.

Slice away the top from each tomato. Using a curved, serrated knife, cut out the central cores and with a fingertip scoop away the seeds and juice. Place the tomatoes

112

on the prepared tray and fill them with the stuffing. Cook them for 20–25 minutes.

With a fish slice transfer the crisp-topped tomatoes on to plates and offer the mayonnaise at the table.

Variation

Chopped marjoram and cooked prawns, instead of anchovies and parsley.

Horseradish and orange mayonnaise

¾ pint (425 ml) mayonnaise	2 tablespoons finely chopped onion
3 tablespoons grated horseradish	Grated rind and juice of 1 orange

Tip the mayonnaise into a bowl, add the horseradish, onion and orange. With a wooden spoon blend the flavours together.

Boned leg of pork marinated in wine and herbs, slowly cooked and served with reduced wine sauce, garnished with a delicately tinted gooseberry purée

The sweetness of pork will be balanced and enhanced by resting it in a flavouring of wine and a suggestion of herbs and spices.

1 × 5 lb (2.5 kg) boned leg of pork

Marinade

1 large unpeeled onion
1 garlic clove
1 orange
2 teaspoons dried thyme
½ nutmeg, grated
6 peppercorns
2 pints (1 litre) red wine
1 pint (570 ml) chicken stock

Gooseberry purée

½ pint (275 ml) Port wine
1 lb (450 g) frozen gooseberries
2 oz (50 g) butter
Salt and pepper
Honey

Red wine sauce

Reduced marinade
½ pint brown sauce (see page 209)

Redcurrant jelly
Coarse grain mustard and cream

Using a single-sided razor blade, cut the rind down the centre of the leg of pork, about ⅛ in (3 mm) deep and then cut across the rind at ½ in (1 cm) intervals. Place the scored pork in a large mixing bowl or a stainless steel fish kettle.

Slice the onion across into thin rounds. Peel the garlic clove and slice it into thin slivers. Quarter the orange.

Place all the dry ingredients around the meat and pour the wine and chicken stock over. Cover the meat with a folded sheet of greaseproof paper and the open bowl with a tea-towel. Leave the flavours to mingle for 2–4 days in a cool area, and turn the meat twice daily.

113

To cook

Set the oven to gas mark 3, 325°F, 170°C.

Take the meat out of the bowl and dry it thoroughly with a cloth. Roll the leg, pressing it to a long compact shape and tie up the meat with string, looping and pulling it tight at 1 in (2.5 cm) intervals. Check the weight and allow 30 minutes per pound (450 g).

Cover a wire rack with foil and using a fingertip, push 4 or 5 holes through and rest it on top of a shallow baking tray, half filled with hot water. Place the pork on the covered rack and being careful not to spill the water, cook the pork in the centre of the oven for about 2½ hours. The meat will feel firm to the touch and the juices will run clear.

Let the pork rest for 15 minutes, while all the garnishes are gathered together. Untie the string and slice down the central score line, cut and lift away each half of the rind. Place the pork on a large serving plate and ladle a glaze of red wine sauce over the surface, replace the rind and present it at the table with buttered potatoes and mustard cabbage, the red sauce and tinted gooseberry purée close by.

Gooseberry purée

In a small saucepan reduce the wine to ¼ pint (150 ml). Allow the gooseberries to defrost and then cook them gently with the butter until tender. Stir in the reduced wine and blend together in the liquidizer. Taste, season and taste again.

Red wine sauce

Pour the marinade through a sieve into a large saucepan. Set the liquid on a low heat to boil, then using a slotted spoon, remove the scum as it rises to the surface. Leave the flavoured wine to reduce by half, but do not go far away as the liquid boils over very quickly. Strain into a clean saucepan, add the brown sauce and redcurrant jelly, stir or whisk until smooth. Taste, twist in black pepper and taste again.

Coarse grain mustard and double cream swirled in at the last minute will create a lovely rich sauce.

Cabbage in mustard sauce

1½–2 lb (750 g–1 kg) hard white Dutch
    cabbage
1 pint (575 ml) mustard sauce (see page 96)

Peel away any blemished outer leaves of the cabbage. Slice the cabbage down through the core and lay the pieces cut side down on a board. Slice both in half lengthways, cut out the hard core and shred the cabbage as finely as you can. Bring lightly salted water to boil in a large saucepan and cook the shredded cabbage in boiling water until just tender, but still crisp. Tip the cabbage into a colander, run cold water over it and when it is cool enough to handle, move the shreds around until cold. Leave to drain.

Spoon the cabbage into a mixing bowl and using a wooden spoon, stir in the sauce. Transfer to an ovenproof serving dish and smooth the surface level. Cover with buttered greaseproof paper and seal with foil. Heat the cabbage for 45 minutes at gas mark 3, 325°F, 170°C.

For a crispy topping, heat the cabbage with an even coat of breadcrumbs. The hard core of the cabbage is delicious cut into strips and eaten raw with salt or mayonnaise.

Curd cake

This is a selection of sweet flavourings blended together with curd cheese. As a garnish I suggest small bunches of pale green seedless grapes would complement the richness of this tasty dessert and add delicate colour; or for complete contrast pour coffee sauce over each portion (see page 85).

6 oz (175 g) chopped crystallised fruit
3 tablespoons dry sherry
5 egg yolks
3 tablespoons water
½ oz (10 g) gelatine (1 packet)
6 oz (175 g) butter

6 oz (175 g) caster sugar
1½ lb (700 g) *dry* curd cheese – Ricotta
1 teaspoon rose water
½ pint (275 ml) double cream
10 in (25.5 cm) spring clip cake tin

Soak the crystallised fruit in the sherry overnight. Brush the inside of the tin lightly with oil and then line it with clingfilm.

In a small saucepan bring ½ pint (275 ml) water to the boil. Turn off the heat and add the yolks (whole). Cover the pan with its lid and leave the yolks to cook and harden for about 5 minutes. Using a slotted spoon lift the yolks on to a plate.

Set the oven to the lowest setting.

Spoon 3 tablespoons of water into a small pan. Sprinkle gelatine over evenly and leave to soak and melt at the bottom of the oven.

In a large mixing-bowl, beat the butter with the sugar until the mixture is pale and fluffy. Set a sieve over and pass the cheese and egg yolks through into the bowl, a little at a time, with the help of a wooden spoon. Add the rose water and fruit with sherry and beat the mixture thoroughly until smooth.

With a plastic spatula stir the gelatine until all the crystals have dissolved. Set to one side to cool.

Whisk the cream until it forms soft, floppy peaks and using a metal spoon, fold it into the cheese, followed by the cooled gelatine. Fill the lined tin with the cheese mixture, pressing it gently into the sides. Refrigerate for 3 hours or overnight.

To serve

Pull the spring clip to release the side of the cake tin and carefully lift it up and away. Place the serving dish over the top of the dessert and invert the two. Lift off the base and unwrap the curd cake.

Serve completely plain with either of the suggested garnishes to hand.

Forward preparation

4 days before

Marinate the pork.

The day before

Prepare

Soak crystallised fruit.
Soak anchovies.
Skin the pistachio nuts.
Breadcrumbs.

The morning

Prepare

Potatoes. Keep them covered with cold water.

Make

Curd cake.
Coffee sauce or prepare grapes.
Stuffing for tomatoes – cover with clingfilm.
Cabbage in mustard sauce.
When cold wrap the dish ready to reheat.
Flavour mayonnaise.

Early evening

Set the oven to gas mark 3, 325°F, 170°C.

Prepare

The pork for cooking and work out the times.
Tomatoes – cooked at the lower heat they will take 5–10 minutes longer.
Brown the stuffing under a hot grill.
Cabbage – 45 minutes.
Hollow out and fill the tomatoes.
Reduce the marinade and make the sauce.
Unwrap the curd cake and have the garnish close by.

Have ready

Potatoes in lightly salted water. Wine sauce and gooseberry purée in saucepans.
Spoon the horseradish mayonnaise into a bowl.

Beetroot and tomato soup

1 lb (450 g) cooked beetroot	2 teaspoons powdered cumin
1 ½ lb (700 g) tomatoes	1 teaspoon cinnamon
½ lb (225 g) onions	½ pint (275 ml) medium dry sherry
4 oz (110 g) butter	3 pints (1.5 litres) chicken stock
4 cloves	Salt and pepper to finish

Garnish

Lemon slices or double cream

Cut the beetroot into thin slices. Slice the unpeeled tomatoes in half. Top and tail the unpeeled onions and cut them in half vertically. Cut the halves across into thin slices. Melt the butter in a large saucepan, add the onions and cook until transparent, but not coloured. Add the beetroot, tomatoes, cloves, cumin, cinnamon and sherry. Give the vegetables a good stir. Turn down the heat as low as possible.

Cover the vegetables with a sheet of greaseproof paper and put the lid on the saucepan. Cook for 30–40 minutes, until tender. Take the saucepan from the heat, and pour in the chicken stock.

Have ready by the liquidizer, a plastic container. You need one large enough to hold the soup and allow the sieve to rest on top. I find a gallon ice cream container, with lid, perfect. Ladle the soup, a little at a time, into the liquidizer and work until smooth. Pour the purée through the sieve into the container, with the help of a wooden spoon. Taste. Add salt and pepper. Let the soup completely cool, then refrigerate. Serve the soup with a slice of lemon or a little double cream swirled into each bowl.

Variation: Beetroot and black cherry soup

Use ½ lb (225 g) tomatoes and 2 lb (900 g) cooked beetroot.

Prepare and cook with the same spices. Liquidize and sieve. When reheating the soup, add pitted black cherries.

A general description of lamb

Unwrap a fresh leg of lamb as soon as you get it home. Rub oil all over the meat to stop the surface drying out and put it on a cake rack placed over a tray, so that the air can circulate around. As with all meats, put it in the coolest part of the refrigerator. Lamb will keep well up to 4 days.

There are many flavours that complement lamb; marjoram and thyme are my favourites. Rosemary is very good, but bear in mind it can be too strong when used in quantity. Some cooks stud a leg of lamb with slivers of garlic cloves before setting it to roast. I think this confuses and overpowers the cooked meat, yet a small single clove, placed in the cooking juices, will add an inviting, subtle hint of flavouring.

Roast leg of lamb

For a roast leg of lamb, whatever the flavouring, I always prepare and cook it the same way.

Most butchers remove the pelvic bone to make carving easier. Trim away any excess fat and tie the leg up loosely with string, looping it at 3 in (7.5 cm) intervals.

Weigh the lamb to calculate the cooking time; you need 15 minutes at gas mark 7, 425°F, 220°C, 15 minutes per pound (450 g) at gas mark 4, 350°F, 180°C for medium pink roast, 20 minutes if you prefer well cooked, and 15 minutes resting. In a small bowl mix together chopped fresh or dried herbs, black pepper and enough oil to form a paste. Make about a dozen slits in the fat, using a pointed knife and with your fingers rub the herbs into these and all over the meat. After 20 minutes roasting pour in 2 fl oz (50 ml) water or white wine, and add the garlic clove. Baste the meat with the juices every 30 minutes. The meat should feel firm when it is cooked; check with a skewer, the juices should be pale pink.

Transfer the lamb to another warm baking tray, remove the string, leave it to rest and settle while you make the gravy and dish up accompanying vegetables.

Gravy

Add ½ pint (275 ml) wine or stock to the cooking juices in the baking tray and bring to the boil. Stir and scrape with a wooden spoon to blend all the juices into the wine, then carefully pour the mixture into a saucepan through a sieve to achieve a smooth gravy. Fat will rise to the surface in the cool pan, spoon it off and throw it away. Set the liquid over a high heat and reduce it a little. Stir in brown sauce to colour and thicken, taste, add seasoning and 1 teaspoon of redcurrant jelly, taste again. Whisk until smooth and pour into a jug.

Carving the lamb

To enable you to present an even selection of sliced meat on each plate, the joint has to be turned several times, so select a large serving plate for the lamb. Before you take it to the table for carving, lay the lamb so that the rounded, meatiest side is uppermost, rest a very sharp knife and a two-pronged fork to one side.

Position the plate so that you can cut the meat away from yourself. Using the curved back of the fork to steady the lamb, start carving down through the rounded side of the meat and carve away 8 thin slices. Turn the lamb to rest, cut side down, and slice away any unwanted fat, then carve thin horizontal slices from this side. Turn the meat again and move the fork to enable you to slice smaller pieces from the shank end. Transfer the slices to the plates and glaze them with the gravy, leaving one side uncovered.

I have always found it slightly daunting to carve a whole leg of lamb before guests, perhaps that is why I tend to offer mainly boned and packaged, parcelled food, but I do hope that this brief description of carving is helpful. If you like to marinate meat try using coffee with lamb as I have done for fillet steak, or add to the spiced wine that I used to marinate pork (see page 113).

Another way of cooking lamb is to seal the meat in a frying pan and then to cook it on a bed of vegetables with wine, covered, in the oven.

The flavouring again is a personal choice, but for this recipe I have chosen thyme, celery and a touch of ground ginger.

Leg of lamb cooked in wine, flavoured with a hint of thyme, ginger and chopped root vegetables, served with a garnish of red plum purée

I 6 lb (3 kg) leg of lamb	2 cloves
I teaspoon chopped thyme	I onion
½ teaspoon ground ginger	I small clove of garlic
Black pepper	2 oz (50 g) butter
Sunflower oil	¾ pint (425 ml) red wine
I carrot	I sprig of thyme
4 sticks of celery with leaves	

To garnish and serve

Plum purée

The juice of ½ orange or lemon	2 lb (I kg) stoned plums
Brown sauce	½ pint (275 ml) red wine
A sprig of thyme	6 tablespoons redcurrant jelly
	I teaspoon cinnamon
	2 cloves
	Grated nutmeg
	Ground ginger to taste
	2 tablespoons coarse grain mustard
	2 tablespoons orange juice

Lamb

Cut away all the unpalatable excess fat. Tie the lamb up loosely with string to form a compact roasting shape. Weigh it to calculate the cooking time; allow 15 minutes at gas mark 7, 425°F, 220°C, 15–20 minutes per pound at gas mark 3, 325°F, 170°C, and 15 minutes resting.

Mix the chopped thyme, ground ginger and twists of black pepper together in a small bowl. Stir in enough oil to form a paste. Using your fingers, rub this mixture all over the meat.

Cut the carrot across into slices about ¼ in (5 mm) thick. Slice the celery sticks across into 1 in (2.5 cm) lengths. Press the cloves into the unpeeled onion and place them with the garlic at the bottom of a baking dish large enough to hold the lamb comfortably.

Heat the butter in a frying pan set over a high heat and put in the lamb. Brown the meat all over, turning it with the help of a fork and your fingers. Transfer the meat rounded side up to the prepared baking tray. Add the wine to the frying pan and with a wooden spoon, stir the liquid until it comes to the boil, pour it over the lamb and lay the thyme on the browned skin. Wash the frying pan while it is still hot as you will find it much easier to clean.

Cover the lamb with lightly buttered greaseproof paper and seal with foil. Cook at the high heat for 15 minutes and then lower the heat for about 2 hours. Check after 1¾ hours, feel the lamb through the foil with your fingertips, if it doesn't wobble and is firm to the touch, unwrap it and test with a skewer. Cook a little longer if necessary.

Transfer the meat to another baking tray and remove the string. Leave it to rest while you make the gravy and dish up the accompanying vegetables. Strain the cooking juices through a sieve into a cold saucepan and set it over a high heat to reduce it a little. Adjust the flavour with orange or lemon juice and twists of black pepper. Whisk in a little brown sauce if you prefer to serve a thicker gravy and pour it into a jug. Set

119

the lamb on a large, warm, serving plate and decorate with the sprig of thyme.

Carve the meat into slices and serve it with the gravy and plum purée to add inviting colour to the plates. Let your guests help themselves to the casserole, green french beans and lemon-buttered cauliflower.

Plum purée

Cooked plums brought together with a delicious blend of flavours. Use fresh, dark red plums if you can, or tinned Victoria plums, strained. Three fresh figs cooked with the plums will add a slightly different texture and flavour. Covered, the purée will keep for 1 week in the refrigerator.

Cook the stoned plums in the wine until tender, add the redcurrant jelly and stir it with a wooden spoon until it has dissolved. Ladle the cooked fruit with wine into the blender and lightly purée and mingle the fruit together. Pour the purée into a plastic container that has a lid.

Assemble the rest of the ingredients and blend them into the warm purée.

Vegetables

See page 103 for Potato casserole.
See page 49 for Lemon butter to accompany the cauliflower florets.

A basket of fruit and a selection of cheeses

The fresh contrast and texture of fruit and cheese will bring the meal to a pleasing close. I suggest apples, pears, a bunch of seedless grapes and refreshing pineapple wedges.

For cheeses: Cheddar, Stilton and cream cheese and herb pâté.

Cream cheese and herb pâté

5 oz (150 g) butter
1 lb (450 g) cream cheese
1 egg yolk
2 tablespoons mixed chopped herbs and parsley. If you use freeze-dried mixed herbs, add them to the melted butter.

1 clove of garlic
Black pepper
Sesame seeds

Melt the butter in a small saucepan set over a low heat, pour it into a jug and leave to cool.

Unwrap and place the cheese in a large mixing bowl, add the yolk and herbs. Peel the garlic clove and crush it over the assembled ingredients.

Rest the bowl on a damp tea-towel and using a wooden spoon, vigorously beat the mixture together until you have a smooth, soft texture. Gradually blend in the cool butter, taste, twist in black pepper and taste again. Cover the surface with clingfilm and chill for about an hour until firm enough to form shapes. Line a flat tray with greaseproof paper, spoon sesame seeds on to a plate. Rinse your hands in cold water and roll pieces of cheese into 1 in (2.5 cm) balls. With dry hands, roll the balls, one at a time, in the mound of seeds and use your palms lightly to secure the coating. Arrange them in a single layer on the prepared tray and chill.

120

To serve and decorate pineapple wedges

Using a stainless steel knife, slice away the top and base from the pineapple. Cut the fruit in half lengthways. Place them, cut sides down, on a board. Cut each half into 3 long sections and cut away the core from each strip. Slice the sections of trimmed pineapple across into even sized wedges. Arrange them close together, skin sides down on a plate and garnish one side with 3 small bunches of mint.

Set the grapes off centre on the cheese board with the Cheddar and Stilton close by. Put the polished apples and pears in a napkin-lined basket. On a cake stand arrange the cheese balls; when the surface is covered, pile the rest on top of the first layer.

Provide finger-bowls with rose-petals floating on the surface of the warm water.

Forward preparation

The day before

Make

Beetroot and tomato soup.
Plum purée.
Lemon butter.
Cream cheese and herb pâté.

The morning

Prepare

Lamb. Brown the leg and place it on top of the vegetables. Cover it with a tea-towel.
Potato casserole. Please see recipe on page 103 but make it with a flavouring of nutmeg instead of thyme. Seal the dish with clingfilm.
Cut the cauliflower into florets, top and tail the beans. Keep them in kitchen-paper-lined containers covered with a tea-towel.

Early evening

Prepare the fruit and cheese, leave them at room temperature.
Work out the cooking times. Set the oven.
Heat up the wine for the lamb and pour it over.
Cover with greaseproof paper and seal with foil.
Start to cook the lamb.
The potato casserole should be put into the oven when you lower the heat. It can then be browned at a high heat while the lamb is resting.

Have ready

Soup in a saucepan.
Plum purée in a small pan.
Lemon butter in a bowl to melt in the oven at the last minute.

121

STILTON PÂTÉ
served sliced with mango, garnished with mustard dressing

LAMB FLAVOURED WITH GREEN PEPPERS
wrapped and cooked in puff pastry, served with lemon butter
and a purée of red peppers

CAULIFLOWER
GREEN SALAD

BLACK COFFEE AND TIA MARIA JELLY
decorated with frosted grapes

Stilton pâté served sliced with mango, garnished with mustard dressing

---

This smooth pâté wrapped in dark green spinach leaves looks particularly attractive when served sliced with a garnish of mango, crisp lettuce and mustard dressing.

8 oz (225 g) soft ripe Stilton	5 oz (150 g) soft butter
9 oz (250 g) cream cheese	Grated rind of 1 orange
1 egg yolk	Black pepper
1 teaspoon brandy	4 oz (110 g) young spinach leaves
	2 mangoes
	2 oz (50 g) Iceberg lettuce
	Mustard dressing (see page 211)

Chop the Stilton in the food processor until you have a smooth paste and then scrape it into a large mixing-bowl, add the cream cheese and egg yolk. Place the bowl on a damp tea-towel and, using a wooden spoon, beat the cheeses together until smooth and creamy. Mix in the brandy and butter, then the orange rind. Taste, season with black pepper, cover loosely with clingfilm and chill for about 1 hour until firm enough to roll.

Wash the spinach leaves and cut away any hard stems. Bring a pan of lightly salted water to the boil. Add the spinach and as soon as the water returns to the boil, drain the leaves into a colander and run cold water over them. Carefully spread the leaves out on paper towels and pat them dry. Brush a large sheet of clingfilm very lightly with oil, spoon on the pâté at one end and fold the clingfilm over. Using your fingers, roll and mould the cheese to a smooth compact cylinder shape 9 in (23 cm) long and 2 in (5 cm) in diameter. Arrange the spinach leaves slightly overlapping each other to form a green blanket the same length as the cheese. Unwrap and lay the pâté at the end of the spinach and carefully press the leaves on to the cheese as you roll it up. Wrap it securely in clingfilm and refrigerate for 2 hours (what would we do without clingfilm and kitchen paper?!).

To serve

Use a stainless steel knife to cut the lettuce and mango and have a bowl of hot water to dip the blade in as you slice the pâté; this prevents it from sticking.

Slice the Iceberg and place into a small bowl. Score the skin of the mango into four, lengthways, and gently pull or peel each section of skin away. Mangoes have a large flat stone. Stand the fruit upright on the board and cut the flesh down as close as you can either side of the stone. Cut each section of fruit into six long slices. Cut the rest of the fruit away from the stones, mix these small pieces with the lettuce and set in mounds on one side of each plate. Allow three thin slices of pâté per portion. Prop the slices of pâté, overlapping each other, against the mound of lettuce. Arrange the mango slices to fan out and position them on the plate opposite the pâté. Remember to shake the dressing well before it is used. Pour a ribbon of dressing from one side of the plate to the other, at an angle to blend the arrangement together. Serve immediately.

Variations

Here are three simple, but delightful, expressions of flavour and colour:
Stilton pâté with sliced avocado and garnished with strawberry vinaigrette.
Stilton pâté with smoked salmon and avocado mayonnaise.
Roll the pâté into small balls and coat half of them with chopped parsley and the others with chopped, toasted nuts. Chill until firm and then serve them nestled in the folds of a pastel-coloured napkin to accompany chilled sherry.

Lamb flavoured with green peppers, wrapped and cooked in puff pastry, served with lemon butter and a purée of red peppers

4 × 2½ lb (1 kg) best end of English neck of
    lamb. When boned and trimmed they will
    each weigh 7 oz (200 g).
Oil to seal the lamb
1 lb (450 g) puff pastry
Beaten egg to coat the pastry

Green pepper paste

1 large green pepper
1 in (2.5 cm) cube of crystallised ginger
1 teaspoon of chopped onion
¼ clove of garlic
Olive oil

Red pepper purée

6 red peppers
4 ripe tomatoes
2 onions
4 oz (110 g) butter
½ pint (275 ml) medium dry sherry or chicken
    stock

Lemon butter (see page 49 for method)

4 oz (110 g) butter
Juice of 1 lemon
Black pepper

Lay one best end of lamb, fat side up, on a board and carefully slice away the outer layer of fat until you can see that underneath is a long, round strip of lamb and, using a sharp knife, cut downwards following the shape of the bones until you can separate the meat. Repeat the same process with the other three. Trim away all the fat from the lamb and then cut each one in half. Each piece will be 2½ in (6.5 cm) to 3 in (7.5 cm) long.

In a frying pan heat enough oil to cover the base and over a medium heat lightly seal the lamb, four pieces at a time. Lay them on a tray covered with kitchen paper and chill.

Green pepper paste

Slice the pepper in half, cut away the stem, seed and pith, then cut each half into four. Place the chopped pepper, ginger, onion and garlic into the food processor/blender and chop them finely. Spoon the paste into a small bowl and stir in a little olive oil, just enough to give the pepper paste a sheen.

Red pepper purée

Cut each pepper in half, cut away the stem and remove the seeds and pith. Slice the flesh into even-sized cubes. Cut each tomato into quarters. Peel the onions, slice them in half and cut them into pieces about the same size as the peppers; this will ensure even cooking.

Melt the butter in a saucepan and, over a low heat, gently cook the onions, add the peppers and tomato and pour in the stock or sherry. Give the vegetables a good stir to coat them with butter, cover them with a sheet of greaseproof paper and lid. Turn down the heat as low as possible and cook for about 30 minutes until very tender. Liquidize into a purée and with the aid of a wooden spoon, push it through a sieve. Taste and season.

These quantities will give you 2 pints (1.2 litres) of purée. Keep covered in the refrigerator for 2–3 days.

To assemble the lamb parcels

Roll the pastry out as thin as possible to form a large square. Have a knife, pastry brush, a small bowl of water and a pastry wheel or a pair of scissors to hand.

Take the lamb pieces out of the refrigerator and spread the chopped green peppers on top of each to form a line down the centre. Cut the pastry into 8 rectangles 4 in (10 cm) wide and 9 in (23 cm) long. Place the lamb, paste side up, at one end of the rectangle. Brush water round the edges and fold the pastry over the meat, press the borders together with a pastry wheel, trim off the edges, cutting through the border. Use your fingertips to press and imprint the cut edge to form a pattern and firmly seal together. Repeat this procedure with the rest of the lamb and pastry. Make a very small slit in each parcel to allow the steam to escape, cut 8 stars out of the pastry scraps, dampen with water and press one on to the side of each parcel. Place them on a greased and floured baking tray as far away from each other as possible. Chill them for at least 30 minutes.

To cook and serve

Set the oven to gas mark 7, 425°F, 220°C.

Brush the parcels with beaten egg and cook them near the top of the oven until golden and crisp – 15–20 minutes for medium-cooked lamb. Pour a little lemon butter on to each plate and place the golden brown pastry on top, ladle the purée to fall over a small corner of pastry and then on to the plate to mingle with the yellow. Arrange crisply cooked cauliflower florets close by.

Present the salad at the table.

Green salad

Choose a round, mild lettuce and serve it sprinkled with lemon juice; the soft leaves will provide contrasts of texture and colour, with a very delicate background flavour.

Select a shallow glass bowl. Separate the lettuce into individual leaves, wash and dry them. Arrange the large, darker leaves around the bowl to resemble the outer petals of an open rose. Continue arranging the leaves in progressively smaller and lighter coloured circles, until in the centre you have the almost white heart.

Black coffee and Tia Maria jelly, decorated with frosted grapes

Fortified wines and spirits to me come in the same category as garlic; I like to use them in small quantities so that they add flavour to the dish that I am preparing, but do not overpower the original taste. Just a touch of Tia Maria added to the jelly enhances the coffee flavour.

8 oz (225 g) caster sugar
8 tablespoons of water
2 pints (1.2 litre) freshly brewed strong coffee. Replace 1 tablespoon of coffee with Tia Maria.

2½ pkts of gelatine soaked in 4 tablespoons of water
1 lb (450 g) black and green grapes
1 egg white
About 4 oz (110 g) caster sugar for coating the grapes

Small paint brush

In a large saucepan dissolve the sugar and water. Boil until you have a light amber syrup. Draw the pan away from the heat and pour in the coffee. Return to the heat and stir until smooth, ladle a little coffee syrup on to the soaked gelatine, mix it together, then pour it back into the saucepan and stir again. Leave in a container until quite cold.

Brush the inside of a 2 pint (1.2 litre) mould lightly with oil, making sure that you coat all the crevices. When the jelly is just starting to set, but still at the pouring stage, ladle it carefully into the mould. Leave overnight to set completely.

Wash and dry the grapes and cut them into bunches of three. Beat the egg white lightly with a fork, to break it down but not to create a froth. Put the caster sugar for coating into a bowl. Paint the grapes with the egg white and gently roll them in the sugar. Lay the coated grapes on a tray lined with greaseproof paper and allow them to dry in a cool place.

To serve

Place the serving dish upside down over the mould. Invert the two, giving them a good shake. Carefully lift away the mould to reveal a beautiful, quivering jelly. Arrange the bunches of grapes on the dish to decorate.

Forward preparation

The day before

Prepare

Puff pastry. If you use frozen, leave it to defrost in the refrigerator overnight.

Make

Black coffee jelly.
Mustard dressing.
Red pepper purée.
Green pepper paste.

The morning

Make

Stilton pâté.

Prepare

Lettuce; Iceberg for garnish and I suggest 2 round lettuce for the salad; keep them in polythene bags.
Coat the grapes with egg and sugar.
Lamb; leave the pastry-wrapped lamb on a prepared baking tray in the refrigerator.
Cauliflower.

Early evening

Have ready

Turn out the jelly and keep it chilled. Arrange the grapes on the dish just before serving it. Slice the mangoes and have them ready in groups of three, covered loosely with clingfilm. Arrange the green salad, have lemon juice close by.
Set the oven to gas mark 7, 425°F, 220°C.
Mix the small pieces of mango with Iceberg lettuce and arrange on the plates.
Unwrap the Stilton pâté. Remember to give the mustard dressing a good shake before serving.

Beaten egg with pastry brush to hand.
Mustard sauce and red pepper purée ready to heat.
Lemon butter in a bowl ready to melt in the oven.

CRABMEAT
with garlic mushrooms and horseradish mayonnaise

TRIMMED BONED BEST END OF LAMB
coated with breadcrumbs, lightly sautéed, sliced on to
Madeira sauce and garnished with blackcurrant and mint

RUNNER BEANS
CREAMED POTATOES
MIXED SALAD

BAKED CREAM
with strawberry purée

Crabmeat with garlic mushrooms and horseradish mayonnaise

If you use button mushrooms, bleached white with lemon juice, and mix them lightly with crabmeat and lettuce at the last moment you will achieve a light, tasty and clean-looking first course. Although I have suggested a mayonnaise flavoured with horseradish as a garnish you may prefer a blander one, perhaps avocado. Don't feel it is essential to use as much, or indeed any, garlic with the mushrooms and bear this in mind if you choose a different dressing. Fresh crabmeat can be difficult to buy at certain times of the year. If you use frozen, allow it to defrost overnight in the refrigerator.

1 lb (450 g) white crabmeat	Tabasco sauce
A little French dressing	½ teaspoon caster sugar, only if you use garlic
½ lb (225 g) brown crabmeat	6 tablespoons olive oil
2 teaspoons brandy	1 tablespoon creamed horseradish
Salt and pepper	1 teaspoon grated lemon rind
1 lb (450 g) button mushrooms	4 oz (110 g) Iceberg lettuce, thinly sliced
3 cloves of garlic	2 teaspoons chopped parsley
Juice of 1 lemon	½ pint (275 ml) plain mayonnaise

Flavour the white crabmeat with a little French dressing. Mix the brown crabmeat with brandy, season and cover both meats loosely with clingfilm and chill.

Wipe the mushrooms clean using a damp cloth. Trim the stalks level with the caps and reserve them for brown sauce. Unless the caps are baby size, cut each one into quarters and place them into a container that has a lid (another use for plastic ice cream tubs). Crush the garlic over, add lemon juice and a shake of Tabasco, caster sugar and olive oil. Put the lid on top and, making sure that it is secure, give the container a good shake to allow the flavouring to coat all the mushrooms. Set to one side. Throughout the day, whenever you can remember, shake the mushrooms to ensure they are evenly marinated.

Mix horseradish cream and lemon rind with the mayonnaise.

To serve

Place the sliced lettuce into a large mixing bowl, add white crabmeat and parsley. Toss them lightly together using a metal spoon. Tip and gently mix in the mushrooms and then divide between the plates. Spoon a little brown crabmeat on top and to one side in a line, and then the mayonnaise to form a second strip of colour. Serve immediately and offer brown bread and butter at the table.

Variations using flavoured mushrooms

The mushrooms should be added only at the last moment. Cook a mixed selection of seafoods, flame them with brandy while they are still warm and mix in a little French dressing. If you have included scallops, remove their corals and use them to flavour mayonnaise. Sliced avocado with prawns is delicious with these mushrooms – garnish with lemon cream. Add segments of grapefruit to crabmeat and serve with honey mayonnaise.

Trimmed, boned best end of lamb, coated with breadcrumbs, lightly sautéed, sliced on to Madeira sauce and garnished with blackcurrant and mint

Lamb lends itself to simple sautées and is at its best when it is still pink. Madeira is a natural choice and blackcurrants a contrast of taste and colour.

4 x 3 lb (1 kg 350 g) English best ends of neck of lamb. When boned and completely trimmed, they will each weigh just over 9 oz (250 g).

To coat

Flour, 3 eggs, salt, anchovy essence and breadcrumbs
Oil for frying.

Madeira sauce

2 oz (50 g) butter
1 onion chopped, with the skin left on to give extra colour to the sauce
1 bay leaf
1 teaspoon dried thyme
12 fl oz (330 ml) Madeira
1 pint (570 ml) lamb stock
1/4 pint (150 ml) brown sauce
1/2 oz (10 g) butter to finish

Blackcurrant and mint sauce

3/4 lb (350 g) blackcurrants, fresh or frozen
1 tablespoon caster sugar
5 tablespoons red wine vinegar
1 tablespoon redcurrant jelly
2 tablespoons cassis
1/2 pint (275 ml) chicken or lamb stock
1 tablespoon chopped mint

I have found it best to trim the lamb and, with the bones, make a stock for both sauces the day before. This allows plenty of time for the fat to set on top of the liquid. If time is too short to make homemade stock, use measured amounts of water in the sauces and add stock-cube flavouring at the end of reducing time.

Lay one best end, fat side up, on a board and carefully slice away the outer layer of fat until you can see that underneath is a long round strip of lamb. Using a sharp knife cut downwards, following the shape of the bones, until you can separate the meat. Repeat the same process with the other three. Lay the four fillets of lamb on a tray, cover them loosely with clingfilm and chill.

Make a light lamb stock (see page 208).

Madeira sauce

Melt the butter in a saucepan. Lightly cook the chopped unpeeled onion. Add the bay leaf and thyme and pour in the Madeira. Turn up the heat and reduce the liquid by half. Now pour in the lamb stock and again reduce liquid by half. Stir in the brown sauce and slowly bring to the boil. Strain through a sieve into a container. When ready to serve, heat up and whisk in the butter to give the sauce a sheen.

Blackcurrant sauce

Put half the blackcurrants, 1 tablespoon of water and the sugar in a saucepan and cook until tender. In a small saucepan reduce the vinegar and redcurrant jelly to a syrup. Pour this over the cooked blackcurrants, add the cassis and chicken stock. Bring to the boil and simmer for a few minutes. Remove from the heat and liquidize and sieve. Add the rest of the blackcurrants and the chopped mint. Cover when cold.

The lamb

Whisk the eggs with 2 tablespoons of water or milk, add a pinch of salt and flavour with anchovy essence. Fill separate long dishes with flour, whisked eggs and breadcrumbs. Coat each piece of lamb with flour and shake away the excess, now dip each one in egg and then into the crumbs. Rub away the crumbs sticking to your fingers, but do not rub them back into the breadcrumbs! Coat the lamb completely, pressing the crumbs on to the meat using the palms of your hands. Lay them on a tray lined with greaseproof paper and chill for about an hour.

To cook

Use two frying pans. The lamb should be cooked in plenty of oil. If you use too little, the coating may come away. Heat about ¼ in (5 mm) of oil in both pans and fry the lamb over a high heat to seal all sides, lower heat and cook for 3–4 minutes on each side. They should be pink on the inside and brown on the outside. Drain on plates lined with kitchen paper. Let them rest while you reheat the sauces.

Variation

The coated lamb may be sealed over a high heat in the frying pan and then baked.
  Preheat the oven to gas mark 7, 425°F, 220°C. Arrange the browned best ends on a cake rack set on a large baking tray and cook them near the top of the oven for 6 minutes.

To serve

Cut each piece of lamb across in half and then cut the halves into 3 at long angles. Pour the Madeira sauce on to the plates and arrange the lamb slices close together on top with the fruit sauce to one side.
  Serve a casserole filled with fluffy creamed potatoes at the table.
  I suggest you serve a salad made with cos lettuce, tomato and cucumber, lightly tossed with plain French dressing. Perhaps this should be eaten after the main course to provide a crisp contrast before the rich, creamy dessert. Garnish with crisp slices of runner beans.

Baked cream with strawberry purée

Years ago my husband and a friend came home full of enthusiasm about a dessert they had had at a dinner. After a lot of description we found that they had eaten and enjoyed crème brûlée and this was my first introduction to cooked dessert creams. Since then I have heard crème brûlée called the 'hostesses' disaster', but if the recipe is followed carefully, allowing plenty of time for the cream to set, and if the cream is placed over ice during the caramelisation process, you will be able to serve a delicious and spectacular custard. After that introduction here is my well-tried version.

Purée

½ lb (225 g) strawberries
3 tablespoons caster sugar
3 tablespoons of brandy

Custard

1½ pints (800 ml) double cream
6 egg yolks
6 tablespoons caster sugar
1 teaspoon rose water

Topping

4 oz (110 g) caster sugar

A shallow oval heatproof dish that will hold 2 pints (1 litre) of liquid.

First make the purée. Liquidize the strawberries, sugar and brandy together. Pass the mixture through a sieve and spread it over the base of the dish.

Pour the cream into a large saucepan and set it over a low heat and bring to the boil. In a china mixing bowl, put the egg yolks and sugar and using a wooden spoon, mix until almost white. Allow the cream to boil for 2 minutes, then pour it over the beaten eggs. Mix together until smooth and pour it back into the saucepan. Do not let the cream boil now or it will separate. With a wooden spoon, stir the custard until you can see bubbles appear around the edges and the cream coats the back of the spoon. Immediately pour it back into the mixing bowl, stir gently to make sure that you have a smooth cream, add a touch of rose water and carefully spoon it over the purée to cover completely. Leave it to chill and set in the refrigerator overnight.

Two hours before serving, heat the grill at the highest setting. Sprinkle the caster sugar evenly over the chilled cream. Place ice cubes in a large ovenproof dish, choosing one that will fit under the grill, and set the cream dish over. Place it under the heat and watch it brown to a smooth gloss. You may have to turn the dish around to achieve an even caramel. Chill until just before serving.

To serve

The cream needs no decoration, it will look very good with the dish cradled in a folded napkin. To break the caramel topping, tap it lightly with the back of a spoon.

130

Forward preparation

The day before

Prepare

Lamb.
Use the bones to make stock.

Make

Mayonnaise.
Strawberry purée and cream.
Brown breadcrumbs.

The morning

Prepare

Flavour the crabmeat.
Marinate mushrooms.
Potatoes.
Beans. Buy young runner
beans about 6 in (15 cm) long,
they need only topping and
tailing before slicing. The older
ones should have the strings
from both sides removed. Cut
the beans into very thin
diagonal slices and then they
will need little cooking. After
slicing, with a stainless steel
knife, keep them in a
polythene bag.
Lettuces and keep in a
polythene bag in the
refrigerator.
Skin the tomatoes and keep in
a bowl sealed with cling film.

Make

Madeira and blackcurrant
sauces.
Coat lamb with breadcrumbs
and chill.
Check you have plenty of ice.

Early evening

Have ready

Heat the grill, caramelise the
sugar and chill the cream.
Chop parsley and have to
hand with lettuce.
Crabmeat, mushrooms and
mayonnaise.
Cook and cream the potatoes,
keep them warm covered
with foil.

Oil ready in frying pans.
Prepare salad, but leave the
dressing until the last minute.
Sauces ready to reheat.
Bread and butter.

SAUTÉED MUSHROOMS
with cream, served on toast spread with orange butter

LEG OF LAMB
filled with minty crabmeat

NEW POTATOES
CARROT AND CORIANDER PURÉE
crisply cooked French beans

SPICED APPLE CHEESECAKE

Sautéed mushrooms with cream served on toast spread with orange butter

Mushrooms are at their best on the day they are bought. Always choose only fresh white ones. Don't be tempted to keep them in the refrigerator: lay a few layers of kitchen paper on the bottom of a plastic container and tip the mushrooms on top – the paper will absorb any moisture. Keep them cool until ready to use.

2 lb (900 g) button mushrooms
1 garlic clove
6 capers
8 rounds of brown bread
2 oz (50 g) butter
1 tablespoon chopped mixed herbs, parsley, chives and marjoram
Salt and pepper
1 tablespoon plain flour
½ pint (275 ml) double cream
Juice of 1 lemon

Orange butter

2 anchovy fillets, soaked in milk to remove excess salt
4 oz (110 g) butter
Black pepper
½ teaspoon anchovy essence
Pinch of mace
Grated rind of ½ orange

To make the orange butter, chop the anchovies. Put the butter in a mixing bowl and beat until smooth, then add the rest of the ingredients. Mix well together and chill.

Carefully wipe the mushrooms clean, cut off the stalks level with the caps and cut them into 4 lengthways. Chop the garlic and capers finely.

Cut the bread into 3 in (7.5 cm) rounds and toast them on both sides. When the toast is brown and still hot, spread with orange butter.

Melt the butter in a large frying pan, and over a medium heat, cook the mushrooms until the juices run out, about 2 minutes. Add the herbs, seasoning, capers and garlic. Sprinkle the flour over and stir in with a wooden spoon so you won't damage the mushrooms, mix well and pour in the cream, still stirring until the sauce is thick and bubbling. Take off the heat, pour in the lemon juice and give a quick stir.

Spoon on to the toasts. Serve immediately.

132

Leg of lamb filled with minty crabmeat

A boned leg of lamb with a light spiced crabmeat stuffing gently pressed into the space left by the bones, neatly tied and parcelled with fine string. The surface of the prepared lamb is quickly browned and set to cook on sliced vegetables in wine, surrounded with bones to provide extra richness to the sauce. As the lamb is cooking, the crabmeat lends a touch of its own character to the meat.

I have been cooking lamb with crabmeat for many years; it was my first attempt at serving something different to our guests and I hope you will enjoy this unusual combination offering contrast of texture and flavour in every slice.

1 5 lb (2.5 kg) boned leg of lamb – keep the bones for cooking
2 sticks of celery
1 onion

1 carrot
A little butter for sealing
¾ pint (425 ml) white wine

Stuffing

4 oz (110 g) white crabmeat
4 oz (110 g) brown crabmeat
1 teaspoon mild curry powder
1 egg yolk
Salt and black pepper
2 sprigs of mint

Needle and fine string

Sauce

¼ pint (150 ml) brown sauce
1 teaspoon redcurrant jelly

Place the white and brown crabmeat in a mixing-bowl, add the curry powder, egg yolk, salt and twists of black pepper. Finely chop the mint leaves and add them to the assembled ingredients. Blend the flavoured mixture together with a wooden spoon.

Wipe the meat with a damp cloth and using a small, sharp knife, trim away all the fat from the inside of the lamb.

Thread a needle with fine string, fold the skin over the shank end. Make a neat line of oversewing stitches to enclose one end of the pocket, tie a knot and cut off the surplus string. Spoon the stuffing into the open pocket, pressing it gently to fill all the space at the bottom. Stitch the cut ends of the lamb together, securing the crab in place. Tie and loop string around the leg at about 1½ in (4 cm) intervals.

Weigh the leg and allow 15 minutes, high roast, gas mark 7, 425°F, 220°C; 20 minutes per pound (450 g) low roast, gas mark 4, 350°F, 180°C, and 15 minutes resting.

Cut the celery across into 1 in (2.5 cm) strips. Slice the unpeeled onion and carrot across into thin rounds and spread them over the base of a large baking tray.

Heat the butter in a frying pan, add the lamb and quickly brown all the skin. Use two wooden forks or spoons to transfer the meat to the prepared tray and place the reserved bones around. Pour the wine into the hot frying pan, bring it to a boil and carefully pour it over the lamb. Cover the meat with butter-brushed greaseproof paper and seal the dish with foil. Set it to cook at the high heat and after 15 minutes reduce the heat to gas mark 4, 350°F, 180°C.

The lamb should be cooked after about 1¾ hours of roasting. 15 minutes before time, press the meat through the foil to feel for firmness; if it feels done, unwrap the lamb and test with a skewer.

Transfer the cooked meat to a dish to rest and settle. Remove the bones and pass the cooking juices through a sieve into a saucepan, then set it over a high heat to

133

reduce a little. Stir in the brown sauce and redcurrant jelly, taste, twist in black pepper and taste again. Leave it over a low heat while you prepare the vegetables for the table.

Cut and pull the string off the leg. Place lamb on a warm serving plate. Pour the sauce into a jug. Slice across the lamb, carving 8 thick slices and serve a portion for each guest; glaze the meat with the sauce as you do so.

Carrot and coriander purée

2 lb (900 g) carrots	Salt and pepper
8 oz (225 g) onions	2 tablespoons coriander
4 oz (110 g) butter	½ pint (275 ml) sherry

Top and tail the carrots; if the carrots are new, there is no need to peel them. Slice the carrots. Chop the onions.

Melt butter in a large saucepan, add the onions and cook over a low heat until they are transparent, tip in the carrots and the seasoning, stir until the vegetables are coated with butter, pour in the sherry, cover with greaseproof paper and top with a tight-fitting lid. Lower the heat as far as possible. Cook for about ¾ hour, until very tender, then leave to cool a little. Chop until smooth in the blender and put into a baking tray, cover with buttered greaseproof paper and seal with foil, ready to heat up.

It takes about 40 minutes to reheat on gas mark 4, 350°F, 180°C.

Spiced apple cheesecake

I use the Robot coupé blender to make this cheesecake.

Base	Topping
2 oz (50 g) butter	2 tablespoons lemon juice or brandy
8 oz (225 g) digestive biscuits	2 tablespoons water
	½ oz (10 g) gelatine
	3 eggs
	8 oz (225 g) cream cheese
	2 oz (50 g) caster sugar
Decoration	6 oz (175 g) apple purée
	Pinch of ground ginger
½ pint (275 ml) double cream, lightly whipped	1 teaspoon cinnamon
	1 teaspoon grated nutmeg
10 in (25.5 cm) cake tin with a loose bottom and	½ pint (275 ml) double cream
spring clip ring	

The base

Melt the butter gently without burning. Chop the biscuits in the blender and pour in the butter. Mix well together. Lightly grease the bottom of the cake tin and spread the biscuit mixture evenly over.

Cook the base for 10 minutes at gas mark 4, 350°F, 180°C, then leave to cool.

The topping

Set the oven to the lowest temperature.

Put the lemon juice or brandy and water into a small saucepan, sprinkle the gelatine evenly over. Leave to soak and melt at the very bottom of the oven. You should always be able to put your hand on the bottom of the pan, as gelatine should melt slowly; just leave it alone for about 5 minutes and it will be ready to use.

Separate the eggs. Put the cream cheese in the blender and work until smooth, add the egg yolks, sugar, apple purée and flavourings. Set the blender in motion again and pour in the double cream. Blend until smooth.

In a large mixing bowl whisk the egg whites until stiff. Pour the gelatine liquid into a jug, start the blender and pour in the gelatine, blending all the time. Gently fold the cheese mixture into the egg whites using a metal spoon.

Lightly grease the sides of the cake tin and spoon in the cheesecake. Leave to set in the refrigerator.

To decorate

Fit a star nozzle in the piping bag and fill it with lightly-whipped cream. Pipe a little cream on the cake stand to prevent the cheesecake slipping.

Run a thin knife around the edges of the apple cheese, pull back the clip to release the sides of the tin and lift it away. Place one hand underneath the base, lift it up and slide a palette knife between the biscuit and tin and gently ease and slide the cake on to the stand.

Using even pressure, pipe the cream in tight overlapping loops around the sides and then three straight lines off centre, on top.

Serve at the table.

Forward preparation

The day before

Make

Orange butter.
Carrot purée.

Base for cheesecake.
Apple purée.

The morning

Prepare

Fill the lamb with crabmeat. Weigh it so you can work out your timetable for cooking. Seal the lamb and leave ready on the vegetables and wine,

covered with greaseproof paper.
Potatoes.
French beans.

Make

Cheesecake.

Early evening

Cover the lamb with foil ready to cook.
Decorate cheesecake.
Have everything ready for sautéed creamed mushrooms.
Take the orange butter out of

the refrigerator.
Allow 40 minutes for the carrot purée to warm through.
Have potatoes and beans ready to cook.

PEA, APPLE AND HAZELNUT SOUP

CHOPPED LAMB
flavoured with marjoram, shaped with a cream cheese and
herb pâté centre, wrapped around with bacon, sautéed,
served on Madeira sauce

LIGHTLY COOKED CARROTS WITH YOGHURT
AND MINT
COURGETTES
NEW POTATOES

COFFEE-FLAVOURED SPONGE
with orange cream

Pea, apple and hazelnut soup

½ lb (225 g) onions
1 lb (450 g) eating apples
4 oz (110 g) butter
2 lb (900 g) fresh or frozen peas
¼ of a nutmeg, grated
½ pint (275 ml) sherry

3 pints (1 ½ litres) of chicken stock
Salt and pepper
Caster sugar
2 tablespoons ground hazelnuts
Double cream, to swirl on top

Peel and finely chop the onions. Cut the unpeeled apples in half and then across into thin slices.

Melt the butter in a large saucepan, add the onions and cook until transparent, but not coloured. Now add the apples, peas, nutmeg and sherry. Give the vegetables a good stir. Turn down the heat as low as possible and cover the peas and apples with a sheet of greaseproof paper. Put the lid on the saucepan and cook for 30 minutes until tender.

Take the pan from the heat and remove greaseproof paper. Pour in the stock. Have ready by the liquidizer a plastic container. You will need one large enough to hold the

soup and allow the sieve to rest on top – I find a gallon ice cream container with lid is perfect.

Ladle the soup, a little at a time, into the liquidizer and work until smooth. Pass the purée through the sieve into the container with the help of a wooden spoon. Taste, add salt, pepper and a little sugar. Let the soup cool completely and then refrigerate.

Serve the soup reheated with ground hazelnuts and a little double cream swirled into each bowl.

Variation

Cook mint with the soup, omit hazelnuts and garnish with sliced lemon

---

Chopped lamb flavoured with marjoram, shaped with a cream cheese and herb pâté centre, wrapped around with bacon, sautéed, served on Madeira sauce

---

I could not make up my mind whether to call these lambburgers or patties as the name could be off-putting, therefore, in the title I have described them as chopped lamb. Prepared and cooked well, ideally on the rare side, they make an excellent meal and if you conceal a stuffing in them it gives an element of surprise. I usually make cream cheese and herb pâté for this, but you may prefer a mixture of chopped nuts, anchovies and hard-boiled eggs. Choose almost anything that will provide a contrast.

As with all burgers, remove every scrap of fat and gristle. Do not mince the meat as it will become bruised, without flavour and tend to stick together too much when cooked. The trimmed and cubed meat should really be chopped by hand, this task is a little daunting when you see the amount required for eight portions, but personally I find it quite pleasurable. The meat can also be chopped in a food processor or blender, but only if you can control the pace of chopping. Do not be tempted to chop the lamb too finely – I like to see even-sized pieces of meat that will add texture to the cooked burger.

6 lb (3 kg) leg of lamb, boned. This will give
  2–2½ lb (1 kg) trimmed lamb.
2 oz (50 g) brown breadcrumbs
1 teaspoon cumin
2 tablespoons chopped fresh marjoram or 1
  tablespoon if dried
1 teaspoon chopped parsley

Black pepper and salt
2 eggs
3–4 tablespoons double cream
Water or wine
8 rashers of bacon to wrap around
Breadcrumbs to dust top and bottom
Oil for sautéing

Fine string

Cream cheese and herb pâté

Very small clove of garlic
2 oz (50 g) butter
½ lb (225 g) cream cheese
Black pepper
1 egg yolk
1 tablespoon mixed chopped herbs. If using
  freeze-dried herbs add them to the melted
  butter first

Madeira sauce

2 oz (50 g) butter
1 onion, chopped
1 bay leaf
1 teaspoon dried thyme
12 fl oz (330 ml) Madeira
1 pint (570 ml) brown stock – beef or lamb
¼ pint (150 ml) brown sauce
½ oz (10 g) butter to finish

Cream cheese and herb pâté

Make the pâté first and leave it to chill while you prepare the lamb.

Crush the garlic and melt the butter. Put the cream cheese, seasoning, egg yolk, garlic and herbs into a mixing-bowl and, using a wooden-spoon, beat until smooth. Gradually pour in the butter, mixing it in gently. Cover with clingfilm.

Lamb

Cut the boned leg into slices and trim away all the fat and gristle. Cube the lamb ready for chopping. To do it by hand you need two very sharp pointed knives identical in weight and shape. Spread out the meat in a single layer on a board and, holding a knife in each hand, chop the meat, using the knives alternately, keeping the point of the blade on the board. The meat will spread out as it is being chopped so use a knife to fold it over and back to the centre, keeping the lamb together. Continue chopping until the meat has a uniform texture.

Tip the meat into a large mixing-bowl, add the crumbs, herbs, salt and pepper. Lightly beat the eggs and pour them on to the meat. Using your fingers mix well together, handling the meat lightly. Lastly, mix in the cream a little at a time.

Divide the mixture into eight portions and form each one into a ball. Wet the surface of the board and gently press each ball flat. Put a 1 in (2.5 cm) cube of pâté into the centre of each. Rinse your hands in water or wine to stop the meat from sticking to them and fold the lamb around the pâté. Reshape them with a flat bottom and top. Wrap the sides in bacon and secure with string. Dip the meat in a little wine and dust the wet surface with breadcrumbs. Chill them for not less than one hour on a tray lined with greaseproof paper.

Madeira sauce

Melt the butter in a saucepan. Lightly cook the onion, add the bay leaf and thyme and pour in the Madeira. Turn up the heat and reduce the liquid by half. Now pour in the brown stock and again reduce the liquid by half. Stir in the brown sauce and slowly bring to the boil. Strain through a sieve into a container.

When ready to serve, heat up and whisk in the butter to give the sauce a lovely sheen.

To cook and serve

Use two pans to sauté the lamb; heat oil in both and when hot quickly seal both sides. Lower the heat and cook them gently for 3 to 4 minutes on each side. Drain them on crumpled kitchen paper, untie the string and serve on the Madeira sauce.

Cut the courgettes into long thin strips, cook them very quickly and serve them on plates as garnish.

Gently heat the yoghurt with chopped mint and pour it over the carrots. Serve them with the potatoes at the table.

Variation

You can use the hot frying pans to make a simple and delicious sauce. Keep the lamb warm and pour away the oil, leaving the dark juices behind. Pour in white wine and over a high heat, using a wooden spoon, scrape the pan until the bottom is clean. Lower the heat and let the sauce thicken. Taste and add seasoning. Whisk in a little butter or red wine butter and pour into a jug. An advantage to de-glazing; the pans are easier to wash!

138

Coffee-flavoured sponge with orange cream

8 oz (225 g) soft butter
8 oz (225 g) caster sugar
4 eggs
8 oz (225 g) self-raising flour
Pinch of salt

Coffee flavouring

5 fl oz (150 ml) fresh, strong coffee
3 fl oz (75 ml) rum, Tia Maria or brandy
1 teaspoon of Camp coffee

Orange cream

1 pint (570 ml) double cream
6¼ fl oz (178 ml) frozen concentrated
    orange-juice
Grated rind of 2 oranges
1 tablespoon caster sugar

10 in (25.5 cm) cake tin with loose bottom

Decoration

3 slices of orange
Small sprig of mint

Sponge cake

Preheat the oven to gas mark 5, 375°F, 190°C. Place the butter in a large mixing bowl or electric mixer with beater attachment. Beat the butter until it becomes pale and gradually spoon in the sugar, beating all the time, until it is almost white in colour. Now add the eggs one at a time and continue mixing until the eggs are thoroughly blended.

Always mix the flour in by hand, so if you have used the electric mixer remove the bowl and place it on a damp tea-towel, sieve the flour into the bowl and using a metal spoon, fold it in. I have found that if you beat the mixture too much when the flour is added it can produce a heavy-textured cake. Spoon the mixture into the prepared tin and spread it over with the back of the spoon. Swirl the centre to produce a slight dent.

Cook for 35–40 minutes in the preheated oven until golden brown. Lightly press the centre of the cake and if it springs back test it with a skewer. If it comes out clean the cake is cooked.

Place the tin on a cake rack and leave it to cool for 5 minutes, during which time the cake will shrink slightly from the sides of the tin. Remove the cake tin, cover the rack with greaseproof paper, then turn the cake out on to it and leave to cool.

Do not wash the cake tin but line it with clingfilm; I use two strips to cover it completely with an overlap. Return the cold cake to the lined tin. Mix the coffee flavouring together and evenly pour it over the cake, starting around the outside and working in progressively smaller circles to the centre. Cover with the overlap of film and place the tin on a plate to catch any drips.
Leave the cake to soak and chill for a few hours.

139

To decorate and serve

Unwrap the cake and place it face down on a cake stand – this will allow any excess liquid to run back into the cake and not be wasted.

Whip the cream with the orange flavouring until soft peaks form. Use a spatula to spread the cream over the top and sides of the cake, using circular strokes to create an attractive rippled finish. Chill the cake until ready to serve. At the last minute decorate with a twist of 3 orange slices and a small sprig of mint laid in the folds of slices.

Variation: Whipped cream cheese

If you have tried and enjoyed the whipped cream cheese, use it instead of the orange cream to cover this soaked sponge as the flavours of lemon and coffee go well together.

8 oz (225 g) cream cheese
Nutmeg
Grated rind of I lemon
¼ pint (150 ml) sugar syrup
½ pint (275 ml) double cream

Beat the cream cheese until smooth, add the seasoning and sugar syrup. Gradually pour in the double cream and whisk until thick.

Forward preparation

The day before

Make

Soup.
Cream cheese and herb pâté.
Madeira sauce.

Cake. Soak in coffee and keep well covered with clingfilm.

The morning

Prepare

Chop and prepare lamb and lay the shaped lamb on a tray

lined with greaseproof paper.
Keep chilled.
Potatoes and carrots.

Early evening

Decorate the coffee sponge and keep it in the refrigerator until you serve the soup. Potatoes and carrots: cook ahead of time. Keep the potatoes warm in a dish with butter, covered tightly with foil. Wrap the carrots in foil and place the parcel in the bottom of the oven with the potatoes.
Cut the courgettes into strips at the last minute, but have the basket and boiling water in the pan ready.
Have crumpled kitchen paper on plates to hand.
The Madeira sauce needs to boil for a minute or two and then butter is whisked in as you serve.
Frying pans with warmed oil.
Orange slices and mint for cake.
Do not boil the yoghurt and mint dressing, warm it gently and pour over the carrots when you dish them up.

HOT CRABMEAT AND AVOCADO PARCELS
garnished with slices of flavoured lemon

SAUTÉED KIDNEYS
served in a sauce flavoured with port and mustard

A COLOURFUL SELECTION OF VEGETABLES
served with a coating of flavoured dressing

A LIGHT CHESTNUT SPONGE
flavoured and rolled with raspberry purée

Hot crabmeat and avocado parcels garnished with slices of flavoured lemon

---

The lively addition of flavoured lemon slices provides the contrast to a delicate mixture of crabmeat and avocado encased in a crisp coat of puff pastry.

1 oz (25 g) butter
2 teaspoons plain flour
4 fl oz (110 ml) single cream
1 tablespoon dry sherry
2 teaspoons lemon juice
12 oz (350 g) crabmeat, all whitemeat or an
   equal mixture of white and brown meat

1 small avocado
1 tablespoon brandy
Black pepper
12 oz (350 g) prepared puff pastry
1 egg white
Lemon slices

A large baking tray, lightly greased and floured

In a small saucepan heat the butter and using a wooden spoon, mix in the flour and cook gently, stirring all the time, for one minute. Add the cream and whisk to a smooth paste and continue whisking until the sauce comes to the boil. Draw the pan to one side and stir in the sherry and lemon juice. Spoon the sauce into a mixing bowl and mix in the crabmeat.

Using a stainless steel knife cut the avocado in half lengthwise, remove the stone and carefully peel away the skin. Place the halves, flat side down on a board, cut the flesh evenly across into slices and gently mix with the crabmeat. Pour the brandy into a ladle, hold it over a medium heat until the liquid flames and while it is alight mix with the crabmeat and avocado. Taste and season with black pepper. Set to one side.

On a floured surface roll out the pastry as thin as possible, about ⅛ in (3 mm), and cut it into eight 4 in (10 cm) squares. Divide and place the crab mixture on to the centre of each pastry shape. Brush the edges of the pastry with water and fold each square into a triangle. Using your fingers press the edges together to encase the filling. With a pair of scissors, trim the sealed edges to a curved shape and crimp the cut pastry firmly with thumb and forefinger to give a neat, rippled finish. Place the parcels on to the prepared tray and chill.

To cook and serve

Set the oven to gas mark 7, 425°F, 220°C.

Whisk the egg white with a little salt. Make three small slits in the top of each pastry and to give them a sheen, paint each parcel with the whisked egg. Bake them near the top of the preheated oven for 12–15 minutes until the parcels are crisp and brown in colour.

Meanwhile garnish each plate with overlapping flavoured lemon slices topped with curls of lemon peel. Use a fish slice to slide the parcels on to the prepared and decorated plates.

Variations

Add thinly sliced, cooked pigeon breasts, duck fillets or smoked ham to the crab and avocado mixture. Or prepare and poach about 12 oz (350 g) of prawns and scallops, mix them with 6 oz (175 g) of mushrooms that have been sliced and sautéed in butter and lemon juice. Use the cooking juices to make the binding sauce.

The combinations are inexhaustible as there are so many delicacies that can be brought together in pastry parcels. Try not to confuse the flavours, so choose no more than 4 ingredients at a time. Use the same amount of butter, flour and liquid to make the mixing sauce, otherwise the pastry may leak, but it is rather nice to serve a complementary sauce, cooked separately, spooned on to each plate and topped with a crisp pastry parcel.

Lemon slices flavoured with syrup and herbs

These lemons are excellent to eat with plain, cold chicken or with fillet of sole, cut into strips and sautéed. This makes a delicious first course.

3 oz (75 g) caster sugar	A pinch of mustard seeds
3 fl oz (75 ml) water	2 allspice berries
2 coriander seeds	Small sprig of tarragon
1 in (2.5 cm) cinnamon stick	6 lemons

In a small saucepan, over a low heat, dissolve the sugar in the water, add the flavouring and boil together until thick and syrupy. Take the pan away from the heat and leave the liquid to cool.

Choose one unblemished lemon, using a small sharp knife peel away the thin skin in spirals and cut the strips into long thin threads. Place them in a sieve and pour boiling water over the peel. Refresh them with cold water and leave them to drain.

Peel the lemons, cutting away all the white pith and cut them across into thin rounds, removing any pips. Arrange them in overlapping slices on a shallow, china dish and sprinkle the blanched rind on top. Pour the flavoured syrup through a sieve to fall over the lemons and place the dish in the refrigerator.

Serve chilled.

Kidneys

Kidneys have a delicate flavour when they are really fresh. As they are usually sold without their coating of creamy white suet, choose the kidneys that look shiny and bright. Keep them in a bowl loosely covered with clingfilm for up to 2 days in the coldest part of the refrigerator.

They are delicious and tender when they are quickly sautéed over a high heat. The only disadvantage with this method is that the pan juices tend to take on a mottled appearance and as I prefer to serve a smooth, clean-looking sauce it is better to leave the kidneys to drain in a sieve while the sauce is made. Just before serving, the kidneys are gently reheated in the sauce without boiling, as too much heat will toughen the meat.

Sautéed kidneys served in a sauce flavoured with port and mustard

These kidneys are cut lengthways down their backs, almost in half, then opened out to form a flat shape, sautéed, served with a flavoured sauce and garnished with a topping of mustard mayonnaise for each kidney.

An alternative sauce may be made by omitting the brown sauce and redcurrant jelly and adding extra port wine, cream and mustard.

You need two sieves; one to drain the kidneys, the other to strain the sauce.

24 lambs' kidneys – they usually weigh between
  1½–2 oz (40–50 g) each, so I have allowed
  for 3 per portion

Port wine, brown sauce and cream sauce	**Port wine and cream sauce**
I medium onion, chopped	4 oz (110 g) butter
4 oz (110 g) butter	I medium onion
¼ pint (150 ml) port wine	½ pint (275 ml) port
½ pint (275 ml) brown sauce	12 fl oz–¾ pint (330–425 ml) double cream
I teaspoon redcurrant jelly	2 tablespoons coarse grain mustard
I tablespoon coarse grain mustard	Black pepper
7 fl oz (200 ml) double cream to finish	Salt
Black pepper	
Salt	

Garnish

½ pint (275 ml) mayonnaise flavoured with a
  pinch of powdered ginger and coarse grain
  mustard to taste.

To sauté the kidneys

Cut each kidney lengthways down the back almost in half and using your fingers peel off the transparent skin. Open them out and snip away the white central core with a pair of scissors.

Peel and finely chop the onion. Melt 2 oz (50 g) butter in a large heavy-based frying pan. When it is sizzling, drop in half of the kidneys and over a high heat sauté them until they lose their pinkness, about 4 minutes, turning them once. Using a slotted spoon, transfer the kidneys into a sieve set over a mixing bowl. Sauté the other 12 kidneys and add them with their juices to the kidneys in the sieve. Leave them to drain while you make the sauce.

Port wine, brown sauce and cream sauce

Heat the rest of the butter in the pan, fry the onion until it is transparent, pour in the measured port and bring it to the boil, scraping the residue from the bottom of the pan using a wooden spoon. Allow it to reduce a little and then whisk in the brown sauce and redcurrant jelly. As the pan is hot it will heat up very quickly. Tip the hot, bubbling,

143

flavoured liquid through a sieve set over a saucepan large enough to hold all the kidneys and using a wooden spoon press all the juices out of the chopped onion. Set it over a low heat, stir in the mustard and cream and taste, twist in black pepper and salt, taste again. Add the drained kidneys and gently reheat them without the sauce coming to the boil.

Port wine and cream sauce

Sauté and drain the kidneys. Heat the rest of the butter in the frying pan and sauté the onion until soft. Add the port and bring it to the boil, scraping the residue from the bottom of the pan using a wooden spoon. Allow it to reduce a little and pour in the cream. Over a high heat stir the liquid continuously until it has reduced and thickened, then pour it through the sieve into a saucepan large enough to hold all the kidneys and using a wooden spoon press all the juices out of the onion. Add the drained kidneys to the sauce and when they have warmed through, take the pan from the heat, taste, add the mustard, twists of pepper and salt, gently stir these flavourings into the sauce and taste again.

To serve

Spoon the kidneys and sauce on to warmed plates, tip away the liquid that has gathered in each kidney shell and using a teaspoon refill them with the mustard mayonnaise.

The cold vegetable salad served at the table will add colour and a delightful crisp contrast of textures.

Variations

Slice the kidneys in half, sauté and reheat them in either of the suggested sauces. Spoon a ribbon of spinach purée over each serving and garnish with crisp-fried bread cubes. For spinach purée recipe, see Sole fillets spread with smoked salmon paté (page 18).

Sauté halved kidneys, prepare the sauce, using brown sauce with chicken stock instead of port. Bring the strained sauce to a boil, draw the pan aside and whisk in crumbled Stilton cheese to taste, until smooth. Gently reheat the kidneys and sauce, stir in mustard and cream.

Garnish

Crisp-fried strips of bacon drained on kitchen
  paper to dry, mixed with chopped parsley
  and then sprinkled over each serving.

A colourful selection of vegetables served with a coating of flavoured dressing

Vegetables chosen for their colour as well as flavour cooked until tender but still crisp, chilled, then attractively arranged on a shallow plate and served coated with a sparkling dressing, are delicious and I hope this will encourage you to make many selections of your own.

The prepared vegetables are cooked in lightly boiling chicken stock with a little oil and then plunged into cold water to refresh them. A vegetable-basket is the ideal thing to use. Have a large bowl of cold water close to the cooker and change the water each time it is used. If you cook the vegetables in the order I have listed the same chicken stock can be used throughout down to blanching the tomatoes for skinning. Have 5 bowls ready to keep and chill the cooked vegetables separately.

2 pints (1 litre) of light chicken stock
1 tablespoon sunflower oil
16 button onions
16 florets of cauliflower
6 carrots
6 courgettes
8 tomatoes
2 bunches of watercress

A large serving dish

Dressing

4 tablespoons lemon juice
1 teaspoon sea salt
A few twists of black pepper
8 fl oz (220 ml) light olive oil
1 teaspoon of chopped marjoram and mint

Preparation and cooking times of the vegetables

Onions

Top and tail the onions and cover them with boiling water for a minute to loosen their skins, drain the onions and run cold water over them. When they are cold, peel away the skin and the slippery layer underneath.
8 minutes in boiling stock.

Cauliflower

Cut the stems across level with the florets.
4 minutes.

Carrots

Peel them and cut across to form thin circles.
2 minutes.

Courgettes

Cut across to the same thickness as the carrots.
1 minute.

Tomatoes

Cut around the stem of the tomatoes to loosen their skins.
Draw the pan away from the heat, place the tomatoes in the stock, slowly count to ten, then using a slotted spoon lift them out and drop them into cold water.
When the tomatoes are cold, drain the water away.

Cover the cold vegetables, chill and make the dressing.

Dressing

Vinaigrette can be made with lemon juice, a light wine vinegar or a mixture of both. I think the dressing made with lemon juice and flavoured with herbs adds a pleasing sharpness to the crisp vegetables.

Pour the lemon juice into a small mixing-bowl, add the sea salt and black pepper. Stir

145

the juice with a wooden spoon until the salt has dissolved, gradually add the oil, then the herbs. Leave the dressing to soak in the flavour of the herbs.

To serve

Strain the flavoured dressing into a jug.

Pull away any yellow leaves and stems from the watercress and cut the stems short.

Arrange the onions in the centre of a plate, leave a narrow space and form a circle with the cauliflower florets. Use the watercress to make a dark green bushy hedge between the onions and cauliflower. Peel the tomatoes, cut them in half and place them, cut side down, around the florets.

In alternate order, arrange the courgettes and carrots to form the last circle. Glaze the vegetables with dressing just as the dish is taken to the table.

A light chestnut sponge flavoured and rolled with raspberry purée

8 oz (225 g) raspberries	6 eggs
3 tablespoons caster sugar	6 oz (175 g) caster sugar
3 tablespoons brandy	½ pint (275 ml) double cream
15.5 oz (439 g) tinned unsweetened chestnut purée	15 petal-shaped flaked almonds

10 × 14 in (26 × 36 cm) baking tray

Liquidize the raspberries with the caster sugar and brandy and strain through a sieve into a bowl.

Line the baking tray with foil, brush lightly with melted butter and dust with flour.

Set the oven to gas mark 6, 400°F, 200°C.

Using a wooden spoon, beat the chestnut purée until smooth and mix in 3 fl oz (75 ml) of the sieved raspberries.

Warm the mixer bowl and whisk attachment.

Separate the eggs, the yolks into the warm mixing-bowl and the whites into a large china or copper mixing-bowl. Reserve 2 tablespoons of caster sugar, add the rest to the yolks and at a high speed, beat until thick, white and fluffy – about 8 minutes.

Whisk the egg whites until they form soft, floppy peaks, gradually add the reserved caster sugar and continue whisking until stiff. Using a metal spoon fold the chestnut purée into the egg yolks and then gently fold the chestnut egg mixture into the egg whites. Pour the sponge into the prepared tin, smoothing over so that it will cook evenly.

Bake for 20 minutes until the sponge is springy to the touch. Cover the cooked sponge with a folded, damp, tea-towel tucking it into the edges. Leave until cool, then refrigerate overnight.

To decorate and serve

Whisk the cream to the floppy peak stage, add the raspberry purée and whisk until thick. Remove the tea-towel. Cut a shallow groove along a short side of the cake about 1 in (2.5 cm) from the edge; this will make rolling easier. Spread two-thirds of the flavoured cream over the cake. Fold the sponge over the groove and start to roll, peeling away the foil as you do so. Cut the rolled edges so they are even and carefully set the roll on a serving dish with the seam underneath. Fit an icing bag with a star nozzle, fill it with the remaining cream and using even pressure, squeeze the cream into tight loops along the centre of the cake. Pipe three star shapes on the side of the dish at 1 in (2.5 cm) intervals and press five petal-shaped flaked almonds on to each star to form flowers.

Forward preparation

The day before

Prepare

Raspberry purée
Kidneys. Keep them loosely covered in the coldest part of the refrigerator.
Slice and flavour the lemons.

Make

Chestnut sponge, cover it immediately with a damp tea-towel and refrigerate when cold.
Puff pastry (or leave ready-made frozen pastry to defrost overnight in the refrigerator).
Dressing.

The morning

Prepare and make the crabmeat parcels, set them on a greased and floured tray and chill.
Cook the vegetables and leave them covered in their individual bowls in the refrigerator.
Blanch the tomatoes and leave them to peel later.
Flavour the mayonnaise.
Prepare and trim the watercress and keep in a polythene bag.

Strain the flavoured dressing into a jug.

Peel and slice the tomatoes. Arrange the vegetable salad. Keep it loosely covered with clingfilm and dress it just before serving.

Fill, roll and decorate the dessert.

Set oven to gas mark 7, 425°F, 220°C.

Whisk the egg white with salt and have the pastry brush to hand, the lemon slices close by.

Kidneys; gather together pans, sieves and other utensils, sauce ingredients and mustard mayonnaise.

The parcels take 12–15 minutes to cook – this time can be used to sauté and drain the kidneys, make the sauce and strain it into a large saucepan.

The frying pan can be washed while it is still warm, or you can prepare the kidneys and sauce before the parcels are painted with egg white and set to cook, leaving 12–15 minutes free.

Bring the sauce to the gentle bubbling stage, stir in the flavourings, taste, season and taste again. Lower the heat, add the kidneys and warm them through without letting the sauce boil. I am aware that I have said this often, but it is important as it takes only seconds for the texture to turn rubbery.

MELON
filled with flavoured prawns and topped with a
curry mayonnaise

ISABELLA'S POLPETTONI
a blending of veal and cheese brought together with a coating
of crumbs, sautéed and served with a purée of tomatoes

A SELECTION OF CRISP SALADS

CHOCOLATE RUM CAKE

Melon filled with flavoured prawns and topped with a curry mayonnaise

---

A refreshing and pleasant blend of flavours.

4 Ogen or Charentais melons
I lb (450 g) cooked and peeled prawns
¼ pint (150 ml) French dressing
Juice of ½ lemon
½ small Iceberg lettuce, sliced down through
   the heart

Curry mayonnaise

---

2 tablespoons tomato purée
¼ pint (150 ml) hot water
I small onion
I clove of garlic
2 tablespoons olive oil
2 tablespoons curry powder
I tablespoon redcurrant jelly
2 lemon slices
½–1 pint (275–570 ml) mayonnaise
Black pepper
Lemon juice

To garnish
8 lemon slices with pips removed
Paprika

Curry mayonnaise

In a small bowl and using a wooden spoon, blend the tomato purée with hot water.
Peel and finely chop the onion and garlic clove. Pour the oil into a small saucepan, set
the pan over a low heat, add the onion and garlic and cook them gently until they
soften. Blend in the curry powder, then gradually pour in the tomato water. Bring the
sauce to a gentle bubble and stir in the redcurrant jelly and lemon slices.

   Turn down the heat, draw the pan half off the heat and leave the flavours to merge
for 45 minutes, stirring it frequently to prevent the mixture sticking to the bottom of
the pan. Set a sieve over a mixing-bowl and pour the curry sauce through, pressing the
onions and lemon slices with a wooden spoon to ensure all the flavours pass into the
bowl.

Remove the sieve and blend the mayonnaise into the warm sauce until the curry reaches a strength of flavour you enjoy. Taste, twist in black pepper and if it needs a lively addition stir in lemon juice. Taste again. Keep the flavoured mayonnaise in a container that has a lid.

The filling

Place the peeled prawns in a shallow dish, flavour them with French dressing and the lemon juice. Cover with clingfilm and chill.

Remove any discoloured outer leaves from the Iceberg and without separating the leaves wash it in cold water, shake away the surplus water and wrap the halved Iceberg in a tea-towel to dry.

Trim a sliver of skin away from the top and bottom of the melons to steady them; using a stainless steel knife, cut them in half horizontally and scoop out the seeds and membrane. In the centre of each cut surface press a melon baller firmly into the flesh, twist the cutter in a circle, lift it away and let the melon ball fall back into the hollow. Work your way around each rim, forming a linking chain of balls. Twist black pepper in the cavities and place them on a tray, cover the surface with a sheet of clingfilm and chill.

To serve

Spoon the mayonnaise into a jug and whisk it gently. Set the melons on plates. Make sure the lettuce is dry and place it, cut side down, on a board. Using a stainless steel knife slice the lettuce across into fine shreds, working towards the core, throw away the core. Place the crisp shreds into a mixing-bowl, add the prawns with their juices and lightly toss them together. Spoon the mixture into the melon cavities, letting the lettuce shreds fall naturally over the sides. With the handle of a teaspoon, scoop a touch of paprika into the centre of each lemon slice and place one on the rim of each plate. Pour the mayonnaise over the prawns and serve.

Variations

Halved melons provide a clean and light-tasting contrast for many unlikely and unusual fillings. Here are a few suggestions to encourage you to create a theme of endless variations which I think is the essence of my approach to cooking:
Prawns and onion in cream cheese, or cream cheese and herb pâté, spooned into the cavity of each melon and coated with Stilton dressing just before serving.
Crabmeat or lobster, mixed with grapefruit segments and lightly tossed in French dressing, served in halved melons, coated with pink mayonnaise or avocado dressing.

Isabella's Polpettoni – a blending of veal and cheese brought together with a coating of crumbs, sautéed and served with a purée of tomatoes

---

It is not really necessary to chop the veal by hand for this recipe (see Chopped lamb, page 138) as the prepared pale pink flesh, cheese and bread lose their individuality during a longer cooking period, making you more aware of combined flavours rather than textures.

I suggest that you need crisp, crunchy salads to contrast with the meat; please choose your own selection, bearing in mind the bright colour of tomato purée.

2 garlic cloves
1 ½ lb (700 g) veal tenderloin, very well
    trimmed and chopped, either by hand or a
    controllable food processor or blender
4 oz (110 g) brown breadcrumbs
½ lb (225 g) grated goat's cheese
4 tablespoons chopped parsley
4 egg yolks
1 teaspoon of salt
Black pepper
24 capers
3 oz (75 g) Mozzarella cheese
3 oz (75 g) Mortadella or ham

Oil for frying
Tomato sauce or purée – see Spiced lentils,
    page 47

To coat

Red wine
Breadcrumbs

Peel and finely chop the garlic cloves, place them in a mixing-bowl with the prepared veal, breadcrumbs, grated cheese and parsley. In a small bowl, blend the yolks and salt lightly together using a fork and pour them on to the assembled ingredients. Twist in black pepper.

Have the red wine close to hand and using your fingers, blend the chopped mixture evenly together, adding the wine a little at a time. Be careful not to overwork the mixture as it can toughen the meat – the blended ingredients will leave the sides of the bowl clean when you have added just the right amount of wine. Divide the mixture into eight portions and form each one into a ball. Wet the surface of the board and press each ball flat. In the centre of each, place 3 capers, a little Mozzarella cheese and sliced strips of Mortadella.

Pour the coating wine into a shallow bowl and spread the breadcrumbs on a plate. Rinse your hands in the wine to stop the meat sticking to them and one at a time, rest a polpettoni in the palms of your hands and close the meat around the centre. Reshape them to resemble fat sausages and roll each one in wine. Dry your hands and then coat the wet surface of the shaped meat with breadcrumbs.

Place the polpettoni on a greaseproof-paper-lined tray and chill for at least 2 hours.

To cook and serve

Use two frying pans to sauté the veal. Cover the bottom of each with a generous amount of oil and set them over a high heat. When the oil is hot add the polpettoni and fry them for 3 minutes, then carefully turn them over, supporting them with your fingertips. Seal the second side for a further 3 minutes. Lower the heat and cook them very gently for 3–4 minutes more on each side. Drain them on a crumpled kitchen-paper-lined tray and leave them to rest and settle while you reheat the sauce.

Arrange the polpettoni on a bed of tomato sauce or purée and serve them with bowls of complementary salads.

Variations

Use fillet steak or venison instead of veal.

Roll the prepared mixture into 1 in (2.5 cm) balls, coat them with grated Parmesan cheese and breadcrumbs. Crisp fry the nuggets of meat; put them on a napkin-lined dish and serve them with apéritifs.

Chocolate rum cake

A dark-coloured chocolate cake, sliced in horizontal layers, brushed with orange-flavoured rum and stacked together with custard and marinated sliced bananas. After reading the recipe through you will see that there seem to be many separate ingredients required to assemble the cake, so make sure you have everything to hand before starting.

4 eggs
10 oz (275 g) caster sugar
10 tablespoons milk
12 tablespoons corn oil
10 oz (275 g) plain flour
4 teaspoons baking powder
2 oz (50 g) Rowntrees cocoa
Salt

Flavouring

1 orange – rind and juice
¼ pint (150 ml) spiced rum
1 teaspoon Camp coffee
3 tablespoons brown sugar
4 bananas

Custard

2–3 oz (50–75 g) caster sugar
6 egg yolks
1 pint (570 ml) milk
3 oz (75 g) flour
1 oz (25 g) butter

To serve

½ pint (275 ml) double cream
Sugared rose petals or chocolate filigree

2 × 10 in (25.5 cm) cake tins with loose bottoms; lined with buttered greaseproof paper and flour-dusted.

Set the oven to gas mark 4, 350°F, 180°C.

Separate the eggs – the whites into a large mixing-bowl and the yolks into the electric mixer bowl. Add the sugar to the yolks, reserving two tablespoons and using the whisk attachment, whisk the mixture at a high speed for about 5 minutes until light and creamy. Lower the speed, pour in the milk and oil and mix to a smooth batter. Remove the bowl, set a fine sieve to rest on top, sift the flour, baking powder and cocoa into the bowl and fold in, using a metal spoon.

Place the mixing-bowl on a damp tea-towel, whisk the whites with a pinch of salt until light and fluffy, spoon in the reserved sugar and continue whisking until firm. Using a pliable spatula scrape and pour the chocolate batter on to the whites, then with a metal spoon, cut down into the centre of the mixture, draw it along the bottom, up the sides over the surface and back to the middle. Continue folding the whites from the bottom of the bowl over to the top until all the ingredients are blended, whilst slowly rotating the bowl towards you. Spoon the mixture into the prepared tins and spread it over with the back of the spoon. Swirl the centre of the cakes to produce a slight dent in each.

Bake for 30 minutes in the preheated oven.

Lightly press the centre of the cakes and if they spring back, test with a skewer; if it comes out clean the sponges are cooked.

Place the tins on a cake rack and leave them to cool for 5 minutes, during which time the cakes will shrink slightly from the sides of the tins. Remove the tins and cover the rack with greaseproof paper, turn the cakes out one at a time on to your hand, place them on the lined rack and carefully peel the lining papers away.

Line one cake tin with clingfilm, using two strips to cover it completely with an overlap and set it to one side.

The flavouring and custard

Grate the rind of the orange, using the fine side of the grater, over a small bowl. Squeeze in the juice, add the rum, Camp coffee and brown sugar and stir the flavoured liquid until the sugar has dissolved.

Peel the bananas, slice the flesh across into thin rounds, immerse them in the flavoured liquid and completely seal the bowl with clingfilm. Leave to one side while you make the custard.

In a large mixing-bowl and using a wooden spoon, beat the sugar and egg yolks until thick and creamy in colour. Place a sieve over the bowl and gradually sift in the flour, stirring it to blend.

Bring the milk to a boil in a large saucepan, then slowly pour it in a steady stream on to the sugar and yolk mixture. Whisk until smooth, then transfer it back to the milk pan. Stir the custard continuously, moving the wooden spoon in a figure of eight and bring to the boil, turn down the heat and stir until thick. Strain the custard through the sieve back into the mixing-bowl and whisk in the butter. Stir occasionally until ready to use.

To assemble

Cut each cake horizontally into 3 layers.

You need custard in each layer to sandwich the cake together, but I leave it to you to decide whether you want perhaps two layers of concentrated banana slices or arranged sliced bananas throughout the cake.

Set one slice of cake, cut side up, in the lined cake tin and using a pastry brush paint the surface with a little juice. With a pliable spatula spread one fifth of the warm custard evenly over. Starting 1 in (2.5 cm) in from the edge of the sponge arrange a thick or thin layer of banana. Continue stacking the cake brushing each layer of cake with juice then spreading with custard and distributing the bananas, ending up with sponge which should be saturated with any remaining juice.

Cover the top with clingfilm and chill for 3–4 hours until firm.

To serve

Peel away the clingfilm from the surface and invert a cake stand over the sponge and tin. Turn the tin and stand over together, lift off the ring and base, carefully unwrap the cake to reveal the pale custard and dark sponge layers.

Whisk the double cream until it forms thick peaks, fit an icing bag with a thin ribbon nozzle and fill with cream. Hold the bag at a 45° angle and with the nozzle flat side on the cake, pipe ribbons of cream at ½ in (1 cm) intervals across the top. Turn the cake slightly and pipe over the bands to form a diamond criss-cross pattern. Leave the sides plain to show the contrast of colour and texture in their even layers.

To complete the decoration arrange 3 filigree chocolate butterflies or sugared rose petals in a cluster to one side of the cake.

For chocolate filigree, please see recipe for Little pots of chocolate (page 166).

Sugared rose petals

Caster sugar
1 egg white
A cluster of large rose petals

A fine paint brush
Cake rack lined with waxed paper
An airtight tin lined with greaseproof paper

When rose petals drop they always seem to fall into attractive shapes and it is rather nice to transfer these clusters to use as cake decorations. To preserve their beauty however, they must be coated with egg white and sugar, observing two simple rules: use only dry petals and the egg wash must completely cover the surface to prevent discoloration.

Spoon 3–4 tablespoons of caster sugar on to a plate. Blend the egg white together using a fork, and checking that the petals are dry, paint both sides of each one. Lay them one at a time on the mound of sugar and using your fingers, scoop the sugar over to coat. Carefully lift each dusted petal on to the cake rack and leave it to dry a little. Dust both sides of the petal again with caster sugar and return it to the rack to dry completely. Shake off any excess sugar from each petal, place them in the lined tin and secure the lid. They will keep for 1–2 days.

Sugar-dusted violets and daffodils also make very attractive colour-contrast garnishes.

Variation: Rose flavoured syrup

Rose petals add a delicate, perfumed flavour to sugar syrup. Wrap about a dozen petals in muslin and tie the parcel with fine string. Make the syrup as usual, turn down the heat until the liquid is just bubbling, immerse the rose package and leave the flavours to mingle for 10 minutes. When you remove the parcel, squeeze out all the liquid with your fingertips.

Variation: Black cherry and rum cake

Poach stoned cherries in the rum, orange and sugar marinade, strain the cooked fruit, reserving the liquid to soak the sponge.

Spiced bananas topped with flavoured whipped cream

Pour and spoon the measured rum, sugar, Camp coffee and orange juice with rind into a small saucepan, set it over a low heat and using a wooden spoon, stir the liquid until the sugar melts. Leave the flavourings to cool.

Peel the bananas and using a stainless steel knife, slice the flesh across into rounds, letting them fall into a shallow glass dish. Pour the cool rum liquid over the fruit, seal the bowl with clingfilm and leave them to flavour for about 30 minutes. Shake the bowl every so often to ensure every slice is well coated.

To serve

Lightly whisk 1 pint (570 ml) double cream, strain the banana juices in and whisk to incorporate the flavours.

Taste, add and mix in a little more rum, Camp coffee or orange if necessary. Taste again and then whisk the cream to hold its shape. Place the bananas into glasses and spoon the flavoured cream over, shaping it into high, coffee-coloured peaks. Decorate with sugared rose petals and serve immediately on napkin-lined plates.

These flavoured bananas and cream are also delicious when served as a filling in oatmeal meringue.

Forward preparation

The day before

Make

The cakes and seal them with clingfilm.

The morning

Prepare

Orange, rum and sugar flavouring.
Peel the cooked prawns and leave them to marinate in French dressing and lemon juice.
Iceberg lettuce.

Make

Polpettoni and chill them on a greaseproof-lined tray.
Curry mayonnaise.
Tomato sauce or purée.
Flavour the bananas.
Make the custard.
Assemble the cake and chill.

Early evening

Prepare

Melons and cover with clingfilm.
Salads to accompany the veal.
Unmould and decorate the cake.
Slice the Iceberg and mix it with the prawns.
Spoon the mayonnaise into a jug and have the whisk close by.
Place the melons on plates.

Have ready

Oil in the frying pans.
A tray lined with crumpled kitchen paper.
Tomato sauce or purée in a small saucepan.

STEPHENS

SMOKED SALMON MOUSSE
BLACK OLIVE TOASTS

FILLET STEAK
in sherry and cream or coffee and cream

MANGETOUT
SAUTÉED POTATOES WITH BACON VINAIGRETTE

CHAMPAGNE ORANGE AND RASPBERRY TRIFLE

Smoked salmon mousse

12 oz (350 g) smoked salmon trimmings
1½ tablespoons lemon or lime juice
7 fl oz (200 ml) single cream
Grated nutmeg and black pepper to taste
¾ pint (425 ml) double cream
1 tablespoon aspic dissolved in 8 fl oz (225 ml)
   boiling water
1 tablespoon dry sherry

To decorate

8 sprigs of rosemary
8 parsley leaves
8 ramekins

Chop the smoked salmon and place into the food processor or blender. Work until you have a very smooth paste, now add lemon or lime juice and single cream. Mix together and add the seasoning. Pour the double cream into a mixing bowl and whisk until you have soft, almost floppy peaks. Count 6 tablespoons of liquid aspic into the salmon and mix until completely smooth, then immediately fold into the cream using a metal spoon. Carefully spoon the mousse into dishes. Smooth the top with a palette knife and chill.

Mix 1 tablespoon of sherry with the liquid aspic and have the rosemary and parsley to hand. If the aspic hardens while you are waiting for the mousses to set do not worry, it can easily be made liquid again by heating it gently. You need a thin layer of aspic on top of each mousse, just enough to give a light sheen. Spoon a little on to one, swirl the ramekin around so the aspic covers the top and tip the surplus on to the next mousse, add a little more and repeat the swirling process until they are all coated. One by one, dip the rosemary into the remaining aspic and arrange to one side of the mousse. Dip a parsley leaf and place it on the sprig. Chill until ready to serve.

To serve

Serve on doily-lined plates and place crisp triangles of toast spread with black olive paste to one side.

Variations

Grated orange rind added to the mousse.

Lightly grease the ramekins, turn the set mousses out onto plates and serve them with strawberry vinaigrette poured over one half.

Spread orange butter on triangles of toast.

It is also pleasant to find a concealed centre, e. g. chopped prawns, avocado or a contrasting mayonnaise.

Black olive paste

Served on crisp brown toast and used as a garnish with most mousses and fish, this paste adds an unusual contrast of flavour. It will keep for 2 weeks, as long as you store it covered and chilled.

Soak the black olives in a tablespoon of olive oil, then use it to cook the onions. You need ¾ lb (350 g) of olives – when stoned they will weigh about ½ lb (225 g). Use a cherry stoner; sometimes there is one on the end of a garlic crusher.

I tablespoon olive oil	I teaspoon tomato purée
½ lb (225 g) peeled and chopped onion	I oz (25 g) butter
I clove of garlic	I teaspoon honey
Stoned olives	Sea salt and black pepper
6 fl oz (175 ml) red wine	

Drain the olive oil into a saucepan, add the onions and crush the garlic over. Set over a low heat to cook while you chop the olives, add these with the wine and tomato purée. Cook until nearly all the wine has evaporated – this will take about 10 minutes. Turn off the heat and leave to cool before tipping it into the processor or blender. Add the butter and honey. Work until fairly smooth, then taste and season. Turn into a container and cover when cold.

Fillet steaks

The choice is yours: fillet steak that has been marinated in sherry and a sauce flavoured with Worcestershire sauce and cream, or for a more unusual and equally pleasing taste, fillet marinated in coffee and the sauce flavoured with mustard and cream.

Whichever you choose, both the sauces are made using the meat flavouring left in the pans, and that makes for easier cleaning! I suggest you use two frying pans large enough to spread the steaks out, otherwise they will start to sweat and braise instead of fry.

Allow the steaks to come to room temperature and when you fry them, let the pan and the oil, or butter, get very hot first. Quickly seal the meat on all sides then lower the heat, turn them every 2 or 3 minutes, allowing them to brown and ensure even cooking.

I find the best way to tell how much a steak has cooked is by touch. Press the steak lightly down into the pan; if it springs back immediately the steak is rare and usually it has cooked for 3 minutes each side at the lower heat. If the steak is not quite so bouncy it will be medium, 5 minutes on each side, and if it is firm you have a well cooked steak, 8 minutes each side. The minute timings are for a 2 in (5 cm) thick fillet steak. Telling by touch comes with experience. I am sure that when I first began to cook, the fried steaks were very much smaller than when they started as the only way I could tell how they were cooked was to slice a little away and look, then cut again to make sure.

Many people enjoy the sight and sound of sizzling steak on a plate, but I think, like all meat it benefits from a rest.

8 fillet steaks

Either with sherry and cream

Marinade	Sauce
½ pint (275 ml) medium dry sherry	2 oz (50 g) butter
1 oz (25 g) peppercorns	½ pint (275 ml) medium dry sherry
	2–3 tablespoons Worcestershire sauce
	8 fl oz (225 ml) double cream
	Black pepper

Or with coffee and cream

Marinade	Sauce
½ pint (275 ml) fresh cold coffee	2 oz (50 g) butter
1 clove of garlic, crushed	½ pint (275 ml) fresh coffee
1 oz (25 g) peppercorns	1–2 teaspoons caster sugar
	6 fl oz (175 ml) double cream
	2 teaspoons coarse grain mustard

To fry

A little oil and butter

Find a suitable plastic container that will hold the steaks closely together, pour the chosen marinade over and cover loosely with clingfilm. Leave them to flavour for not less than 5 hours, turning them twice.

To cook

Bring the steaks to room temperature, leaving them in the marinade.

Heat the oil and butter in the pans, pat the steaks dry with kitchen paper and over a high heat, quickly seal them on all sides. Turn down the heat and cook them to preference.

Take the fillets out and keep them warm. To one hot pan add the sauce liquid and to the other, butter. Bring the liquid to boil, scraping the residue from the bottom of the pan using a wooden spoon, then carefully pour this on to the bubbling butter. Allow the sherry or coffee to reduce over a high heat until you have a brown syrupy sauce. Add the flavouring and cream. Leave it to reduce a little and then taste and season. Lower the heat while you dish up the steaks.

To serve

This is one of the few dishes where I like to see sauce poured over meat and if you have allowed it to reduce long enough, the sauce will give the steaks a rich colourful glaze.

Garnish each plate with a bundle of crisp mangetout and serve the sautéed potatoes with bacon vinaigrette at the table.

If you prefer a salad with steak, heat the bacon vinaigrette until bubbling and pour it over a large bowl of mixed salad; serve immediately.

Bacon vinaigrette

I small onion
6 streaky rashers Canadian-style bacon. This is
  usually sold without rind and is very good
  when crisply fried.

I teaspoon oil
5 fl oz (150 ml) French dressing

Peel and chop the onion, cut bacon into thin strips and separate them to make for
easier frying. Heat the oil in a large frying pan and cook the bacon strips until crisp.
Turn off the heat. Stir in the onion, followed by French dressing. Tip into a jug, cover
loosely with clingfilm and keep in a cool place.

This hot dressing has many delicious uses; the two that I have suggested for this
menu and also others throughout the book. You will find by using different types of
bacon you can vary the flavour of the same dish. For instance: hot, bubbling smoked
bacon vinaigrette, poured over a chilled sliced avocado is an excellent first course. If
the dressing is made with unsmoked bacon it will impart a totally different flavour and
subtle alterations can be made by the addition of prawns or other shellfish.

Champagne, orange and raspberry trifle

I like to see distinct layers in a trifle: sponge and biscuits usually soaked with a
fortified wine, but in this case, orange juice, a layer of fruit purée, then jelly
with fruit, and a topping of custard. Any purée can be used, chosen to
complement the jelly and fruit, but jam is equally as good.

¼ pint (150 ml) fresh orange juice
1½ pkts gelatine ¾ oz (20 g) – see Pineapple
  mousse, page 178
I oz (25 g) caster sugar
Juice of 2 oranges
2 oz (50 g) whisked sponge
12 ratafia biscuits
6 oz (175 g) raspberry purée or 3 tablespoons
  jam
½ bottle champagne at room temperature
I lb (450 g) frozen raspberries – these are
  excellent if they are used straight from the
  deep freeze

Custard

I pint (570 ml) double cream
4 egg yolks
4 tablespoons caster sugar
Orange flower water

To decorate

Candied fruit

The base and jelly

Pour the ¼ pint (150 ml) orange juice into a small saucepan and sprinkle the gelatine
over. Leave it to soak, set the oven to its lowest setting and place the soaked gelatine
in at the bottom to melt.

Put the caster sugar and the juice of the oranges into a pan, set it over a low heat
and stir until the sugar has dissolved. Switch off the heat and leave to cool. The
gelatine should have melted by now; give it a gentle stir, pour it into a jug and set to
one side until cool.

Cover the bottom of a deep glass bowl with pieces of sponge and pour the orange syrup over, add a layer of biscuits and then a layer of purée or jam. Open the champagne, carefully pour into a bowl and stir in the gelatine. Add the frozen raspberries and almost straight away the jelly will start to set. Allow it to become almost solid before adding to the trifle. If liquid jelly is poured over the sponge and biscuits it will soak through and they will become flabby and similar in taste.

The custard

Pour the cream into a large saucepan and set it over a low heat to boil. In a mixing-bowl put the egg yolks and sugar. Using a wooden spoon mix until almost white in colour. Allow the cream to boil for 2 minutes then pour it on to the beaten eggs. Mix together until smooth and then pour it back into the saucepan. Do not let the mixed cream boil or it will separate. Stir the custard over a low heat until you can see little bubbles appear around the edges and immediately pour it back into the mixing-bowl. Stir gently to make sure you have a smooth custard. Taste, add a little more sugar if necessary and a touch of orange flower water. Leave to cool and then ladle it carefully over the set jelly. Refrigerate for at least 2 hours or, better still, overnight.

To decorate and serve

For more flavour the trifle needs nothing; however there is a lot of bare white custard, so perhaps just before serving arrange strips of candied fruit into a pattern.
Serve the trifle with a large spoon to ensure all the layers are together on the plates.

Forward preparation

The day before

Prepare and cook potatoes for sauté.

Make

French dressing
Trifle
Black olive paste

The morning

Make mousses and decorate.
Marinate steaks.
Cook bacon vinaigrette.

Early evening

Bring the steaks to room temperature.
Decorate trifle and keep chilled.

Have ready

Bread to toast. Black olive paste.
Just before you serve the mousses, sauté the potatoes until crisp and keep them warm on a tray lined with kitchen paper, then wash the pan and have it ready with the other one to cook steaks. When they are cooked and the sauce is reducing use the free pan for heating bacon vinaigrette.

ASPARAGUS MOUSSE
served with a delicate peach dressing and a crisp garnish of celery

SIRLOIN STEAKS
filled with mushrooms and smoked ham, pan fried and served with a trio of garnishes

BUTTERED ROAST POTATOES
COS LETTUCE

A LIGHT BUT RICH CHOCOLATE CREAM
served in individual ramekins and decorated with chocolate filigree

---

Asparagus mousse served with a delicate peach dressing and a crisp garnish of celery

---

1 lb (450 g) asparagus
½ oz (10 g) gelatine (1 pkt)
½ teaspoon caster sugar
1 tablespoon red wine vinegar
Black pepper
2–3 drops of Tabasco
8 oz (225 g) cream cheese
1 teaspoon grated onion
5 fl oz (150 ml) double cream

Peach dressing

3 soft, ripe peaches
1 tablespoon lemon juice
1 tablespoon mango chutney
7 fl oz (200 ml) light olive oil
2 fl oz (50 ml) red wine vinegar
Black pepper

Garnish

2 heads of celery
A shallow clear glass bowl that will hold 3½
   pints (2 litres) of water

Have salted boiling water in a saucepan.

Using a stainless steel knife trim off the white, almost woody, base from each asparagus stalk and then peel a thin layer of skin away, starting at the bottom working to the tip. Slice each stalk across into rounds, putting the tips to one side.

Cook the sliced stalks in the water, just enough to cover them, for 3–4 minutes until tender. Drain the slices into a sieve resting over a large bowl, shake the sieve to remove excess liquid and tip the asparagus on to a kitchen-paper-lined tray to dry. Return the cooking liquid to the saucepan and replace the sieve over the bowl. In the saucepan reboil the cooking liquid, add the asparagus tips to cook briefly until tender but still firm. Drain them well.

Spoon 3 tablespoons of the cooking liquid into a small saucepan and sprinkle the gelatine evenly over the surface.

161

Measure ¼ pint (150 ml) of the asparagus water back into the larger saucepan. Throw the rest away. Bring the water to a boil and pour it over the soaked gelatine. Using a plastic spatula sitr until all the crystals have dissolved, and transfer to a jug.

Gently pat the asparagus slices completely dry with fresh kitchen paper and spoon them into the food processor or blender, work until smooth adding the sugar, vinegar, pepper and Tabasco as you blend.

Put the cheese into a mixing-bowl, place a damp tea-towel underneath and using a wooden spoon, beat the cheese until smooth. Mix in the gelatine liquid and the grated onion.

Pour the cream into another mixing-bowl and whisk it until you can see the whisk shapes in the cream. With a metal spoon, fold the asparagus purée into the cheese, then, still using a metal spoon, gently mix in the cream and drained asparagus tips. Taste for any extra seasoning, then spoon the mousse into the glass bowl and using a plastic spatula, smooth the surface level. Place it into the refrigerator to set.

Peach dressing

Select a small dish that will hold the peaches together in a single layer and pour boiling water over them. Slowly count to 10, drain and cover them with cold water. Free the skin at the stem and carefully pull it away in strips. Hold the peaches, one at a time, over the liquidizer and using a stainless steel knife, cut the peaches into the jug. Add the rest of the ingredients and liquidize until smooth. Taste and then pass and press the purée, with the help of a wooden spoon, through a sieve into a bowl. Pour the dressing into a container that has a lid. Keep in a cool dark place.

Variation

Serve this delicious and delicate dressing with hot poached asparagus accompanied with lemon cream (see page 87).

Celery garnish

I suggest two heads of celery, so the clean-tasting crisp sticks can be eaten throughout the meal. Using a stainless steel knife, cut off each root and remove any damaged stalks. Pull away their strings and leaves, keeping the pale green ones for decorating the mousse. Wash the celery in cold water and pat dry with kitchen paper. Slice the stalks across into 2 in (5 cm) lengths and arrange them on a napkin-lined plate.

To serve

Pour the dressing into a sauceboat. Rest the mousse on a napkin-lined plate. Arrange a band of small celery leaves down one side of the mousse.

At the table, spoon the mousse on to the plates, ladle a little dressing over each portion to provide an attractive colour and flavour.

Offer the celery as a crisp contrast.

Variation: Smoked salmon rolls

Spread slices of smoked salmon with lemon cream and asparagus mousse. Roll the slices into compact cylinder shapes.

Allow 2 rolls per person.

162

Sirloin steaks filled with mushrooms and smoked ham, pan fried and served with a trio of garnishes

I suggest these steaks are served medium-cooked so that the filling will warm through. The cooking time, after the initial high heat for a ¾ in (2 cm) thick stuffed sirloin, is 2–3 minutes each side; press the meat with your fingertips and it will slowly bounce back into place (see Fillet steak with sherry and cream, page 157). Use two frying pans large enough to spread the steaks out, then they will brown easily.

Seasoning is important when serving steaks that have little or no sauce, but salt and pepper should only be added to the meat when it has been completely sealed at a high heat. When the steaks are cooked leave them to rest and settle for a few minutes; they will be more tender to eat.

8 5–6 oz (150–175 g) sirloin steaks, ¾ in (2 cm)
    thick
Oil to prepare steaks

String and needle

Stuffing

1 medium onion
8 oz (225 g) mushrooms
2 oz (50 g) butter
Salt and black pepper
1 tablespoon chopped parsley
1 teaspoon chopped marjoram or thyme
Juice of ½ lemon
8 oz (225 g) smoked ham

To fry

2 oz (50 g) butter
4 tablespoons oil
Sea salt and black pepper

Glazing sauce

2 oz (50 g) butter
½ pint (275 ml) red wine or beef stock

Trio of garnishes:

Green mayonnaise

4 oz (110 g) spinach leaves
2 oz (50 g) watercress leaves – 2 bundles
Nutmeg
1 pint (570 ml) mayonnaise

Avocado dressing

2 large ripe avocados
4 fl oz (125 ml) lime or lemon juice
1 tablespoon hazelnut oil
Sea salt and black pepper
A few shakes of Tabasco
1 teaspoon dry sherry

Chopped tomato chutney

Juice of ½ lemon
1 Granny Smith apple
1 medium onion
1 clove of garlic
8 very firm tomatoes
2 tablespoons red wine vinegar

2 tablespoons light olive oil
1 teaspoon caster sugar
Grated rind of 1 orange
1 tablespoon chopped mint leaves
1 tablespoon horseradish sauce
Black pepper

To make the garnishes:

Green mayonnaise

Trim away the stem at the base of each leaf and wash the spinach in lots of cold water to remove any grit.

Wash the watercress bundles quickly in cold water and shake the surplus away. Pick off the dark green leaves and put them with the cleaned spinach. Bring a saucepan of salted water to boil and over a high heat cook the leaves for 2 minutes.

Strain them in a sieve placed over a large container. Throw away the hot water and refresh the leaves with plenty of cold. Squeeze the leaves dry in the palms of your hands, squeeze again and drop the green bundle into the food processor or blender. Work until fine, then with the help of a pliable spatula, pass the purée through a sieve into a mixing-bowl.

Blend in the mayonnaise, taste, grate in a little nutmeg and taste again. Keep it in a container that has a lid.

Avocado dressing

Cut the avocados in half, peel away their skins and remove the stones. Place the flesh in the food processor or blender with the juice, oil, salt and pepper and a touch of Tabasco. Work until you have a smooth purée and taste. Scoop the avocado into a container that has a lid, carefully spoon the sherry to lie on the surface and cover with the lid.

Chopped tomato chutney

It is very pleasing to see all the ingredients cut to a uniform size and shape. They must be handled gently during heating and mixing otherwise they could disintegrate and the dressing would be a purée – just as good to eat, but all the careful preparation would have been wasted.

Pour water with the lemon juice into a small bowl. Hold the apple steady and using an apple corer, push it through the stem to the base, pull it out, throw away the core and put the fruit in the lemon water.

Slice the top and bottom of the onion, peel away the skin and the first fleshy layer. Cut the onion in half and then into even-sized cubes. Peel the garlic clove and slice it into very thin strips.

Cut around the stem of the tomatoes to loosen their skins. Select a bowl that will hold the tomatoes together in a single layer. Pour boiling water to cover and slowly count to 10. Tip away the water and run cold water over the tomatoes until they are cold. Peel away the skins, cut the tomatoes in half horizontally and using your fingertips, scoop out their seeds. Cut the flesh into small even shapes.

Take the apple out of the lemon water and dry it with kitchen paper. Using a stainless steel knife, cut it in half, then into cubes.

In a saucepan, place the prepared onion, garlic, apple and tomatoes. Pour in the vinegar and oil, spoon in the sugar. Set the pan over a low heat and using a wooden spoon, gently stir until it heats through, about 2–3 minutes.

Take the saucepan to one side and carefully mix in the rind, mint and horseradish sauce. Taste. Twist in black pepper and taste again. Transfer to a bowl and when the dressing is completely cold, cover and seal with cling film.

Keep all three dressings in the refrigerator.

The stuffing

Top and tail the onion, remove the skin, the first fleshy layer and cut it in half. Finely chop the halves. Using a stainless steel knife chop the mushrooms with their stalks to a similar size.

Melt the butter in a large frying pan and cook the onions gently for about 5 minutes, add the chopped mushrooms, raise the heat and stirring with a wooden spoon, cook the mixture until all the juices have disappeared. Season with salt and pepper, stir in the parsley and herbs with the lemon juice. Continue cooking and stirring until the lemon juice has evaporated. Transfer the stuffing to a mixing-bowl.

Slice the ham into very thin strips and mix it with the cold stuffing. Cover and pat clingfilm over the surface.

The steaks

One at a time, lay the steaks on a board with the border of fat facing away. Press your hand on top of the meat to steady it and using a sharp pointed knife, make a small horizontal slit in the centre, halfway up, through to the fat. Slide the blade along to one side without cutting through. Pull the knife out, then back in with the blade facing the other way, cut towards the other side and carefully pull the knife out again.

You now have a small opening to a large pocket. Fill each pocket with the stuffing, using the handle of a small teaspoon to push it to the far edges. Gently pat the steaks even and over-sew the cut, finishing with a loose knot. Brush both sides of the steaks with oil and arrange them on a tray. Cover with clingfilm and chill.

To cook and serve

Bring the steaks to room temperature.

Mix and spoon the dressings into bowls and take them to the table. On the highest setting, heat equal amounts of oil and butter in the pans; when the oils are hot and sizzling add the steaks, standing them up to colour the fat, then quickly seal them over the high heat. Turn down the heat, season with a sprinkling of salt and twists of black pepper and cook for 2–3 minutes on both sides. Using a fish slice, lift the steaks on to a baking tray, cut and pull away the string and leave them to rest.

To one hot pan add the butter, to the other, the wine or beef stock. Scrape the residue from the bottom of the pan using a wooden spoon, then carefully pour the liquid on to the bubbling butter.

Dish up the steaks while you allow the liquid to reduce to a syrupy sheen. Pour a little sauce over each steak and serve with the roast potatoes at the table and plain Cos lettuce leaves arranged standing upright in a glass bowl.

Variation

Prepare the stuffing as I have described but instead of ham, use thin slices of smoked salmon. It adds a faint fishy taste to the meat which is surprisingly pleasant.

Buttered roast potatoes

16 medium sized waxy potatoes
3 oz (75 g) butter
2 dessertspoons of oil

Set the oven to gas mark 7, 425°F, 220°C.

Peel and shave the potatoes to egg shapes, making one long side flat to prevent rolling during cooking. Hold one 'egg' between your thumb and forefinger and using a small stainless steel knife, slice down and through almost to the flat side at even ⅛ in (3 mm) intervals. Repeat with the other potatoes.

Heat the butter and oil in a baking tray until very hot. Add the potatoes, baste each one with the hot fat and cook them near the top of the oven for 45 minutes until they are golden, crisp fans. Spoon the hot oils over the potatoes at least twice during the cooking. Using a slotted spoon lift them onto a kitchen-paper-lined tray to drain.

A light but rich chocolate cream served in individual ramekins and decorated with chocolate filigree

---

Tracing a design on silicon paper, following the lines with piped chocolate, leaving them to dry, then placing them at a jaunty angle on a simple dessert such as this, will make the presentation exciting. I have drawn a pattern for you to trace and give you ideas. Then all you need is a metal fine plain nozzle, piping bag and a steady hand.

Chocolate cream

I lb (450 g) Terry's or Bournville plain chocolate
7 fl oz (200 ml) freshly brewed coffee
4 medium eggs

8 small ramekin dishes

Chocolate filigree

4 oz (110 g) plain chocolate
A touch of butter, less than ¼ teaspoon.
A simple pattern traced 10 times on to a sheet
of silicon paper. I always make more than I
need in case one breaks.

A fine plain metal nozzle fitted with a small bag.

Chocolate cream

Break the chocolate into a medium sized saucepan and pour in the coffee. Set the pan over a low heat and using a wooden spoon, stir until smooth and then leave to cool.

Separate the eggs, the yolks into a small bowl and the whites into a large mixing-bowl. With a fork beat the egg yolks until they are blended together, pour the mixture through a sieve into a jug and stir the sieved yolks into the cooled chocolate. Whisk the egg whites until they form soft peaks. Scrape all the chocolate on to the whisked whites and then with a metal spoon, fold it in.

Ladle the mousse into the ramekins, arrange them on a tray and chill.

Chocolate filigree

Using double sided tape, secure the silicon paper to a flat board.

Break the chocolate into pieces. Put the pieces closely together on a plate that will lie comfortably over a saucepan. Fill the pan half full of water and bring it to the boil. Switch off the heat and rest the plate on top. Leave the chocolate to melt gently. Put the plate down on a tea-towel, as the underneath will be wet. Add the butter and with a pliable spatula, blend the chocolate until completely smooth, then scoop it into the prepared bag.

Hold the nozzle just above the tracing and using gentle even pressure follow the lines of the drawings.

Leave the filigree decorations in a cool place to dry and then store them on the paper in an airtight tin. Use within two days.

To serve and decorate

Place each mousse on a napkin-lined plate and with a palette knife transfer the chocolate drawings.

Variations

1 teaspoon grated orange rind stirred in the melted chocolate and coffee.
Brandy soaked sponge set in the bottom of each ramekin.

Forward preparation

The day before

Make

Peach dressing.
Tomato chutney.
Green mayonnaise.
Chocolate filigree decorations.

The morning

Prepare

Potatoes, but do not slice them, keep covered with cold water.
Celery and Cos lettuce. Put them in polythene bags.

Make

Asparagus mousse.
Chocolate cream.
Mushroom stuffing and fill and sew the steaks.
Avocado dressing.

Early evening

Bring the steaks to room temperature.
Arrange celery and lettuce.
Set oven to gas mark 7, 425°F, 220°C.

Have ready

Baking tin with butter and oil.
2 trays, 1 lined with kitchen paper.
Butter and oil in the frying pans.
Butter and wine for the sauce close by.
Mix and dish up the salad

garnishes. Keep them covered with clingfilm and serve chilled.
Whisk the peach dressing and pour into a sauceboat.
Dry and slice the potatoes.
Decorate asparagus mousse.
Place the filigree decorations on the chilled chocolate creams just before serving.

SAUTÉED SMOKED MUSSELS
with hot bacon dressing

A CASSEROLE OF BEEF
garnished with vegetables and topped with sliced potatoes

CELERY AND WALNUT SALAD

APRICOT AND ALMOND TART

Sautéed smoked mussels with hot bacon dressing

All my smoked mussels and salmon are purchased from Loch Fyne Oysters Ltd., Ardkinglas, Cairndow, Argyll, Scotland, telephone: 04996-264/217.

The delicate and individual flavour of smoked mussels mingled with a hot bacon dressing and poured over fans of cold crisp Iceberg lettuce will produce a light beginning to a meal.

I lb (450 g) smoked mussels
½ lb (225 g) green bacon rashers
2 onions
Sunflower oil for frying

½ pint (275 ml) French dressing
½ lb (225 g) button mushrooms or mangetout peas
I small compact Iceberg lettuce

Carefully examine each mussel, removing any pieces of shell and using a pair of tweezers, take out their beards. Place the mussels in a bowl, coat them with a little oil and cover the surface with clingfilm.

Cut the rind off the bacon and slice each rasher across into fine strips. Top, tail and peel the onions, remove the first fleshy layers, cut them in half and chop the halves into small, even shapes.

, Cover the base of a frying pan with a film of oil, set it over a high heat and crisp-fry the bacon. Add the onions and using a wooden spoon, mix them together. Draw the pan to one side, blend in the French dressing and tip the mixture into a bowl.

Cut away the earthy base from the mushroom stalks and wipe the caps clean. Cut the mushrooms down into four and place them in a kitchen-paper-lined container.

Unless the mangetout peas are very young and tender, trim both ends of the pods and pull away their strings. Immerse them in boiling water for one minute. Drain the peas into a colander and rinse them with cold water, gently moving the peas around with fingertips to ensure every pod is cooled. In a shallow container, layer them between kitchen paper towels.

Peel away any discoloured leaves from the Iceberg lettuce, cut it in half, wash briefly in cold water and pat it dry in a tea-towel.

To serve

If you have chosen to include mangetout peas, layer them in a sieve set over a saucepan half filled with boiling water to warm them through. Using a stainless steel knife, slice each half of Iceberg into 4 even wedges. Place one on each plate and with the palm of your hand, gently press them down to fan out their leaves. Heat a thin layer of oil in a large frying pan, add the mussels and slide the pan backwards and forwards over the flame to spread and heat them through.

Using a wooden spoon, stir in the bacon dressing and continue stirring until the liquid bubbles. Lastly add the warmed pods or mushrooms. With a slotted spoon, transfer the mussels and vegetables on to the Iceberg fans, pour over the dressing and serve immediately.

Variations

Instead of Iceberg wedges, allow a quarter of a peeled and sliced avocado per person. Sprinkle fried breadcrumbs over the sautéed mussels to provide a crisp contrast.

Sauté fillets of poached poultry or game and use smoked bacon to flavour the dressing.

Beef

I have found no quick, foolproof way of knowing how tender beef will be when it is cooked. I always rely on my butcher's advice and trust him to sell me meat that he has selected and hung well. To enable you to cook beef correctly, it is good to find out how your butcher cuts his meat and which part of the animal it comes from. If a joint contains more used muscles it will need more cooking. If it is cut from a part where the muscles are not used so much, then it will need less time.

Unless you are marinating beef, it will keep well for 2 days in the coolest part of the refrigerator, on a cake rack, with a tray underneath to catch the drips. If you are storing steaks, brush them with oil, lay them out on a plastic tray and cover loosely with clingfilm.

A casserole of beef, garnished with vegetables and topped with sliced potatoes

4 lb (2 kg) Rump steak
2 onions
1 pint (570 ml) Guinness or red wine
1 garlic clove
3–4 oz (75–110 g) butter
1–2 tablespoons flour
Nutmeg

Garnish

16 button onions
1 lb (450 g) carrots
A small turnip
Butter

6 pints (3 litres) casserole

Topping

2 lb (1 kg) potatoes
1 pint (570 ml) milk
1 garlic clove, peeled
Nutmeg and salt
Butter to glaze

Set oven to gas mark 3, 325°F, 170°C.

Rump is usually sold in 1 inch (2.5 cm) thick slices. Using a sharp knife, cut away all the fat and gristle. Slice the trimmed pieces into 24 × 2 in (5 cm) triangle shapes.

Peel the onions, remove the first fleshy layer and cut them in half. Place the halves, cut side down on a board and cut them across into thin slices. Peel the garlic and cut it into slivers. Pour the beer into a jug. Place a mixing-bowl near, or on, the stove.

In a frying pan and over a high heat melt a third of the butter. Add 5–6 triangles of meat and allow them to brown and turn them with a pair of large tongs to brown the other sides. Transfer them to the bowl, add more butter to the pan and continue to fry the meat in batches.

Fry the onions and garlic until soft and using a slotted spoon, lift them to the bowl. Heat the rest of the butter in the pan, stir in enough flour to absorb it and stirring all the time, gradually pour in the beer or wine. Bring the liquid to a boil, scraping the residue from the bottom of the pan and draw the pan off the heat. Leaving the meat juices in the bowl, arrange the beef and onions in the casserole and grate nutmeg over each layer.

Pour the thickened beer through a sieve into the mixing bowl, blend it into the juices and ladle it over the meat. Cover the surface with a double layer of greaseproof paper and seal the casserole with foil.

Cook in the lower part of the oven until tender. Check after 2 and 2½ hours. Remove the foil and keep the casserole in a cool place overnight.

Vegetable garnish

Top and tail the onions and cover them with boiling water for a minute to loosen their skins, drain the onions and run cold water over them. When they are cold, peel away the skin and the slippery layer underneath.

Peel and cut the carrots and turnip to a similar size and shape as the onions. Immerse the vegetables in boiling water for a few minutes and using a slotted spoon, lift them to a colander. Rinse them with cold water and dry them in a tea-towel.

Heat a little butter in a frying pan and sauté the vegetables to give them a glaze. Leave to cool and gently stir them into the casserole with a seasoning of salt and black pepper.

Potato topping

Peel the potatoes. Cut each one across into thin slices and wrap them in a tea-towel.

Slowly heat the milk with the garlic clove and grated nutmeg in a large saucepan, add the potatoes and gently cook the slices for 15 minutes.

Strain the potatoes into a colander and throw away the milk and the garlic. Arrange cold potato slices over the meat, overlapping both the slices and rows to completely cover the surface. Using a pastry brush, paint a thin coating of butter over the top layer and reheat the casserole for an hour at gas mark 4, 350°F, 180°C, raising the heat for the last 15 minutes to brown the potatoes.

To serve

Serve the meat and potatoes directly from the dish, using a large spoon and fork. The celery and walnut salad will provide a crisp clean-tasting contrast. Offer warm brown rolls nestling in the fold of a napkin-lined basket.

Variations

Gently poach soaked prunes in red wine, fill each one with a rolled anchovy fillet which has been soaked in milk to remove excess salt and rinsed. Stir the stuffed prunes into the cooked beef casserole before reheating.

Present the casserole without the layered potato topping and garnish each portion with celery and walnuts that have been sautéed lightly in butter.

170

Celery and walnut salad

2 heads of celery
4 oz (110 g) shelled walnuts
1 hard-boiled egg yolk
Juice of 1 lemon

¼ teaspoon sea salt
4 tablespoons hazelnut oil
1 teaspoon chopped parsley
Black pepper

Using a stainless steel knife, cut off the bases from the celery and remove any damaged stalks. Pull away their strings and leaves, keeping the pale green ones for garnish. Wash the celery in cold water and pat dry with kitchen paper. Slice the stalks into fine strips about 2 inches (5 cm) long and place them in a large glass bowl with the walnuts.

Chop the egg yolk.

Put the lemon juice into a mixing-bowl and add the sea salt. Stir the juice with a wooden spoon until the salt has dissolved. Slowly pour in the oil and stir gently until blended together. Twist in black pepper, add the chopped yolk and parsley, and taste again.

To serve

Blend the dressing together again, pour it evenly over the salad and arrange a hedge of celery leaves at one side of the bowl.

Apricot and almond tart

Pastry

4 oz (110 g) butter
1 tablespoon lemon juice
1 egg yolk
1 tablespoon cold water
8 oz (225 g) flour
Pinch of salt
2 tablespoons caster sugar

Filling

1½ lb (700 g) fresh apricots
Apricot or gooseberry jam

Sponge

6 oz (175 g) soft butter
6 oz (175 g) caster sugar
3 eggs
4 oz (110 g) self-raising flour
2 oz (50 g) ground almonds
A few drops of almond essence

The topping

6 oz (175 g) icing sugar
Lemon juice
A long piece of thin lemon ribbon *or* blanched
   lemon rind
A small cluster of grapes

10 inch (25.5 cm) loose-bottomed flan tin, brushed lightly with oil and dusted with flour

Pastry

Make sure the bowl and the ingredients are cold.

Cut the butter into small cubes. Mix the lemon juice, egg yolk and water together in a jug. Sift the flour, salt and sugar into a mixing-bowl resting on a tea-towel. Add the butter and rub the mixture between your fingers and thumbs until you have a fine crumble. Make a well in the centre, pour in the liquid and using a spatula, cut and fold it in. Hold the bowl, and with your free hand gather the mixture together, gently pressing and rolling it into a smooth ball. Wrap and chill the pastry in clingfilm. (Some people whose hands are always hot, find it difficult to make pastry in the traditional way as it needs to be kept cool. However, pastry can be made in the blender which keeps the mixture cool and also has the merit of making the preparation very much quicker.)

On a lightly floured surface, roll out the pastry to a thin layer about 1 in (2.5 cm) larger than the flan tin.

Fold the pastry in half and lift it into the tin. Unfold the pastry and gently press it in place. Using your thumb and forefinger, fold and pinch the pastry edge over to make a raised border. Trim away the excess pastry and recrimp into firm ruffles. Prick the base and the sides of the case with an even-pronged fork. Chill for 30 minutes.

The filling

Cut the apricots in half and remove their stones. Cover the base of the flan with a layer of jam. Arrange the apricots on top, skin side down.

Using a wooden spoon, beat the butter and sugar together in a mixing-bowl until white, light and fluffy. Blend in the eggs one at a time with a tablespoon of flour. Sift the rest of the flour and almonds on to the mixture and fold it in with a metal spoon. Lastly stir in the essence. Spoon the mixture on to the apricots. Using a wet spatula spread the sponge. Encourage it to fill the apricot cavities and smooth it to the edge of the pastry shell.

Bake for 35–40 minutes or until a skewer slipped into the sponge comes out clean. Leave the pastry to cool in the tin.

To decorate and serve

Pass the icing sugar through a sieve into a bowl and using a pliable spatula, blend in the lemon juice until the icing reaches a pouring thickness.

Set the flan tin on an upturned mixing-bowl and gently push down the sides of the tin. Spoon a little icing on to the cake stand to stop the pastry slipping. Lift the flan with its base to rest in one hand, slide a spatula between the pastry and the tin base and ease the tart on to the cake stand.

Pour the icing in a continuous stream, backwards and forwards over the sponge. Tie a small bow or knot of ribbon around the stem of the grapes and place them on the stand.

Using a sharp knife, cut the flan into wedges, lift out each portion with a cake slice and use the knife to slide it onto the plates.

Variation

Drained poached black cherries and black cherry jam instead of apricots and jam.

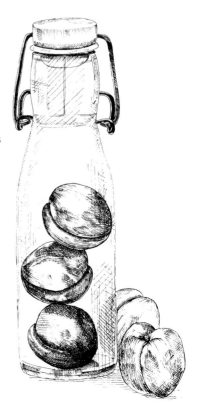

Forward preparation

The casserole can be cooked 2 days ahead of time. After leaving it overnight in a cool place, keep it refrigerated.

The day before

Make

Pastry.

The morning

Prepare

Mussels and mix them with a little oil.
Vegetable garnish. Cook them in the boiling water and rinse in cold.
Wash and slice the celery, keep in a bowl sealed with clingfilm.
Potatoes and cook them in milk.
Blanch the peas or prepare the mushrooms.

Make

Bacon dressing.
Apricot and almond tart.
Dressing for the salad.
Mix the vegetables into the casserole and top with potatoes.

Early evening

Set the oven to reheat the casserole.
Cut and wash the Iceberg lettuce.
Make the celery and walnut salad.
Carefully remove the tart from its case, slide it on to a large cake stand and coat the surface with icing. Set the decoration in place.

SAUTÉED APPLES AND ANCHOVIES
served on crisp rounds of brown fried bread

HOME SPICED TOPSIDE OF BEEF
flamed with brandy and cooked slowly on a bed of root
vegetables in wine

RED CABBAGE
BROADBEAN PURÉE
CAULIFLOWER WITH PARSLEY SAUCE

WHISKED SPONGE FILLED WITH PINEAPPLE MOUSSE
coated with lemon icing and served with pineapple purée

Sautéed apples and anchovies served on crisp rounds of brown fried bread

---

Having prepared the fried bread, have everyone sitting down as this is another instant first course.

Juice of 1 lemon
6 crisp eating apples
24 anchovy fillets soaked in milk to remove
  excess salt

4–5 fl oz (125–150 ml) hazelnut oil
8 slices of brown bread cut with a round 3 in
  (7.5 cm) pastry cutter
4 oz (110 g) butter

If you wish to serve a dressing with the sautéed apples, try lemon cream (see page 87) or even clotted cream.

Put about 1 pint (½ litre) water and the lemon juice into a bowl. Core the apples and place them in the bowl.

Take the anchovies out of the milk and dab them dry.

Have ready plates with crumpled kitchen paper.

Heat the oil in the frying pan and fry four rounds of bread at a time on both sides until crisp. Lay them on the covered plates to drain and keep warm. Wipe out the frying pan.

Dry the apples and using a stainless steel knife slice them on to a plate. Heat the frying pan with the butter, add the apples and cook them quickly until brown, trying not to burn the butter. Mix in the anchovies and take the pan away from the heat.

Place a round of bread on each plate and spoon the apples and anchovies on top. Pour a little dressing over to one side, or one teaspoon of clotted cream.

Home spiced topside of beef flamed with brandy and cooked slowly on a bed of root vegetables in wine

This is an excellent way to present a joint of beef. The meat is first flavoured with salt, sugar and herbs, then slowly cooked in red wine. It is at its best when allowed to marinate for 5 days and one advantage of preparing the meat far ahead of time, apart from turning it in the marinade twice a day – it does mean the main course is organised.

I use a stainless steel fish kettle, first to flavour the meat and then for braising. If you haven't got one, use a china or glass mixing-bowl, but you may find the meat will have to be cut in half and marinated in two separate containers.

5 lb (2.5 kg) topside of beef, rolled in a long and thin almost sausage shape, tied up at 1 in (2.5 cm) intervals.

Marinade	For cooking the beef
4 pints (2 litres) water	½ lb (225 g) pork rind
¾ lb (350 g) sea salt	2 carrots, sliced
½ lb (225 g) brown sugar	2 sticks of celery, sliced
½ oz (10 g) saltpetre	2 onions, sliced with their skins left on
1 bay leaf	1¾ pint (1 litre) red wine
1 tablespoon dried thyme	¼ pint (150 ml) brandy
6 peppercorns	1 teaspoon dried marjoram

To serve

Brown sauce.

Marinade

Bring the water to boil in a large saucepan and add the rest of the marinade ingredients, stirring until the salt and sugar have dissolved. Pour it into a large container and leave to cool completely. Place the beef into the fish-kettle and pour the liquid over and cover the top with a double layer of greaseproof paper. Partly cover with the lid and leave it to marinate in a dark, cool place for 3 to 5 days.

Whenever possible turn the meat at about the same time each day, for example 8 a.m. and 8 p.m.

To cook

Set the oven to gas mark 4, 350°F, 180°C.

Cut the pork rind into thin strips. Lay half of the rind at the bottom of the baking dish or kettle. Take the beef out of the marinade, wipe it dry, place it over the rind and arrange the vegetables around it. Cook the beef uncovered for 20 minutes and during that time heat up the wine and brandy. Take the meat out and lower the heat to gas mark 1, 275°F, 140°C. Pour in the hot wine and sprinkle the marjoram over. Cover the meat with rind, a double layer of greaseproof paper and completely seal with foil. Cook it in the lowest part of the oven for 2¾ hours, but check after 2½ hours. Remove the meat, leave it to rest for 15 minutes and then wrap it in foil to keep warm. Scoop away any grease that has formed on top of the cooking liquid and then strain it into a saucepan. Whisk in brown sauce to thicken. Taste and season.

To serve

Unwrap the meat and place on to a warm serving dish. Remove the string and cut eight slices of beef to lay on the dish; slice the rest at the table. Pour a little sauce over the meat to give it a lovely sheen. Arrange lightly cooked florets of cauliflower around and spoon parsley sauce over each piece.

Vegetables

Red cabbage not only tastes good but adds colour to the plate. A purée of broad beans will provide a contrast to the crispness of the cabbage, but if you feel potatoes are necessary, serve them creamed, omitting the purée as the textures are too similar to use together.

Red cabbage

Everyone has a favourite way of cooking red cabbage and this is mine. It can be prepared well in advance and then frozen in convenient amounts.

I red cabbage about I ½–2 lb (700–900 g) in weight	A pinch of thyme
I large onion	2 tablespoons brown sugar
4 eating apples	I tablespoon sultanas
I small clove of garlic	½ pint (275 ml) red wine
4 oz (110 g) butter	¼ pint (150 ml) chicken stock
½ teaspoon grated nutmeg	2 tablespoons red wine vinegar
Grated rind of I orange	Salt and pepper

Peel away any blemished outer leaves of the cabbage. Slice the cabbage in half and cut out the hard core. Shred the cabbage as finely as you can, or use the vegetable slicer on the blender. Peel and slice the onion and apples and finely chop the garlic.

In a large saucepan melt the butter and cook the onions and garlic over a low heat. Add the apples, nutmeg, thyme and orange rind. Mix in the cabbage and stir until well coated with butter. Now add the sugar, sultanas, wine, chicken stock and vinegar. Bring to the boil and then lower the heat. Cover the cabbage with greaseproof paper and the saucepan lid. Cook very gently for 30 minutes. Taste and season.

If you wish to freeze or serve it later, allow the cabbage to cook for only 15 minutes, leave it to cool and then spoon it into suitable containers. Cover the top with greaseproof paper and leave until cold.

Broadbean purée

I use the same method as for soup to make vegetable purée. Reheat this purée in a china or Pyrex dish, otherwise the colour will alter.

8 oz (225 g) onions	½ pt (275 ml) sherry
4 oz (110 g) butter	Salt, pepper and you may like to add a little
2 lb (900 g) frozen broad beans	lemon juice

Peel and chop the onions. Melt the butter in a large saucepan, add the onions and cook them over a low heat until they are transparent. Tip in the beans and seasoning, stir until the vegetables are coated with butter. Pour in the sherry, cover with greaseproof paper and top with a tight-fitting lid. Lower the heat as far as possible.

Cook for about ¾ hour, until very tender and leave to cool a little. Chop until smooth in the blender and put into a dish. Cover with buttered greaseproof paper and seal with foil, ready to heat up. For this menu, with everything cooking at a low heat, it will take about 1 hour.

Parsley sauce

---

1 oz (25 g) butter	Salt and pepper
2 tablespoons flour	½ oz (10 g) parsley, chopped
1 pint (570 ml) milk	

Melt the butter over a low heat in a heavy-based saucepan. Tip in the flour and cook slowly, stirring all the time for 2 minutes. Gradually add the milk. Raise the heat, whisk until smooth and the sauce begins to boil. Lower the heat as low as you can and simmer for 15–20 minutes, stirring often to stop the sauce sticking to the bottom of the pan. Add salt and pepper. Pour into a jug and press clingfilm lightly on to the sauce to stop a skin forming. Add parsley before serving.

Whisked sponge filled with pineapple mousse, coated with lemon icing and served with pineapple purée

---

In this recipe a light pineapple mousse is concealed inside a deep sponge cake. To hold the mousse a hollow is formed by removing the centre and after filling it with pineapple a layer of sponge is placed on top. The cut surface is hidden by a coating of lemon icing. The inside of the cake can be frozen in a polythene bag and then used for trifle another day. This is not difficult, but does require organisation and the end result is worth it.

For the mousse you need half a packet of gelatine and this is the best way to measure the correct amount. Pour the gelatine into a dessertspoon to create an oval shape equal at the top and bottom. Using a palette knife carefully slide away the top half, leaving the bottom layer intact.

1 round sponge cake, 10 in (25.5 cm) by 3 in
  (7.5 cm) deep
1 pineapple

1 tablespoon icing sugar
1 tablespoon brandy
Sugar syrup

Mousse

2 tablespoons lemon juice
½ pkt gelatine
2 whole eggs
1 egg yolk
1 oz (25 g) caster sugar
¼ pint (150 ml) double cream

Lemon Icing

8 tablespoons of icing sugar
2 tablespoons lemon juice

With a sharp stainless steel knife, cut the top and bottom off the pineapple. Cut it in half horizontally and place the halves, cut side down, on a board. Slice away the skin in vertical strips and with the tip of the knife remove the spikes. Now cut the flesh away from the core and then into even-sized chunks. Weigh out 4 oz (110 g) and set the rest to one side for the purée.

Finely chop the weighed pineapple in the food processor with icing sugar and brandy and put it into a saucepan. Do not wash the processor bowl yet.

Light the oven to its lowest setting and pour the lemon juice into a small pan, sprinkle the gelatine over and leave to melt in the bottom of the oven. Cook the purée until it has reduced to just under 3 fl oz (75 ml) and mix it with the gelatine. Pour it into a jug and leave to cool.

Eggs for the mousse will need to be whisked until light, almost white and very fluffy so place the whole eggs and yolk into the warmed mixer bowl and leave them to whisk while you prepare the cake.

You need a long thin sharp knife. Cut a circle 2½ in (6.5 cm) deep and ½–¾ in (1–2 cm) in from the sides. Then ½ in (1 cm) from the bottom push the knife in horizontally to the far side of the circle you have just cut. Now slide the knife blade around the cut to release half of the smaller cake. Take the knife out and with the blade facing the opposite way, repeat the same process the other side. You will now be able to lift out the middle of the cake, leaving a shell ready to fill with mousse. Carefully put this into a cake tin lined with clingfilm and return your attention to the mousse.

Add the sugar, a little at a time to the eggs. Beat the cream in a large mixing-bowl until it forms soft, almost floppy, peaks. Lower the speed of whisking, slowly pour in the pineapple purée and switch the machine off. Fold the egg mixture into the cream using a metal spoon to keep the air bubbles and pour the mousse into the sponge shell. Cut a layer of sponge from the small cake for the lid and put it on top of the mousse. Chill it to set.

Pineapple purée

Weigh the remainder of pineapple; for every pound (450 g) of the fruit you need ¼ pint (150 ml) of sugar syrup. Chop it in the processor and cook it with the syrup until tender. Liquidize the cooked pineapple and chill.

To decorate and serve

Make the lemon icing. Carefully lift the sponge out of the tin and slide it on to a serving dish. Spread the icing over the cake to completely cover the top and let it fall down the sides.

Put the purée into a jug and stir it each time you pour it over a portion.

Forward preparation

5 days before

Prepare and marinate the beef.

The day before

Prepare

Red cabbage and when cold keep covered with greaseproof paper in the refrigerator.

Make

Sponge and keep sealed with clingfilm.
Lemon cream.

The morning

Prepare

Soak the anchovies.
Cauliflower.

Make

Broadbean purée.
White sauce – add parsley just before serving.
Pineapple mousse and leave it to set in the cake.
Pineapple purée.
Work out the cooking times for the beef, including the initial high heat and resting period.
The cabbage and purée. Allow just over an hour to warm through at the low heat.
Toast the almonds.

Early evening

Start to cook the meat.
Unwrap and decorate the sponge.
Pour the pineapple purée into a jug.
Chop ½ oz (10 g) parsley for the white sauce and squeeze it dry between kitchen paper.
Have a large saucepan ready for the beef liquid and the brown sauce close by.
Fry the bread and place on plates lined with crumpled kitchen paper to drain and keep warm. Wipe out the pan and add the butter and oil, leaving ready to heat up.
Take the anchovies out of the milk and dab them dry.
Core the apples and leave them in water and lemon.

179

SALMON FILLETS LAYERED WITH VEGETABLES
set in jelly and garnished with tomato dressing

WHOLE PIGEONS
filled with apricot and nut forcemeat, casseroled in wine

BRAISED CHICORY
BUTTERED NOODLES

APPLE AND GINGER SPONGE MERINGUE

Salmon fillets layered with vegetables, set in jelly and garnished with tomato dressing

---

For this recipe, thin slices of salmon are arranged in horizontal layers with crunchy, bright carrots and beans set in aspic which are then served garnished with raw tomato dressing and broccoli florets. A rather long description for a simple and elegant first course.

14 oz (400 g) filleted salmon with the skin
    removed
1 oz (25 g) butter
1 pint (570 ml) dry white wine
5 fl oz (150 ml) dry vermouth
5 fl oz (150 ml) water
1 heaped tablespoon aspic
3 oz (75 g) French beans
3 oz (75 g) carrots
Broccoli cut into 8 florets
A little French dressing
8 button mushrooms
A little butter

Tomato dressing

3 tomatoes
1 teaspoon lemon juice
¼ pint (150 ml) French dressing

8 ramekins, to hold 5 fl oz (150 ml) of liquid

Lay the salmon on a board, run your fingers over it against the grain to feel for any bones which can be pulled out using a pair of tweezers. Cut the salmon in half horizontally and slide the escalopes on to a sheet of lightly greased clingfilm. Place another sheet over the fish and using a light rolling pin gently flatten the salmon to an even thickness.

Heat a frying pan. Drop in the butter and swirl it around to coat the pan. Set it on a low heat, add the salmon escalopes and cook them for 30 seconds. Turn them over and sauté gently for a further 30 seconds until they are cooked. If you are not sure, gently separate the flakes with a fork and the flesh should be opaque. Carefully lay them on a plate lined with kitchen paper and press the salmon with more paper to remove any excess butter. Leave until cold.

180

Aspic

Reduce the wine to ½ pint (275 ml). Add vermouth and water to make 1 pint (570 ml) of liquid. Bring it to the boil, switch off the heat and stir in the aspic. Continue stirring until completely dissolved. Leave it in a jug to cool.

Vegetables

Top and tail the beans and cut them in half. Peel and cut the carrots into strips the same size as the beans. Cut away the stems from the broccoli.

Bring to a boil lightly salted water and cook the vegetables separately until tender, but still crisp. Drain them into a colander and run cold water over them. Lay the vegetables on kitchen paper to dry.

Brush the cooked broccoli lightly with French dressing, place them on a plate, cover with clingfilm and chill.

Wipe the mushrooms clean and thinly slice them. Sauté the slices in a little butter and lay them on the paper with the other vegetables.

Coat the insides of the ramekins with a light vegetable oil using a pastry brush. Cut the salmon escalopes in half horizontally and then into squares of a size that will fit comfortably in the dishes; you should manage to get 3 per dish. Lay a slice in each mould, divide and arrange the beans on top, pour a little cooled aspic over. Set in place a second layer of fish and top the slice with carrots, add a little more aspic, position the last layer of fish over and then the sliced mushrooms. Ladle in the rest of the aspic to come up to the rim. Using your fingertips, gently and evenly press the layers down. Without spilling the liquid transfer the dishes to a tray and put them in the refrigerator for at least an hour to set.

To serve

Run a thin knife around each jelly. Place the ramekin in one hand and cover it with the other. Invert the ramekin and shake it until you feel the jelly fall on to your hand. Let it drop back into the mould, then quickly turn it out on to a plate. Turn out the others, using the same method. Whisk the dressing and pour it to cover half of each jelly and then to run onto the plates. Place a green floret on each plate on top of the pale red dressing.

Variations

Sliced sole fillets, prawns or chicken breasts may be used and layered with almost any cooked vegetables that will stand out in contrast. Have fun arranging your own pictures in aspic. Choose an almost translucent dressing to accompany the jelly: strawberry, redcurrant or mustard.

Whole pigeons filled with apricot and nut forcemeat, casseroled in wine

These pigeons have their breast bones removed and are then reshaped with stuffing. They can be casseroled in either Port or red wine sauce. Whichever sauce you choose they are both served with braised chicory and ribbon noodles tossed in butter and Parmesan cheese.

Buy ready plucked and drawn pigeons and select ones that have perfect skins. Try not to pierce the skin during preparation.

8 pigeons

Stuffing

1 onion
2 oz (50 g) butter
1 bunch of watercress
8 oz (225 g) smoked ham
12 oz (350 g) hazelnuts
12 oz (350 g) dried apricots
1 teaspoon grated orange rind

Red wine sauce

2 oz (50 g) butter
2 fl oz (50 ml) brandy
1 pint (570 ml) red wine
1 teaspoon chopped marjoram and thyme
1 bay leaf
½ pint (275 ml) stock
½ pint (275 ml) brown sauce
1 teaspoon lemon juice

OR Port sauce

2 oz (50 g) butter
2 tablespoons flour
½ pint (275 ml) Port
1½ pints (just under 1 litre) jellied brown stock
1 teaspoon chopped marjoram and thyme
Redcurrant jelly and cream to finish

Garnish

4 oz (110 g) brown breadcrumbs, fried in
   butter until crisp

Stuffing

First prepare the stuffing. Peel and chop the onion and lightly sauté in butter. Leave to
cool. Carefully check over the watercress and pull away any yellow leaves and stems.
Cut the ham into small cubes.
   Place the watercress, shelled nuts and apricots together in the food processor or
blender and work until finely chopped. Spoon this mixture into a mixing-bowl, stir
in the orange rind, ham and onions with butter and mix well together. Taste for
seasoning – the watercress has a peppery flavour so perhaps you would like to add just
salt. Set the bowl to one side.

The pigeons

Place the whole pigeons on a board, breast side up. Lift the neck skin and with your
fingers, feel for the wishbone. Using a sharp knife, cut the flesh around to release it,
then pull it out. The bones are very fragile and may break as they are handled, so
make sure you remove any loose fragments throughout. Cut down one side of the
breastbone, keeping the blade close to the bone, now follow the bone down from the
leg to the wing until the flesh is completely free. Repeat the process on the other side.
Turn the bird so that the neck is facing you. Place your fingers into the opposite cavity,
lift the upper carcass and with the knife cut away the entire breastbone towards the
neck and wingbone. Cut around the wing joints on both sides. The breastbone will now
be loose and wobbly. Lift it up and cut away the underside to the base of the neck.
Remove both the breastbone and neck together by holding the main carcass flat in one
hand and pulling away with the other. Bone the other seven in the same way.
   Wipe the pigeons and lay them on the board, rub your fingers over the flesh and feel
for any shot. Divide the stuffing between them, build it up high, moulding it with your
hands to the same shape as the breastbone. Fold the flesh and skin over to meet in the
centre.

To sew up and truss the pigeons

Thread a needle with fine string and sew the breasts together to enclose the stuffing. Start from the tail and over-stitch to the neck. Cut the string leaving a 2 in (5 cm) excess. Thread the needle with a second and longer piece of string and push the needle through the lower part of the wing, through the body and the other wing, then pass the needle in the opposite direction through the thighs. Gather and tie the three ends of string into a firm knot. Now pass the last piece of string through the lower part of the legs and body, pulling the legs together and tie a knot.

All this stuffing, sewing and trussing takes time and patience – then you have to find and remove the string! However the cooked birds will look compact and attractive.

Set the oven to gas mark 4, 350°F, 180°C.

To cook in Red wine sauce

Melt the butter in a frying pan, brown the pigeons all over, four at a time and lay them breast side up in a large casserole dish. Flame the brandy and while it is still alight pour it over the birds. Pour a little wine into the frying pan. Over a high heat and using a wooden spoon, scrape the sediment from the bottom of the pan to mix it in with the wine, then carefully transfer the liquid to a large saucepan, add the rest of the wine, herbs and stock and bring it slowly to the boil. Wash the frying pan while you are waiting as the hot pan will be easier to clean. Pour the wine and stock over the pigeons. Cover with lightly oiled greaseproof paper and seal with foil.

To cook in Port sauce

Heat the butter in a large saucepan, brown the pigeons a few at a time and lay them breast side up in a casserole dish. Blend the flour into the butter and cook until brown. Pour in the Port and stock and stir until smooth. Bring slowly to the boil, add the herbs and pour the liquid over the birds, then cover and seal.

Cook the pigeons in the preheated oven for an hour until tender, but not over-cooked. I find the cooking times vary a little as it does depend on the size and age of the birds.

To serve

Carefully take the pigeons out and lay them on a board.

Tip the cooking liquid through a sieve into a large saucepan and bring it slowly to the boil. For Red wine sauce, stir in the brown sauce until smooth, then add lemon juice. For the Port sauce, add redcurrant jelly and cream to taste. Check both for seasoning.

Cut and pull away the strings from each bird. Using poultry scissors, trim the legs if they look untidy and then lightly push the breasts apart to reveal the stuffing.

Pour the sauce to cover the bottom of a warm serving dish. Arrange the pigeons round the sides to form a circle and ladle a little more sauce over them to give a sheen. Press the crisp breadcrumbs on to the fruit stuffing. Place the orange flavoured chicory in the centre.

Serve the rest of the sauce in a jug, Parmesan cheese in a bowl and the buttered noodles in a casserole; it is rather nice to toss them with cheese at the table using a large spoon and fork.

Variation

Fill a boned loin of pork with the delicious apricot and hazelnut stuffing. Serve it sliced with Madeira sauce, garnished with tinted Parmesan noodles and dark green broccoli florets.

Braised Chicory

8–16 chicory
2 oz (50 g) butter

Grated rind and juice of 2 oranges, mixed
   together

Wipe the chicory and pull away any damaged leaves. Cut a thin slice away from the base and using a pointed knife, cut out the bitter core at the bottom. Butter a casserole dish and lay the chicory in a single layer. Pour over the juice, cover with buttered greaseproof paper and seal with foil. Cook in the oven at gas mark 4, 350°F, 180°C for 1 hour.

Buttered noodles

1 tablespoon oil
1 lb (450 g) wide ribbon noodles, green
2 oz (50 g) butter

Butter to finish
Black pepper
2 oz (50 g) freshly grated Parmesan

Bring 6 pints (3 litres) of salted water, with 1 tablespoon of oil, to the boil and add the noodles. Cook for 8 minutes, stirring them often. Only allow 3 minutes if you are cooking fresh noodles. Again I can judge when pasta is cooked by touch; during the cooking time, unless you are sure, lift up a strand and pinch it. The pasta should be tender, but still have a slightly firmer centre.

    Set a sieve over a large container. As soon as the pasta is cooked strain it through the sieve and then tip into a warm casserole. Toss with butter, using two wooden forks, twist black pepper over and serve immediately.

Home-made pasta tinted to a pale, gentle green, by adding finely puréed spinach will blend the dish together with shades of colour. With the addition of purée use a touch more flour in mixing and rolling the pasta.

Apple and ginger sponge meringue

Rounds of meringue flavoured with chopped dried apple and crystallised ginger, baked with a layer of sponge, then brought together with apples and cream.

Meringue

3 oz (75 g) dried apple rings
2 oz (50 g) crystallised ginger
6 egg whites with a pinch of salt
12 oz (350 g) caster sugar
1 teaspoon red wine vinegar
1 tablespoon cornflour

Sponge

6 oz (175 g) soft butter
5 oz (150 g) caster sugar
6 egg yolks
6 tablespoons milk
6 oz (175 g) plain flour, sieved once with
1 teaspoon baking powder

To fill and decorate

Butter
4 lb (2 kg) crisp green eating apples
3 fl oz (75 ml) sugar syrup

¾ pint (425 ml) double cream
2 fl oz (55 ml) sugar syrup

2 11 in (28 cm) loose-bottomed flan tins, lined with lightly greased greaseproof paper.

184

Set the oven to gas mark 3, 325°F, 170°C.

Chop the dried apple and ginger together in the food processor or blender. Set to one side. Do not wash the bowl, use it to make the sponge after the egg whites have been whisked.

Beat the egg whites with salt in the mixer until white, stiff and dry. Add two-thirds of the sugar a tablespoon at a time, add the vinegar and cornflour, then gradually spoon in the remaining sugar. Switch off the machine and remove the bowl. Fold in the apples and ginger using a metal spoon and then spread the meringue evenly in the flan tins.

Now make the sponge. Blend the butter and sugar together until almost white, then add the yolks and milk, working until smooth. Lastly spoon in the flour sieved with the baking powder. Dot the sponge over the meringue and using a pliable spatula, spread the mixture over, working from the centre outwards.

Bake in the middle of the oven for 40–45 minutes. The sponge and meringue should be a light brown colour. Leave them to cool in their cases.

The filling

Peel, core and slice the apples into a buttered saucepan, add 3 fl oz (75 ml) sugar syrup and cover the apples with two layers of buttered greaseproof paper. Cook them over a low heat until tender and almost clear. Shake the pan often during cooking to gently move the slices. Carefully tip the cooked apples into a bowl and leave to cool.

To decorate and serve

Whip the cream. Spread a little cream over the serving dish to stop the meringue slipping. Peel the greaseproof paper away from one meringue and place it on the dish, sponge side up. Sprinkle the sponge with half of the syrup. Mix the apples with two-thirds of the cream and spread it over the cake. Brush syrup over the other sponge, take it out of the tin and position it with the sponge side on to the fruit, pressing it gently down. Pull away the paper and pipe the rest of the cream on top to decorate.

Fill and decorate the meringue no more than 2 hours ahead and then keep it in a cool place.

Variation

You may like to cook and serve the meringue/sponge the other way round. Flour the greased and lined tins, spread the sponge over the bottom and then the meringue over. Cook for 40 minutes at gas mark 4, 350°F, 180°C. Leave them to cool a little and then carefully unwrap, sandwich together with the meringue inside and brush syrup over the sponge just before decorating.

Forward preparation

The day before

Prepare

Bone the pigeons, lay them flesh side up on a tray and sprinkle the meat with olive oil and red wine. Cover them loosely with clingfilm and put them in the refrigerator. Do not be tempted to fill them as the flesh will discolour the stuffing.

Make

Apple purée
Fruit and nut forcemeat
Cook the salmon and keep the escalopes covered and chilled.

The morning

Prepare

Aspic.
Blanch the vegetables ready
for the jelly.
Fill the ramekins with salmon,
vegetables and aspic.
Tomato dressing.
Fill and sew the pigeons,
brown them in butter and set
them in the casserole.
Prepare the oranges.

Make

Make the meringue.
Make the sauce.
Fry the breadcrumbs.

Early evening

Have ready

Prepare the chicory for
braising.
Unwrap, fill and decorate the
meringue.
Allow just over 1 hour to cook
pigeons and chicory at gas
mark 4, 350°F, 180°C.
Grate the Parmesan, have the
butter to hand.

Have the sauce ready to
reheat, pigeons close by with
prepared paper and foil.

```
┌─────────────────────────────────────────────────────┐
│                                                       │
│                  MUSHROOM SOUP                        │
│                                                       │
│                  PIGEON BREASTS                       │
│    wrapped in bacon, lightly cooked and served sliced with game │
│                 and black cherry sauces               │
│                                                       │
│                     CABBAGE                           │
│    filled with Brussels sprouts and chestnut purée topped with │
│              crisp breadcrumbs and almonds            │
│                                                       │
│                  FRENCH BEANS                         │
│                                                       │
│      PINEAPPLE AND MELON OATMEAL MERINGUE             │
│             HOT CHOCOLATE SAUCE                        │
│                                                       │
└─────────────────────────────────────────────────────┘
```

Mushroom soup

Button mushrooms make the soup more pleasing in colour.

2 lb (900 g) mushrooms
½ lb (225 g) onions or leeks
4 oz (110 g) butter
½ pint (275 ml) medium dry sherry

4 tablespoons lemon juice
2 sprigs of mint, chopped
3 pints (1.5 litres) chicken stock
Salt and pepper to taste

Garnish

Anchovy fillets soaked in milk, dried, chopped
   and tossed in parsley

Slice the mushrooms. Peel and chop the onions or leeks finely to enable them to cook evenly with the mushrooms. Melt the butter in a large saucepan, add the onions and mushrooms and give them a good stir. Now pour in the sherry, lemon juice and add the mint. Turn down the heat as low as possible. Cover the vegetables with a sheet of greaseproof paper and put the lid on top of the saucepan. Cook for about 30 minutes until tender.

Take the saucepan from the heat and pour in the chicken stock. Have the liquidizer, sieve and container ready. Ladle the soup, a little at a time, into the liquidizer and work until smooth – mushrooms take very little time. Pour the purée through the sieve into the container with the help of a wooden spoon. Taste. Season with salt and twists of pepper; taste again.

To serve

Place a little of the anchovy mixture in each bowl and pour the hot soup over.

Variation

Use dried coriander or cumin as flavouring instead of mint and lemon.

Pigeon breasts wrapped in bacon, lightly cooked and served sliced with game and black cherry sauce

I like to serve a savoury and a spiced fruit sauce, their colours are good and if they are both poured on to the plate and mingled together, a different flavour can be tasted with each piece of pigeon. The work can be made lighter by marinating the pigeon breasts and making both sauces the day before.

12 pigeons
Salt and pepper
¼ pint (150 ml) Port
2 fl oz (55 ml) olive oil
8 slices long back bacon

String

Game sauce

6 pigeon carcasses
½ oz (10 g) butter
2 onions with a few cloves pressed into them
1 carrot chopped
1 stick of celery chopped
2 tablespoons red wine
A pinch of tarragon
1 tablespoon Worcestershire sauce
1 tablespoon red wine vinegar
1 tablespoon tomato purée
Brown sauce
Salt and pepper

Black cherry sauce

1 lb (450 g) stoned black cherries or frozen
Juice of 2 oranges
Juice of ½ lemon
½ pint (275 ml) red wine
½ teaspoon dried marigold leaves
1 sprig of parsley
6 green peppercorns
Pinch of paprika

3 cloves
½ nutmeg, grated
Salt and pepper
½ teaspoon powdered cinnamon
½ teaspoon powdered ginger
Salt and pepper
½ pint (275 ml) brown sauce to be added when the sauce has reduced

Garnish

Cherries with stalks (I like to find bunches of 3)

Pigeons

Remove the skin from the pigeons and gently slice away the breasts. Trim off any fat and pull out the little white thread from the small fillets. Lay the breasts on to a plastic tray, season and pour the Port and oil over, cover them lightly with clingfilm and keep them in the refrigerator overnight. Keep 6 pigeon carcasses for game sauce.

To cook

Take the rind off the bacon and stretch it widthways using the blunt edge of a knife – the fat can almost double in size. Wipe the pigeon breasts dry and place them into piles

188

of three. Roll the bacon around each portion, slightly overlapping as you roll; try and make sure the ends are covered with bacon. Tie the breasts up with string so they keep their shape during cooking.

Heat ¼ in (5 mm) depth of oil in frying pan and on a high heat, seal the parcels four at a time. Arrange them on a baking tray as far away from each other as possible. Chill for one hour or more.

Set the oven to gas mark 7, 425°F, 220°C. Bake near the top for 20 minutes if you like to eat pigeon on the rare side; 30 minutes and they will be just over medium. Turn the pigeons halfway through the cooking time.

Game sauce

Chop 6 pigeon carcasses. Melt the butter in a large saucepan and fry the chopped bones; keep turning them, allowing them to brown. Add the onions, carrot and celery, then pour in a little wine, scraping the bottom of the pan with a wooden spoon to loosen any residues. Cover with water and bring to the boil. Lower the heat until the liquid is just bubbling. Scoop the scum away using a slotted spoon, pour a little cold water into the centre to encourage more scum to rise and when it does scoop it away. Add the rest of the ingredients and cook for about an hour. Strain the liquid through a fine sieve into a smaller pan and over a high heat reduce the liquid to 1 pint (570 ml). Stir in brown sauce to thicken. Taste and season. Pour the sauce into a jug and when cold cover with clingfilm.

Black cherry sauce

Put half of the cherries into a saucepan with the rest of the ingredients, bring to the boil and reduce by half. Pour through a fine sieve, pushing the cherries through using a wooden spoon and return to the saucepan. Add the brown sauce and bring slowly to the boil, stirring until smooth. Add the rest of the cherries. Taste and season. Pour the sauce into a jug and cover with clingfilm when quite cold.

To serve

Take the breasts out of the oven, let them rest a little and cut away the string.

Heat up both the sauces and ladle them so they lie together on the plate. Leave the cherries in the pan for a moment and using a skewer, run it over the sauces in a zig-zag line to mingle them slightly. Slice each breast into 3 at an angle, place them fan shaped on to the plates. Divide the cherries and put them together by the pigeons. Garnish with cherries on stalks.

Variations

Make chicken liver pâté, well flavoured with brandy. You need about ½ lb (225 g). Lift up the fillets, spread a little pâté under each one and gently press it back on to the breasts. Wrap and cook them as described, or sauté them carefully in butter. Make the game sauce and reheat it with double cream and garnish with any vegetable or fruit purée in this book. For example, a red and yellow pepper purée would be colourful and tasty.

Cabbage with Brussels sprouts and chestnut purée

It is better to serve this in two casserole dishes.

3 oz (75 g) butter
6 oz (175 g) chopped onions
1½ lb (700 g) frozen sprouts
9 oz (250 g) tinned unsweetened chestnut
    purée

¼ pint (150 ml) sherry
Grated nutmeg
Honey to sweeten
Salt and pepper
1 white cabbage

Garnish

Breadcrumbs, fried in butter
Almonds

Brussels sprouts and chestnut purée

Melt the butter in a large saucepan, add the onions and cook them over a low heat without browning. Tip in the sprouts and chestnut purée and stir until the vegetables are coated with butter. Pour in the sherry, cover with greaseproof paper and top with a tight-fitting lid. Lower the heat and gently cook for about 45 minutes until tender. The purée seems to absorb a great deal of liquid so it is best to check often and add a little sherry if need be. Chop in the blender until smooth. Taste and add the seasoning. Put to one side.

The cabbage

Cut away the stem and remove any damaged leaves. Simmer the cabbage in salted water for 15 minutes until the leaves are tender. Take it out of the water and place in a colander. Run cold water over and leave to drain and cool. Butter the casserole dishes. Gently pull the leaves away from the heart of the cabbage and lay them in overlapping circles with the base of the leaves in the centre of the dishes. Fill the hollow with purée, cover the top with a large leaf and gently fold the tips of the leaves over into the centre. You should now have two neat round green parcels. Cover them with buttered greaseproof paper and seal with foil.

As the pigeons are cooked at a high heat, warm the cabbage through in the lowest part of the oven for 30 minutes. Just before serving remove the foil and paper, press crisp breadcrumbs and almonds over the top. Serve the cabbage with a dish of crisp cooked French beans.

Pineapple and melon oatmeal meringue and hot chocolate sauce

I make no excuse for including the oatmeal meringue quite a few times, it is without doubt the most popular sweet.

Every morning when we are open, for the past 11 years, I have made it first and almost in my sleep, in order to get it cooked and out of the way. It amazes me that our customers ask for this time and time again – I sometimes feel that I need only make this to the exclusion of everything else.

8 egg whites
Pinch of salt
1 lb (450 g) caster sugar
2 teaspoons red wine vinegar
2 tablespoons cornflour
3 oz (75 g) toasted oatmeal mixed with
2 oz (50 g) chopped dried fruit, almonds and
    hazelnuts
1 lb (450 g) melon and pineapple, sliced
1 pint (570 ml) double cream

Chocolate sauce

1 pint (570 ml) double cream
15 oz (450 g) plain chocolate
3 oz (75 g) butter

2 11 in (28 cm) loose-bottomed flan tins, lined with lightly greased greaseproof paper.

190

When making a meringue, always resist the temptation to add the sugar too quickly. I find by not having all the ingredients to hand, enough time is allowed between each addition.

Set the oven to gas mark 3, 325°F, 170°C.

Start to whisk the egg whites with the salt and continue beating while you line the flan tins and weigh out the sugar. The whites will now be stiff and dry. Add two-thirds of the sugar, a tablespoon at a time, add the vinegar and cornflour, then gradually spoon in the remaining sugar. Switch off the machine and remove the bowl. Fold in the oatmeal mixture using a metal spoon and then spread the meringue evenly into the lined tins. Cook them just below the middle of the oven for 30–40 minutes. They should be a light brown colour and crisp on top. Leave them to cool in their tins. Keep them in a cool place, but not in the refrigerator.

To serve

Prepare the fruits and leave them to drain in a sieve.

Whip the cream. Spread a little cream over the serving dish to stop the meringue slipping. Peel the greaseproof paper away from one meringue and place it on the dish. Spread cream over, then arrange the fruit on top. Spread cream over the other meringue, take it out of the tin and position it, cream side on to the fruit, pressing it gently down. Pull away the paper and pipe the rest of the cream on top to decorate.

Chocolate sauce

This keeps well in the refrigerator for two weeks. Use it a little at a time:
   to mix with cream before it is whipped;
   to flavour custard;
   when slightly melted to coat éclairs and cakes;
   or, to serve hot as a rich chocolate sauce.
Put the cream and chocolate into a large saucepan, melt over a low heat, stirring all the time and bring to the boil. Draw aside and stir in the butter. When you have a smooth chocolate sauce pour it into a container and leave to cool and set.

Store covered.

The day before

Prepare

Pigeon breasts and marinate.

Make

Game sauce.
Black cherry sauce.
Mushroom soup.
Brussels sprouts and chestnut
purée.

The morning

Make

Meringue.
Chocolate sauce.

Prepare

Cabbage and fill the
casseroles.
Fry breadcrumbs until crisp in
butter and mix in almonds.
Soak anchovies in milk.
French beans.
Wrap the breasts in bacon and
seal them ready to bake.

Early Evening

Fill and decorate the meringue.
Take the anchovy fillets out of
the milk and dab them dry,
chop and mix them with
parsley.

Have ready

Soup.
Game sauce.
Black cherry sauce.
Cherry garnish.
Water in saucepan and French
beans in the vegetable basket.
Oven set to gas mark 7, 425°F,
220°C.
Pigeons – allow 20–30
minutes.
Cabbage with purée – allow
30 minutes.
Chocolate sauce ready to
heat.

Avocado Mousse
served with a vegetable vinaigrette and a faint flavour of prawns

Pheasants
concealed in a wrapping of leaves and cooked with Port and orange

Parsnip and Pear Casserole
garnished with walnuts

CRISP FRENCH BEANS

Oatmeal Meringue with Raspberries

Avocado mousse served with a vegetable vinaigrette and a faint flavour of prawns

---

A dressing with the colourful addition of sliced vegetables and a suggestion of prawns is the complementary background flavour for individual avocado mousses set with a soft cream centre. The avocado flesh tends to react to most metals, so select and use only stainless steel or plastic utensils.

Lemon cream

Juice of ½ lemon
½ teaspoon sea salt
¼ pint (150 ml) double cream

Garnish

Marjoram flowers

8 ramekin dishes, lightly greased

Vinaigrette

4 tablespoons white wine vinegar
1 teaspoon sea salt
A few twists of black pepper
8 fl oz (220 ml) light olive oil

Avocado mousse

3 tablespoons of water
½ oz (10g) gelatine – 1 pkt
2 medium avocados, 1 lb (450 g) in weight
2 tablespoons lemon juice
Salt and pepper and Tabasco
¼ pint (150 ml) hot chicken stock
¼ pint (150 ml) mayonnaise
¼ pint (150 ml) double cream
1 egg white, lightly whisked

Vegetable dressing

4 oz (110 g) stoned black olives
2 small green peppers
8 spring onions
16 cooked and peeled prawns, moistened with a touch of French dressing while they are warm
8 capers
1 tablespoon marjoram flowers and leaves

Lemon cream

Put the lemon juice in a mixing-bowl and add the sea salt. Stir, using a wooden spoon, until the salt has dissolved and gradually add the cream.

Unlike the vinaigrette, the lemon cream for this particular recipe should be refrigerated to allow it to thicken.

Avocado mousse

Put 3 tablespoons of water into a small saucepan, sprinkle the gelatine evenly over the surface and leave it to soak in.

Cut the avocados in half, peel away their skins and remove the stones. Place the flesh in the food processor or blender with the lemon juice, season with salt, pepper and a shake of Tabasco. Work until you have a smooth purée. Pour the hot chicken stock over the soaked gelatine, stir until all the crystals have disappeared and then blend it into the avocado purée. Tip the flavoured avocado into a mixing-bowl and stir in the mayonnaise.

In another mixing-bowl, whisk the cream to soft peaks and using a metal spoon, fold it gently into the avocado mayonnaise. Taste to check seasoning and then to complete the mousse, fold in a lightly whisked egg white.

Ladle two-thirds of the avocado mousse into the prepared ramekins and using the back of a teaspoon swirl a small dent in the centre of each mousse. Fill the hollows with lemon cream and carefully cover and conceal with the rest of the mousse, smoothing it level with a plastic spatula.

Place the filled ramekins on a tray and put them in the refrigerator to set.

Vinaigrette

The method for making the vinaigrette, as you will see, is the same as the flavoured cream.

Pour the vinegar into a small mixing-bowl, add the sea salt and black pepper. Stir the vinegar, using a wooden spoon, until the salt has dissolved and gradually add the oil, stirring to blend together. Pour the dressing into a small container with lid and keep it in a cool, dark place.

Vegetable dressing

Cut each olive down into eight strips. Slice each pepper in half lengthways and remove the core and seeds, cut the flesh into very long strips. Trim the roots away from the spring onions and peel off their soft outer layer, cut across, at an angle to form thin, long, exaggerated ovals. Cut the prawns across into thin rounds. Slice each caper in half.

Pour the vinaigrette into a bowl, add the sliced vegetables, marjoram leaves and prawns. Stir the mixture gently, blending the flavours together.

To serve

Run a thin knife around each mousse. Place the ramekin in one hand and cover it with the other. Invert the ramekin and shake it until you feel the mousse fall on to your hand, let it drop back into the mould, then quickly turn it out on to the plates. Turn out the others using the same method.

Stir to blend the vinaigrette and ladle the vegetables, with a little dressing, over the mousses, allowing the long slices to fall naturally. Garnish each mousse with marjoram flowers and serve immediately.

Variations

The prawns are sliced and served with the dressing as a hint of additional flavour, but the mousse is equally pleasing with a selection of cooked seafoods in vinaigrette; perhaps the concealed surprise could be brandy-flavoured brown crabmeat?

The flavour of avocado can be paired with a range of dressings and here are a few:
Strawberry vinaigrette
Stilton dressing
Horseradish and orange mayonnaise.

Pheasants

Rely on your butcher's advice, particularly when buying game. Tell him when you are going to eat the pheasants and whether you enjoy mild or strongly flavoured meat. Give him enough time to have them plucked and drawn for you. I prefer to buy hens as they are smaller and I think more delicate in flavour.

I find they are more pleasant to handle and prepare when they have been hung for just under a week. Pheasants are at their best during the months of November, December and January.

Pheasants concealed in a wrapping of leaves and cooked with Port and orange

You need a shallow baking dish to cook and serve the parcels.

4 young, prepared hen pheasants
A sprinkling of red wine
8–12 large, perfect cabbage leaves
1 orange
Pepper
1½–2 pints (1 litre) pheasant stock
½ pint (275 ml) Port
2 tablespoons redcurrant jelly

Fine string

Stock

2 fl oz (55 ml) olive oil
2 oz (50 g) pork rind
Pheasant bones, chopped
1 stick of celery chopped
1 onion, sliced but not peeled
1 carrot, chopped
Sprig of thyme
1 bay leaf
1 heaped tablespoon flour
¼ pint (150 ml) red wine
Water

To finish

½ pint (275 ml) brown sauce
1 lemon

Place the pheasants, breast side up, on a board. Gently pull one leg from the body. Cut

195

the skin and feel for the ball-and-socket joint. Using a pointed knife, cut down between the two to release the leg. Carefully peel away the skin from the leg and using a pair of poultry scissors, trim the tip. Repeat the process with the other legs and put to one side.

Using a sharp knife, cut through the skin to one side of the breastbone and cutting against the bone, slice away the breast. Repeat with the other breasts. With your fingers pull away the skin and trim the edges of each breast. Pair the legs with breasts and lay them on a tray. Sprinkle a touch of wine over the meat, cover with clingfilm and chill.

Having prepared and portioned the pheasants, if they look a little too large, I always trim away the surplus meat, sauté the trimmings lightly in butter and when cold, freeze them covered with red wine and oil, for later use; one or two suggestions – mix with crabmeat and avocado in pastry; sauté with smoked mussels and bacon, or if you have a favourite recipe for ham mousse, use these delicious trimmings with, or instead of, ham.

The stock

Heat the oil in a large saucepan, add the rind, bones, vegetables and herbs. Keep stirring them over a high heat until they take on a colour, stir the flour into the pan and let it cook for a minute. Stir in the wine, bring the liquid to a fierce boil and then add enough water to cover the bones. When the water is boiling, turn down the heat and leave the liquid to simmer and flavour for 4 hours.

Set a sieve over a large bowl and pour the liquid through, pressing the bones with a wooden spoon so all the flavoured juices fall into the container. Wash the saucepan and sieve. Set the sieve, lined with a thin, damp tea-towel, over the clean pan and strain the stock again into the saucepan. Reduce the liquid to 1½–2 pints (1 litre).

Refrigerate the stock overnight and the next day, spoon any fat off the surface.

Cabbage leaves

Have ready, a saucepan full of boiling water, a sieve set over a bowl and a large tray lined with kitchen paper.

Cabbage leaves have a thick, domed, central stem. To make them easier to roll and cook evenly, slice away the top curve of each main white stem horizontally. Drop the prepared leaves in the boiling water for 1 minute and then using slotted spoon, lift and place the softened leaves into the sieve to drain. When they are cold enough to handle, spread the leaves on the lined tray and pat them dry with a tea-towel.

To wrap, cook and serve

Preheat the oven to gas mark 3, 325°F, 170°C.

Grate the orange rind and set to one side. Remove the peel and white pith. Hold the fruit in one hand over a bowl and using a sharp knife, cut through to the central core and around both sides of the membrane that separates the segments, allowing the orange slices to fall in the bowl.

Take the prepared pheasant from the refrigerator and lay the breasts, cut side up, on a board. Season each one with twists of black pepper, divide and place orange segments on top. Fold the legs to fit snugly and rest one on each breast. Place one paired pheasant on the trimmed stalk-end of a cabbage leaf, fold over the bottom, then the sides to enclose the meat and roll up the leaf from the core end to make a parcel. Repeat with the others, cutting the spare leaves to cover any exposed flesh.

Tie each parcel up with fine string, finishing with a loosely tied bow to make the cooked pheasant easier to untie. Carefully place them, leg side down, in the baking dish. In a saucepan, bring together the stock, Port and redcurrant jelly and stir until the jelly has dissolved. Add the orange rind and pour the hot flavoured liquid to barely cover the parcels. Top with buttered greaseproof paper and completely seal with foil.

Cook in the preheated oven for 1 hour, but look and test after 45 minutes. Press the meat and if it feels firm and the juices are pale pink, take it out of the oven and leave to rest. Ladle a little juice into a saucepan, add the brown sauce, stir until smooth and hot, taste and twist in black pepper.

Carefully cut and untie the wrapped pheasants, pour the shiny thickened sauce to cover each parcel, allowing it to mingle with the juices in the dish and grate the lemon rind evenly over the surface.

Serve at the table accompanied with parsnip and pear casserole and crisp green beans tossed in lemon juice.

Parsnip and pear casserole, garnished with walnuts

I lemon	Salt and pepper
2½ lb (I kg) parsnips	2 level tablespoons brown sugar
I lb (450 g) dessert pears	½ pint (275 ml) double cream
3 oz (75 g) butter	4–6 tablespoons brown breadcrumbs

Garnish

24 walnut halves
2½–3 pint (1 ½ litre) gratin dish

Have ready a saucepan with lightly salted boiling water, a colander set over a bowl large enough to hold all the cooking water and a smaller bowl filled with cold water and the juice of the lemon.

Peel and slice the parsnips across into even, thin rounds. Drop them into the boiling water and cook the slices for 2 minutes, then pour the liquid and parsnips into the colander and leave them to drain. Tip away the hot water and pour cold water over the slices, moving them with your fingers to ensure each round is refreshed with water.

Using a stainless steel knife, peel the pears, cut them in half lengthways, scoop out the cores with a teaspoon and cut away the thread that runs from the base to the tip of each pear. Cut the halves across into even slices, placing them in the lemon water as you do so.

Melt the butter in a small saucepan and using a pastry brush paint the inside of the dish with a thick coat of butter. Arrange the parsnip slices on the base of the dish in overlapping rows, sprinkle with a little salt, sugar, black pepper and pour on an even coating of cream. Cover the parsnips with a layer of overlapping pears, season and add the coating of cream. Build up alternate seasoned layers finishing with parsnips. Brush the sliced vegetables with the rest of the butter and press breadcrumbs over, spreading them to form an even topping.

As the parsnips are partly cooked and the pears have been soaked in lemon juice, the prepared dish can now be completely sealed with clingfilm and left for a short time in the refrigerator.

To cook and serve

Set the oven to gas mark 3, 325°F, 170°C.

Cook near the top for 45 minutes, raising the heat to gas mark 6, 400°F, 200°C near the end of the cooking time to brown the crumbs.

In a small frying pan heat a little butter, add the walnuts and toss them to give an even, glossy coating. Arrange the warm nuts around the edge of the cooked dish and serve.

Sprinkle grated cheese over each seasoned and cream-coated layer.

As the combination of flavours is so good, I often make a Parsnip, pear and walnut soup. 1½ lb (700 g) sliced parsnips, cooked with ½ lb (225 g) quartered, unpeeled pears and the usual proportions of butter, onion and sherry – see soup recipes.

Add ground walnuts to the puréed soup just as it is about to be served.

Oatmeal meringue with raspberries (Nick's dessert)

The combination of whipped cream and frozen raspberries is a lovely clean, refreshing and cool filling for the oatmeal meringue.

I pint (570 ml) double cream
2 × I I in (28 cm) oatmeal meringues, see
   Pineapple and melon oatmeal meringue, on
   p. 190

I lb (450 g) frozen raspberries, to use
   immediately from the deep freeze

Whip the cream to form floppy peaks.

Fit a flat ribbon nozzle to the piping bag and fill the bag with about a quarter of the cream. Using a spatula, spread a little cream over the serving dish to stop the meringue slipping. Peel the greaseproof paper away from one meringue and place it on the dish. Spread cream over, then arrange the raspberries on top, leaving a ½ in (1 cm) cream border. Using even pressure, pipe loose ribbon loops evenly around the edges of the fruit. Spread cream over the other meringue, take it out of the tin and position it, cream side down, on to the raspberries pressing it gently down. Pull away the paper, fill the piping bag with cream left in the bowl and again, using even pressure, hold the bag at 45° angle, with the nozzle flat side on the meringue and pipe ribbons of cream at ½ in (1 cm) intervals across the top.

Keep the decorated meringue at room temperature for 1 hour before serving to allow the raspberries to soften a little and flavour the cream.

Forward Preparation

The day before

Prepare

Pheasants and make the stock.

Cook

Meringues and when they are cold, cover them with a tea-towel and store in a cool place.
Prawns; moisten them with a touch of French dressing while they are warm. Keep them loosely covered with clingfilm in the refrigerator.

Usually I suggest and list a timetable that involves preparation and cooking the day before and the morning, but for this menu I find it better to prepare for dinner early in the afternoon, leaving the morning free.

Make the avocado mousses. Wrap the pheasants, cover them loosely with clingfilm and keep them chilled.

Have the stock, Port and orange rind ready to heat. Prepare the parsnip casserole. Fill and decorate the meringue. Keep it in the refrigerator. Top and tail the beans and keep them in a polythene bag. Prepare the vegetables for the avocado dressing. Keep them in individual bowls sealed with clingfilm.

Evening

Set the oven to gas mark 3, 325°F, 170°C.

Heat the pheasant cooking liquid.

The pheasants and parsnip casserole are cooked for the same length of time, but leave the casserole in the oven to brown at a higher temperature when the parcels are cooked.

Blend the sliced vegetables with vinaigrette.

Take the meringue out of the refrigerator.

RED WINE PUNCH

TRIPLE MOUSSE
crabmeat, cucumber and smoked salmon

CHRISTMAS GOOSE
with chestnut stuffing garnished with poached pears

ROAST POTATOES AND PARSNIPS
BRUSSELS SPROUTS

MINT ICE
served on half a grapefruit

CHRISTMAS PUDDING
with brandied apricots

I find that the best way to organise a busy timetable is to make a list of everything to be done and I rely on this method all year round in the restaurant. As Christmas is a hectic time in any household, with the preparing of lunch being only one of the many things to think of, you may find it helpful to plan your Christmas meal well in advance, with the help of a checklist. The crossing off of each item on a list provides a great deal of satisfaction, as well as reminding you of small things that might otherwise be forgotten in the rush.

If you make your list as early as September or October, the first item to cross off would be brandied apricots, followed by the Christmas cake and pudding.

Like most people you probably have family-favourite traditional pudding, cake and preserving recipes which you prefer to use for The Day, so I have omitted recipes for these important items of Christmas fare.

Forward preparation

Two days before

Prepare forcemeat.
Skin and cook the chestnuts.

Check that you have

Mayonnaise.
Brown sauce.

Make mint ice. For method see p. 68
Please read about stocks and method of boning chickens, (appendix and page 59)

The day before

Bone the goose.
Start to make the stock early in the day to give it time to chill so that you can remove the surface fat.
Fill the goose, set it in the casserole, cover with a tea-towel and keep it in the refrigerator.
Make the triple mousse.

Prepare the vegetables

Potatoes and parsnips; keep covered with cold water.
Using a stainless steel knife, trim the bases of the sprouts and remove their outer layer of leaves, keep them in a polythene bag in the refrigerator.
Brown the almonds and keep in an airtight tin.

Work out cooking timetable for the next day

The Christmas pudding 3–4 hours reheating.
2¼–2½ hours for the goose and 20 minutes resting.
About 1 hour for the roast potatoes and parsnips.
20 minutes to poach pears.
3–4 minutes to cook the sprouts in rapidly boiling water.

The morning

Preheat the oven.
Brown the goose and set it to cook.
Put the Christmas pudding on to boil.
Make the sauce for the meat, pour it into a jug until ready to reheat.
Collect together the ingredients for the punch.

Start to get ready

Unmould the triple mousse and return it to the refrigerator.
Bread to toast, napkin and basket.
Spoon the brandied apricots into a bowl.
Warm the punch. I would like a drink by now!
Start to roast the potatoes and brown them at a higher heat if

necessary while the goose is resting.
Prepare the pears and start to cook them. Have the brandy close by.
Lightly salted water in a saucepan.
Sprouts in the vegetable basket.
Lemon and butter in a small pan, almonds nearby.
The sauce ready to reheat.
Take the goose out of the oven.

201

Red wine punch

Heat the punch in a non-reactive stainless steel saucepan or fish kettle.

For 10 glasses:

1 litre red wine
1 orange with a few cloves pressed into the skin
1 lemon sliced

1 stick of cinnamon
6 sugar lumps
4 fl oz (125 ml) brandy

Fruit garnish – optional

Sliced apples, oranges and a cube of crystallised
  ginger cut into slivers.

Pour the wine into the pan, add the orange, lemon, cinnamon and sugar. Set it on a low heat, stir until the sugar has dissolved and then keep it at simmering point for 10 minutes.

Heat the brandy in a small pan and when it flames, pour it into the wine. Switch off the heat, let it cool a little and then strain it into a bowl. Add the garnish and serve.

Triple mousse: crabmeat, cucumber and smoked salmon

The layered mousse can be unmoulded and then cut across into slices, or spooned from a glass serving dish, to reveal a delicate array of colours and flavours that will stimulate your guests' appetite for the goose.

If you choose to serve the mousse sliced, you need a plastic oblong container 2½ in (6 cm) deep, that will hold 3½ pints (2 litres) of water, the inside coated with a light vegetable oil (I use a pastry brush). If you want to spoon the mousse, a shallow glass bowl of a similar size.

Both the crabmeat and cucumber recipes each require half a packet of gelatine and this is the easiest way to measure the correct amount: pour 1 packet of gelatine into a dessertspoon to create an oval shape, equal at the top and bottom. Using a palette knife carefully slide away the top half, leaving the bottom layer intact.

My kitchen is not equipped with too many bowls, whisks etc., as I find that the more available, the more I tend to use. For a recipe such as this triple mousse, which includes various stages of preparation, there would be a mountain of washing-up to do at the end if clean utensils are used throughout. For this reason I suggest that you wash your equipment as you finish each separate stage; this also allows each mousse time to set before the next is made.

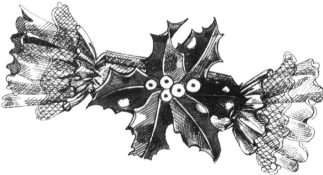

Crabmeat mousse

1½ fl oz (35 ml) white wine
½ pkt gelatine
½ oz (10 g) butter
½ oz (10 g) flour
¼ pint (150 ml) light fish or chicken stock
¼ lb (110 g) white crabmeat
¼ lb (110 g) brown crabmeat
¼ pint (150 ml) pink mayonnaise
2½ fl oz (65 ml) double cream

Cucumber mousse

10 oz (275 g) cucumber
2 tablespoons water
½ pkt gelatine
4 oz (110 g) cream cheese
2½ fl oz (65 ml) boiling water
1 tablespoon red wine vinegar
1 teaspoon caster sugar
Pinch of ground mace
2½ fl oz (65 ml) double cream, lightly whipped
Salt and pepper

Smoked salmon mousse

6 oz (175 g) smoked salmon
3½ fl oz (100 ml) single cream
1 tablespoon lemon juice
Grated nutmeg to taste

7½ fl oz (225 ml) double cream
1 level tablespoon of aspic dissolved in 4 fl oz
  (125 ml) boiling water.
3 teaspoons dry sherry

Garnish

Lemon slices
Parsley

Crabmeat mousse

Pour the white wine into a small saucepan, sprinkle the gelatine powder evenly over and leave it to soak in. Light the oven to the lowest setting and place the saucepan in, at the very bottom. Allow the gelatine to melt completely, but remember you should always be able to place your hand underneath the pan.

Melt the butter in a saucepan and tip in the flour. Gradually add the stock, stirring all the time and bring it to the boil. Whisk until smooth, pour in the gelatine, mixing it in well. Switch off the heat, stir in the brown crabmeat and leave to cool. Spoon the white crabmeat into a mixing-bowl and stir in the mayonnaise.

Pour the cream into another mixing-bowl, place a damp tea-towel underneath and whisk until you can see the whisk shapes in the cream. With a metal spoon, fold the cool brown crabmeat mixture into the crab mayonnaise then, still using a metal spoon, gently mix in the whipped cream. Spoon the mousse into the prepared dish and, using a pliable spatula, smooth the surface level. Place it in the refrigerator to set. Now prepare the cucumber mousse.

Cucumber mousse

Cut the cucumber into cubes, put them into the food processor or blender and work until fine, but not slushy. Spoon the cucumber into a sieve and leave over a bowl to drain.

Put the two tablespoons of water into a small saucepan, sprinkle evenly with the gelatine and leave to soak. In a mixing-bowl and using a wooden spoon, beat the cream cheese until smooth. Pour the boiling water on to the soaked gelatine, stir until all the crystals have disappeared and then blend into the cheese.

Press the remaining juice out of the cucumber with a wooden spoon. Tip the dried cucumber into a small bowl, add the vinegar, sugar and mace and mix it into the cheese. To complete the mousse fold in the cream, lightly whipped. Taste and season with salt and pepper.

Take the set crabmeat mousse out of the refrigerator and pour the cucumber mousse on top. Return the dish to the refrigerator.

Smoked salmon mousse

Chop the smoked salmon and place into the food processor or blender. Work until you have a very smooth paste. Now add lemon juice and single cream. Mix together and add the seasoning. Pour the double cream into a mixing-bowl and whisk until you have soft, almost floppy, peaks. Count 3 tablespoons of liquid aspic into the salmon and mix until completely smooth, then straight away fold it into the cream using a metal spoon.

Gently spoon the mousse on to the set cucumber, smooth the top with a palette knife and chill. Mix 3 teaspoons of sherry with the liquid aspic. If the aspic hardens while you are waiting for the mousse to set, melt it over a gentle heat and leave it to cool. You need a thin layer of aspic on top of the mousse to seal it and to give it a very light sheen. Spoon a little over and swirl the bowl around so that the aspic covers the top.

Chill until ready to serve.

To decorate and serve

If you have made the mousse in a plastic container, run the tip of a knife around the edge of the mould, place a large serving plate upside down on top of the mousse and invert them together. Gently lift away the mould to reveal three even layers of mousse. Decorate the plate with three overlapping slices of lemon, pinned together with a sprig of parsley. Slice the mousse at the table with a thin sharp knife. Catch each portion on a sweet-serving slice and slide it on to the plate with your knife.

If you made the mousse in a glass container, serve it at the table, using a large spoon, so that each portion will have the three layers of mousse. Serve accompanied with warm, crustless brown toast arranged in the folds of a large napkin.

Christmas goose

When you buy a goose, select one that has very little down on the legs, soft yellow feet and fat. Compared with a turkey there is not as much meat on a goose, but the flavour and richness of the flesh is delicious. It is very easy to plain-roast a goose as it is almost self-basting, but I find it can be difficult to carve in front of guests and to organise everything else at the same time. With careful planning to allow time, the goose can be boned, filled with forcemeat to replace the carcass and tied up well in advance. Served surrounded with poached pears that provide contrast of texture, the boned goose will look attractive and can be easily carved into elegant slices.

1 goose 6–7 lb (3 kg)

Stuffing

1 lb (450 g) chestnuts
1 pint (570 ml) stock
1 lb (450 g) trimmed pork fillet (you will need to buy just under 1 ½ lb [700 g])
½ pint (275 ml) double cream
Salt and pepper
Nutmeg to taste
1 tablespoon chopped fresh sage
3 boned and trimmed chicken breasts

Stock

Goose giblets and bones
5 pints (2½ litres) water
2 onions, quartered – leave the skins on to add
   colour to the stock
2 carrots, chopped but not peeled
1 stick of celery, chopped
Few parsley stalks
Thyme for flavouring
6 peppercorns to be added during the last hour
   of cooking

For braising

¼ pint (150 ml) stock made from the bones
1 sliced onion
1 sliced carrot
1 stick of celery, chopped
1 teaspoon chopped sage

For the sauce

¾ pint (425 ml) stock, made from the bones
Brown sauce to thicken
½ teaspoon redcurrant jelly
Dash of Worcestershire sauce
Salt and pepper

Pears

8 pears
Juice of 1 lemon
2 tablespoons of brandy

To prepare the chestnuts and stuffing

Put the chestnuts in a large saucepan, cover them with cold water and bring to the boil. Draw the pan aside, take out the nuts one at a time and remove the outer and inner skins. Throw the water away and return the chestnuts to the pan. Cover them with stock, put the lid on and simmer until tender, about 30 minutes. Drain the cooked nuts in a sieve and when they are cool enough to handle, chop them for the stuffing.

Trim the pork fillet, cut it into cubes and place them in the food processor/blender. Chop the pork until smooth and while the machine is still working, slowly pour in the cream, mixing it in well. Tip the pork into a mixing-bowl, add the seasoning and sage. You will notice that the forcemeat thickens slightly when you add salt. Stir in the chestnuts, cover with clingfilm, pressing it down gently on to the forcemeat and chill.

To bone the goose

Lay the goose, breast side down and using a sharp pointed knife, slice the skin down the back and cut the flesh away from the carcass, legs and wings. That sounds very easy, but please read the detailed description I have given for boning a chicken (page 59). Cover the boned goose with a damp tea-towel and start to make the stock.

The stock

Put the bones and giblets into a large saucepan and pour in 5 pints (2½ litres) of water. Bring it to the boil and then lower the heat until the water is just bubbling. A scum will form on top; scoop this away using a slotted spoon. Pour a little cold water into the centre of the pan and remove the scum that will rise again when the water returns to the boil. Continue until the surface is white and frothy. Add the vegetables, parsley stalks and thyme. Place a sheet of greaseproof paper on top and partly cover the saucepan with its lid. Leave to cook for about 4 hours (adding the peppercorns towards the end), when the stock will have reduced to just under half. Remove the bones and pour the cooled liquid through a fine sieve into a plastic tub. Chill the strained liquid until a layer of fat has formed on top, remove this and throw it away. Keep the stock covered in the refrigerator.

To stuff and roast the goose

Lay the boned goose out flat. Carefully remove the breasts without cutting the skin and put them with the chicken breasts. Cut away the rest of the flesh from the leg and wing area, trim this and mix it with the forcemeat. Slice each goose breast in half horizontally and lay two fillets down the centre of the skin, lengthways. Top them with the forcemeat, smoothing it out with wet hands to form a long sausage. Arrange the other goose fillet on top and cut the chicken breasts to cover the sides, gently pressing them into place. Cut the sides of the skin so they will overlap slightly down the centre of the breasts. Tuck and fold in the skin at both ends to cover the meat and sew the bird neatly together. Tie around with string, looping it at 1 in (2.5 cm) intervals, so it will then keep its shape during cooking. Cutting the breasts and spreading the forcemeat as I have described will ensure that the bird is evenly cooked.

Set the oven to gas mark 4, 350°F, 180°C.

Brush the surface of the goose with a little oil and brown it slowly in a large casserole on top of the oven. Lay the bird on its back and pour in the stock, surround the goose with the onion, carrot, celery and sprinkle in the chopped sage. Bring the stock to boil, cover the breast with a double layer of greaseproof paper and seal the casserole completely with foil. Cook in the oven for 2¼–2½ hours.

About half an hour before the goose is cooked (it will be fairly firm to the touch by now) peel the pears with a stainless steel knife and cut out the threads that run from the core to the stalk, use a teaspoon or melon baller to scoop out the core. Roll the fruit in lemon juice and pop them into the casserole to cook for 20 minutes.

Making the sauce

Do not use the cooking juice of the bird as it is very fatty. Bring to boil ¾ pint (425 ml) of the stock, add the brown sauce to thicken and add the flavourings. Taste and twist black pepper into the sauce just before serving.

To serve

Unwrap the goose, test it with a skewer, the juices should run clear and the bird feel very firm. Carefully take out the pears using a slotted spoon, and lay them on a dish. Heat the brandy in a soup ladle and as soon as it flames tip it over the pears. Cover with foil and keep warm.

Tip away the cooking juices and leave the goose to rest while you dish up the vegetables into serving dishes and reheat the sauce.

Remove the string and place the goose on a large serving plate, pour a little sauce over the skin, letting it fall on to the plate to give a sheen and arrange the pears on top of the sauce.

Roast potatoes with parsnips

2½ lb (1 kg) small potatoes
2½ lb (1 kg) young parsnips
Dripping or butter

Peel the potatoes and parsnips and cut them into barrel shapes, all of a similar size. Boil the vegetables for 10 minutes, drain and dry them thoroughly. Put them into hot fat to roast. Raise the heat while the goose is resting if they need more colour.

Brussels sprouts with lemon butter and almonds

Lay the almonds on a baking tray; as they are served only as a crisp garnish I suggest 4 tablespoons. Bake them in the oven until golden brown. For the lemon butter see page 49.

Brussels sprouts

Cook 2 lb (1 kg) brussels sprouts until tender but still crisp. Drain them and throw away the water. Return the sprouts to the pan and toss them over a high heat to dry. Switch off the heat and pour in the hot lemon butter, shaking the pan until the sprouts are well coated. Add the almonds and tip the glistening sprouts into a warm serving dish.

Grapefruit

With a sharp knife, slice each grapefruit in half, cut around the white core, twist and pull it out. Using a serrated, curved knife, cut around each segment to release the flesh completely. For a simple but effective decoration peel a thin layer of skin away from the cut surface, leaving the first ½ in (1 cm) attached and loop the grapefruit ribbon into a small knot.

Keep the cut and prepared grapefruit covered with clingfilm in the refrigerator until the first course is served.

To serve

Spoon the mint ice on to the grapefruits and tuck a sprig of mint into the yellow skin knot. Serve the fruit nestled in the folds of a napkin.

Appendix

Stocks

In the home kitchen today stock cubes are an excellent time saving substitute; use them for making my soup recipes and for enriching home-made stocks, but do not use them in sauces that have to be reduced as they make them too salty, though you can add a little at the end of reduction if you need extra flavour.

Most home-made stock will keep for up to three days, except for fish, and I like to use that the next day.

This is the way I make my stock.

Brown stock

If you want to make a brown stock, roast the bones in the oven at gas mark 9, 475°F, 240°C, with a little dripping or butter, for 45 minutes, until brown, then follow the recipe.

To make 5 pints, use a large saucepan, one that will hold at least 14 pints of water. Measure to make sure as you do not want the stock to splash over once you have added the bones and vegetables.

4 lb veal knuckle bones, ask your butcher to chop them for you
6 carrots, chopped but not peeled
4 large onions, quartered – leave the skins on to add colour to the stock
I celery chopped with leaves and base
I lb (450 g) pork rind
Mushroom stalks

4 over-ripe tomatoes or I tablespoon tomato purée
Parsley stalks
I also like to use thyme for flavouring
I teaspoon peppercorns – add these to the stock during the last hour of cooking, they can add a bitter taste if cooked too long.

Put the bones and pork rind into the pan and pour in 10 pints (5 litres) of water. Bring it to the boil and then lower the heat until the water is just bubbling. A scum will form on top, scoop this away using a slotted spoon. Pour a little cold water into the centre of the pan and remove the scum that will rise when the liquid returns to the boil. Continue until the surface is white and frothy. Add the vegetables and thyme. Place a sheet of greaseproof paper on top and partly cover the saucepan with its lid and leave to cook for about three hours (adding the peppercorns towards the end) when the stock will have reduced by half. Remove the bones and pour the cooled liquid through a fine sieve into a plastic tub. Chill the strained liquid until a layer of fat has formed on top. Remove this and throw it away. Keep the stock covered in the refrigerator.

Chicken stock

A few things to remember:
Use a large heavy-based saucepan with a lid. Do not be tempted to keep the stock in the pan – as soon as the cooked stock has cooled, it should be strained into a china or plastic container; an ice cream tub is ideal.

Chill the strained stock until a white fat has formed on top. Lift this off with a spoon and throw it away.

It will keep up to three days covered in the refrigerator.

Always boil before using.

4 chicken carcasses
10 pints (5 litres) water
2 carrots, chopped but not peeled
Celery leaves and base
Pork rind if you have any

A few mushroom stalks
Parsley stalks
Sprig of thyme
2 onions with a few cloves pressed into them

Put the bones into the saucepan, pour in the water and bring slowly to the boil. Lower the heat until the water is just bubbling and wait until a grey scum forms on top. Scoop this off with a slotted spoon into a bowl. Pour in a little cold water to encourage more to rise and scoop it off when the water boils again. Continue skimming until the surface is white and frothy. I have always been told to sprinkle the top with salt to make scum rise, but I have found that by adding a little cold water it works as well, if not better.

Add the vegetables and thyme, wait until the liquid is boiling again and partly cover the saucepan with its lid. Leave it undisturbed for two hours.

Lift out the carcasses and keep them for soup. Strain the cooled stock through a sieve into a container.

Whenever a recipe calls for chicken breasts, especially poached, use the carcasses to make a simple stock for cooking the breasts and then, with the addition of vegetables, a soup the next day.

Chicken and vegetable soup

Chicken carcasses: remove the skin from the wings, trim all the meat away and cut it into thin strips.

Choose vegetables that need little or hardly any cooking, for example:

Leeks, the white parts cut across to form thin rings.

Courgettes, cut into thin circles.

Spinach, the leaves rolled together to form a sausage shape and then cut across into thin strips.

Egg noodles can also make the soup interesting; they take four minutes to cook.

Flavouring: Worcestershire or soy sauce.

Seasoning: when you bring the stock to boil add a little salt and freshly ground pepper at the last minute.

Allow 6–7 fl oz (175–200 ml) stock per person. Freeze any left over for later use.

Bring to boil in a saucepan and season with salt and then add the leeks, courgettes, chicken and noodles. Simmer gently for 4–5 minutes and stir the spinach in and allow it to soften a little. Bring the soup back to the boil and add flavouring and black pepper.

Brown sauce

Use this sauce diluted with wine, beef or chicken stock, then flavoured with meat juices. It makes an ideal gravy to serve with any plain roasts. Mix it with minced beef for cottage pie and use it as a base for some of my sauce recipes.

The brown sauce will keep for one week in the refrigerator and then it must be boiled to store for a further seven days. A few days before you make the sauce, keep a container in the refrigerator and use it to collect some of the ingredients together: save the rind from bacon and pork, the stalks from mushrooms and parsley, celery leaves, carrots and over-ripe tomatoes.

209

8 oz (225 g) dripping	5 pints (2½ litres) meat stock
4 onions, sliced but not peeled	I tablespoon dried thyme
8 oz (225 g) pork and bacon rind	Bouquet garni
4 oz (110 g) carrots, not peeled	2 tablespoons tomato purée, or I tablespoon
Mushroom stalks	and a few over-ripe tomatoes
4 oz (110 g) celery	2 tablespoons Worcestershire sauce
8 oz (225 g) flour	

Melt the dripping in a large saucepan and fry the vegetables until brown. Stir in the flour and cook gently for five minutes. Gradually pour in the stock, stirring all the time and bring it to the boil. Now add the thyme, bouquet garni, purée or purée and tomatoes and Worcestershire sauce. Turn down the heat until the sauce is just bubbling. Cover with a sheet of greaseproof paper and cook very gently for about one hour. Strain into a plastic tub. Taste, season and cover the top of the sauce with clingfilm to stop a skin forming.

Mayonnaise

I used to be wary of making mayonnaise. Every time I tried, it seemed to curdle, so I would throw it away and use a commercial variety, which although an adequate substitute, is never as good as home-made.

I have now found that for best results the egg yolks, wine vinegar and lemon juice should be at room temperature. The oil, bowl and whisk, slightly warmer. The same rules apply when using the blender.

Advantages of making mayonnaise in the blender

It takes little time.

It is easier to control the stream of oil.

There is less chance of curdling.

If the mayonnaise has separated when you make it by hand, put a whole egg into the warm blender bowl. Start to work it until smooth, then gradually add the mayonnaise, blending until it has completely mixed together.

The disadvantage of making mayonnaise in the blender

I am sure it tastes slightly different, perhaps a little oily and bland? Try it and decide for yourself.

4 egg yolks	Salt and pepper
2 tablespoons red wine vinegar	I pint (570 ml) olive oil
2 teaspoons lemon juice	

Whenever you are whisking anything by hand place a damp tea-towel under the bowl to keep it steady.

To make sure you separate the eggs completely, pass the egg whites through your fingers, pull away the thread and slide the yolks into the mixing-bowl. Pour the oil into a jug.

Whisk the egg yolks together until smooth and pale, add the lemon juice, vinegar and seasoning. Whisk until you have mixed it all together – this will take a minute or two. Now gradually add the oil, a little at a time to start with. As the mayonnaise begins to thicken, add the oil in a continuous stream.

The mayonnaise is ready when it looks like lightly whipped cream.

Pink mayonnaise

Tomato ketchup mixed with mayonnaise adds a delicate colour and yet still keeps it light in taste. Use a small clove of garlic, as the flavours should mingle together and not have one that overpowers.

4 tablespoons tomato ketchup	6 stuffed green olives, chopped
I tablespoon chopped parsley	I clove of garlic crushed
A shake of Tabasco sauce	I teaspoon lemon juice
I teaspoon Worcestershire sauce	I teaspoon hazelnut oil

Mix well together and add to 1 pint (570 ml) of mayonnaise.

French dressing

Make this dressing in the mixer using the whisk attachment. Keep it in a cool, dark place. Don't be tempted to store the dressing in the refrigerator, as constant contrast of temperatures will eventually spoil the flavour.

I prefer to make a light dressing using sunflower as well as olive oil. The wine vinegar can be flavoured with herbs before making the dressing. Pour the vinegar into a mixing-bowl, add the herbs, choosing only one or two. I tend to use thyme or sage. Cover the vinegar with clingfilm and leave overnight. Pass the flavoured vinegar through a sieve.

I ½ oz (40 g) English dried mustard	½ pint (275 ml) red wine vinegar
2 oz (50 g) caster sugar	½ pint (275 ml) sunflower oil
2½ fl oz (65 ml) boiling water	I pint (570 ml) olive oil

Whisk all the ingredients together.

Mustard dressing

This is an ideal dressing for salad, pâté, mousse and cold meat. It will keep for 2 weeks in the refrigerator.

4 tablespoons brown sugar	I tablespoon coarse grain mustard
6 tablespoons red wine vinegar	Black pepper
¼ pint (150 ml) light olive oil	I container with a tight-fitting lid

Put all the ingredients into the container, make sure the lid is secure and shake well until the sugar has dissolved.

Fruit purée

A fruit purée is delicious served as a garnish with poached fruit, ice cream and cakes, or as flavouring for mousse and cheesecakes.

Apricots, plums, blackberries and blackcurrants should be cooked then puréed. If you wish to use fresh pineapple in a mousse, I have found to my cost that the pineapple has to be cooked first, otherwise the gelatine will not set it. They can all be made using the same method.

Count how many apricots or plums you use then the same amount of stones can be removed at the end of the cooking time.

Variations of flavour

Add a few sprigs of mint to blackcurrants.
Cook apples with blackberries.
Orange or lemon rind can be added to the sugar syrup.
Cinnamon and cloves add a spiced flavour to plums.

1 lb (450 g) fruit
¼ pint (150 ml) sugar syrup

Place the fruit and sugar syrup in a large saucepan.

Cook gently until tender. Small or ripe fruit will only take minutes. Liquidize and sieve the purée. Store in a container with a lid in the refrigerator.

Sugar syrup

It is always useful to have sugar syrup to hand. Use it as I have for fruit purées or to pour over fruit salads. I prefer my syrup to be dark golden amber in colour. Just imagine how good it looks when poured over pineapple and if the fruit is a little tart it makes a good contrast of flavours as well as colour.

Pour ½ lb (225 g) caster sugar into a saucepan and shake the pan so the sugar settles evenly. Pour in ½ pint (275 ml) cold water and bring slowly to the boil. Don't stir it yet. Raise the heat a little and have ready ½ pint (275 ml) boiling water. The syrup will start to turn a pale gold, then amber. Take the pan away from the heat – be careful, as it will be very hot. Pour in the hot water and return it to a low heat. Stir the syrup with a wooden spoon until smooth and boiling gently.

Add grated lemon or orange rind if you wish and leave to cool. Strain or pour into a container. When the syrup is quite cold, seal with a lid.

Lining a cake tin for baking

I tend to cut a batch of cake linings and keep them flat ready for use.

Lay the base of the cake tin on a sheet of greaseproof paper. Steady the base with one hand and with a pencil draw around the outside. Remove the base, now draw a larger circle to cover the sides of the tin. With a pair of scissors cut the paper around the outside pencil line. Cut the paper down from the outer circle to just inside the inner circle, making the cuts 1 in (2.5 cm) apart, so that the paper now looks like a big daisy. Brush the paper lightly with melted butter or oil making sure to cover the thin strips well and arrange it, greased side down, in the cake tin. With your fingers work around the sides pressing the strips of paper flat and brush the paper with a little more butter or oil. Put a spoon of flour into the tin and swirl the flour around until the inside is completely dusted. Tip away the excess flour.

The reader will have noticed my frequent references to thin, very sharp, finely pointed knives. I have found my set of Cook's Knives from the Wilkinson sword Professional range invaluable; indeed, I could not imagine working without them!

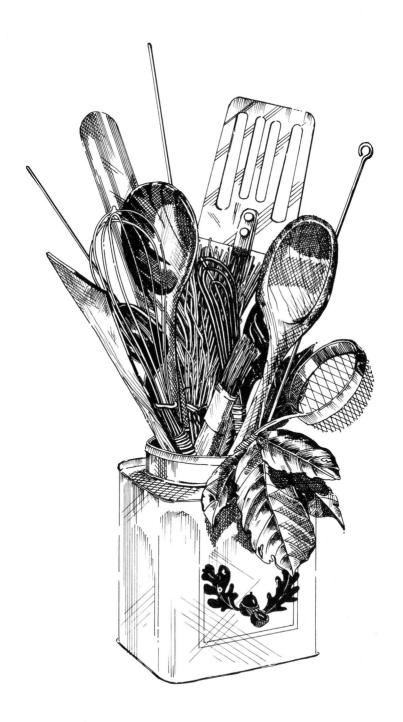

INDEX

mousse – *cont.*
 avocado, 193–5
 crabmeat, 35–6, 202–4
 crabmeat, cucumber and smoked salmon, 202–4
 cucumber, 202–4
 smoked salmon, 156–7, 202–4
 Stilton and pear, 72–3
 whisked sponge with pineapple mousse, 177–8
mullet
 butter-brushed red mullet fillets, 29–31
mushroom
 crabmeat with garlic mushrooms, 127, 128
 pepper, mushroom and walnut salad, 106–7
 salad, 93–4
 sautéed mushrooms, 102
 sautéed mushrooms with cream, 132
 sirloin steaks with mushrooms and smoked ham,
  163–5
 soup, 187–8
mussel
 sauce, 88, 89, 90
 sautéed smoked mussels, 168–9
mustard
 dressing, 28, 29, 122, 123, 211
 mint and apple, 108
 sauce, 96, 114

noodles, buttered, 184

oatmeal
 meringue with raspberries, 198
 pineapple and melon oatmeal meringue, 190–91
olives
 red mullet fillets in wine, with onions and black
  olives, 29–31
 tomato and black olive salad, 14–15
onions, 145
 red mullet fillets in wine with onions and black
  olives, 29–31
orange
 boned chicken with pork forcemeat on a bed of
  oranges, 58–60
 butter, 132
 champagne, orange and raspberry trifle, 159–60
 coffee-flavoured sponge with orange cream,
  139–40
 duckling and orange segments, 28–9
 horseradish and orange mayonnaise, 113
 orange and lemon garnish, 12, 13
 pheasants in port and orange, 195–7
 tomato and orange salad, 37

parsley sauce, 177
parsnip
 and pear casserole with walnuts, 197–8
 roast potatoes with parsnips, 206
pastry
 avocado in, 41–2
 puff, 36, 69, 70, 77, 78, 123, 124
pâté
 cream cheese and herb, 65, 120, 137, 138
 prawns and cream cheese, 74–5
 smoked salmon, 18
 Stilton, 122–3

pea, apple and hazelnut soup, 136–7
peaches
 dressing, 161, 162
 melon with spiced peaches, 85
peanuts
 avocado with sweetcorn and peanuts, 41–2
pears
 parsnip and pear casserole, 197–8
 poached pears with blackcurrant sauce, 25–7
 Stilton and pear mousse, 72–3
pecan nuts
 figs marinated in port with a pecan nut centre,
  15
peppers
 lamb with green peppers, 123–4
 pepper, mushroom and walnut salad, 106–7
 red pepper purée, 123, 124
 yellow pepper dressing, 106, 107
 yellow pepper purée, 53, 54
pheasant in port and orange, 195–7
pigeon
 breasts wrapped in bacon, 188–9
 whole pigeons with apricot and nut forcemeat,
  181–3
pineapple
 pineapple and melon oatmeal meringue, 190–91
 shortbread, 97
 upside-down cake, 55–6
 wedges, 121
 whisked sponge with pineapple mousse, 177–8
pinenuts
 French beans with lemon butter and pinenuts, 85
plum purée, 119, 120
poached
 chicken breasts with mussel sauce, 88–90
 figs marinated in port, 15
 pears with blackcurrant sauce, 25–7
 redcurrants, 32
pork
 chicken with pork forcemeat, 58–60
 duck with pork forcemeat, 60
 escalopes of pork with mint and apple mustard,
  108–9
 marinated in rum, 100–102
 marinated in wine and herbs, 113–14
 with raspberries, 109
port, 72, 73
 figs marinated in port, 15
 pheasants in port and orange, 195–7
potatoes
 buttered roast, 165–6
 casserole, 103
 casserole of beef with vegetables and potatoes,
  169–70
 crisp buttered, 109
 puff pastry potatoes, 77–8
 roast, 85
 roast potatoes with parsnips, 206
praline, almond, 66
prawns
 melon with flavoured prawns and curry
  mayonnaise, 149–50
 prawns and cream cheese pâté, 74–5
 prawns and sesame seed garnish, 31